EMERSON'S
TRANSCENDENTAL
ETUDES

Cultural Memory

in

the

Present

Mieke Bal and Hent de Vries, Editors

EMERSON'S TRANSCENDENTAL ETUDES

Stanley Cavell

Edited by David Justin Hodge

STANFORD UNIVERSITY PRESS

STANFORD, CALIFORNIA

Stanford University Press
Stanford, California

Printed in the United States of America
on acid-free, archival-quality paper

Library of Congress Cataloging-in-Publication Data

Cavell, Stanley, 1926–
    Emerson's transcendental etudes / Stanley Cavell ;
edited by David Justin Hodge.
        p.   cm.
    Includes bibliographical references and index.
    ISBN 0-8047-4542-0 (alk. paper) —
    ISBN 0-8047-4543-9 (pbk. : alk. paper)
    1. Emerson, Ralph Waldo, 1803–1882—Criticism
and interpretation.   2. Transcendentalism (New England)
3. Philosophy in literature. I. Hodge, David Justin.
II. Title.
PS1638.C38 2003
814'3—DC21

                                        2003005750

Original Printing 2003

Last figure below indicates year of this printing:
12   11   10   09   08   07

Typeset by Tim Roberts in 11 /13.5 Adobe Garamond

Contents

Author's Acknowledgments

I have placed myself, as my various citations along the course of the following essays acknowledge, in debt to notable scholars of Emerson. I emphasize here the younger voices who participated in the seminar on Emerson I offered at Harvard in the late 1980s, a number of whom became teaching fellows in the Emerson-inspired course I then developed on Moral (or Emersonian) Perfectionism for the Moral Reasoning stratum of the Harvard Core Curriculum. I have had other occasions and reasons to express my permanent, indeed increasing gratitude to them. That many of them have taken the experience of those times into their subsequent teaching and writing lives is something that does the heart an irreplaceable good.

Often as it had crossed my mind to round up my various texts on Emerson and make a book of them, a good time for it never seemed to present itself until David Justin Hodge, out of his knowledge of and devotion to Emerson, proposed to undertake the editing of such a volume. I knew almost at once that I wanted to take him up on his sense of what the volume should include. What I could not have known then was the extent to which his knowledge of the Emersonian corpus, and his generosity with that knowledge, would produce annotation and an apparatus that so distinctly increase the usefulness of this volume. I am grateful to him for the book's existence.

S.C.

Editor's Preface

Thirty years have passed since Stanley Cavell published his first remarks on the founding of American thinking. At that time, in the context of an investigation of Henry David Thoreau's *Walden*, he asked: "Why has America never expressed itself philosophically? Or has it?"[1] Cavell offered an initial reply to the question with respect to Thoreau and then, several years later, pitched the same question with Ralph Waldo Emerson in mind. Since then, Cavell has produced many celebrated essays and lectures that illustrate his continuous effort to suggest how we might inherit the texts and problems born out of and borne by these American thinkers.

While a number of us who have followed Cavell's writing have managed to track these many pieces to their various sources, it has been easy for others to overlook the extent of pertinent articles, lectures, and chapters of books in this line of his work. One aim of creating this book, then, is to avert the unfortunate possibility that Cavell's substantive writings on Emerson may have failed to present themselves, to those who might welcome them, as the articulate, interwoven, and enduring works that they are. Even readers with some knowledge of the scope of the work may not recognize the degree to which his published writing adds up to a full statement on Emerson as a philosopher, or may suppose that he was, perhaps, leading up to a more balanced book that has not yet appeared. Now, with the appearance of *Emerson's Transcendental Etudes*, such postulation and ambiguity can be well lost. As Cavell attests in his Introduction to this volume, he understands this to be his book on Emerson, the only one he expects of himself.

The thirteen chapters that follow are arranged in chronological order. This serves the important purpose of allowing the reader to experience the way in which Cavell's thinking on Emerson develops over the years. Furthermore, as he does in work on Wittgenstein, Shakespeare, psychoanalysis, and film, Cavell refers liberally to his own past writings. Sequencing the essays chronologically, therefore, affords the reader a chance to accumulate and absorb what will become the intricate reference materials of subsequent chapters.

The last two chapters contain material never before published, and Cavell has written an Introduction to the book. The remaining eleven chapters are reprinted from other publications: 1 and 2 from *The Senses of Walden: An Expanded Edition* (San Francisco: North Point Press, 1981; rpt. Chicago: University of Chicago Press, 1992); 3, 4, and 5 from *In Quest of the Ordinary: Lines of Skepticism and Romanticism* (Chicago: University of Chicago Press, 1988); 6 from *This New Yet Unapproachable America* (Albuquerque: Living Batch Press, 1989); 7 and 8 from *Conditions Handsome and Unhandsome: The Constitution of Emersonian Perfectionism* (Chicago: University of Chicago Press, 1990); 9 from *New Literary History* 25 (1994): 951-58; 10 from *Philosophical Passages: Wittgenstein, Emerson, Austin, Derrida* (Cambridge, Mass.: Blackwell, 1995); and 11 from *The Revival of Pragmatism: New Essays on Social Thought, Law, and Culture* (Durham, N.C.: Duke University Press, 1998).

A complete index of Cavell's direct citations from Emerson's work in this volume can be found online at http://www.sup.org/cavell_index. The online index is a chronological record of Cavell's use of Emerson's writing.

During the course of editing this book, one that included the creation of the citation index, I kept assiduous notes on a number of allusions and references that seem worthy of further attention. In the near future, at Cavell's urging, it is my expectation to write something that highlights the most revealing of the many conceptual correspondences I encountered.

At the end of these remarks, placed here at the beginning of Cavell's, it is sincerely an honor to thank Stanley Cavell for entrusting to me the care of his scholarly writing on Emerson, for being implacably patient in the process of bringing this volume into its present form, and for sustaining me with the inspiration of his example.

D.J.H.
Cambridge, Massachusetts

EMERSON'S
TRANSCENDENTAL
ETUDES

Introduction

Spending my childhood in a musical household—seeming to remember reading notes on a stave before I could read words of my speech—
I learned early that one can turn pages for another playing the piano without being able oneself to match the playing. Because Liszt and Chopin
were the composers my mother loved most to play, I would sometimes, left
to myself, take volumes of their music from the piles at the sides of the piano's music stand, turn the pages looking for sheets dappled with the dens-
est flights and swoops of notes, and wonder when I would be able to play
them. My desire to think of Emerson's essays as transcendental musically
as well as philosophically marks my inability for a long time to hear the
sense of Emerson's sentences within, rather than despite, what seemed to
me their detachable ornaments. And it registers, I know, my recurrent as-
tonishment that two such differently creative creatures as Franz Liszt and
Ralph Waldo Emerson should have inhabited the parlors and auditoriums
of the Western world over essentially the same expanse of years, resulting
in the thought that, when Emerson was writing the most famous of his essays from the late 1830s through the early 1840s, there was perhaps no one
born and brought up on his shores who could play, let alone dream of writing, music such as Liszt's. It also matters to me that only in recent generations are pianists—on both, or other, shores—expected to play the Liszt
Transcendental Etudes for the sake of their music more than for the sake of
their virtuosity.[1] Something I wish my title to suggest, or recall, is that

there is a beauty that is realized only in granting an alarming difficulty. But I do not assume that the difficulty is everywhere of the same kind.

I recognize that this is said somewhat defensively, an attempt to re-draw the image of Emerson in response to having been told so often that Emerson cannot be as hard to fathom as I make out or, not to put too fine a point on it, cannot be as philosophical. I have, for example, taken, in "Self-Reliance," Emerson to be directly alluding to Descartes ("Man is timid, he is afraid to say 'I think,' 'I am' but instead quotes some saint or sage") as well as to Kant, hearing Emerson's aversion to "conformity," which he calls the virtue most in demand, to continue the essential insight of Kant's discovery of what he calls "the reality of duty," namely, that we are called upon to act not merely in conformity with the moral law but for the sake of the law. But readers of Emerson whose expertise I respect have sim-ply denied that such allusions are, even if in some way intended, to be taken as serious philosophical observations on Emerson's part. And the ground of denial has mainly been, I think it is fair to say, that it simply makes no sense to suppose that Emerson, famously intimidated by formal argument, *could*, in principle, mean to be taking on and questioning, or modifying, even per-haps significantly parodying, signature thoughts of Descartes and of Kant. Something of this same sheer vision of, or unrelenting insistence upon, Emerson's inability to think and write rigorously has meant that, for all Nietzsche's explicit praise of Emerson, and for all the practically uncount-able allusions to (I often call them rewritings of) Emerson in Nietzsche's writing, this relationship is forgotten as often as it is discovered. Until Emer-son's own philosophicality is established for oneself, one is *bound* to find it inexplicable, hence bound to forget, that Nietzsche, in his rampage against the uses of Western knowledge and morality and religion, was inspired by, was characteristically incorporating, genteel Emerson.

Still, it is obvious that Emerson does not sound like what, especially in the Anglo-American tradition, we are accustomed to think of as philos-ophy. Why be so insistent? Why not, for example, distinguish (as Heideg-ger does) between philosophy and thinking, and grant thinking but not philosophy to Emerson? In some sense, indeed, I think this is right; but it is right only if the thinking in question is seen to be a criticism of philoso-phy (as it is in Nietzsche and in the Heidegger he, in turn, inspired). In the meantime, my insistence on Emerson's philosophicality is meant to ac-count for Emerson's writing, most immediately for its tireless recurrence to descriptions of itself, or figures for itself. For example, in "Self-Reliance" he shows himself writing *Whim* on the lintels of his door post (a complex image that is taken up more than once in my essays); in "The Poet" words are declared to be horses on which we ride, suggesting both that they obey our intentions and that they work beyond our prowess; in "Fate," as in "Intellect," intellect is said to "dissolve" what it touches, something I take as meant in opposition to the use of the conventional, parliamentary term "resolve," which in the American Constitution heralds the legitimizing of slavery; in "Experience" an Emersonian essay as a whole is allegorized as an embryo, said (according to "Experience") by a celebrated biologist of the period to form itself simultaneously from three points, which for Emerson describes such an essay as a circle, namely, one in search of like-minded readers; in "Circles" it is asserted that around every circle another can be drawn, which suggests further that Emerson's essays are related by encircling each other. And so on.

What commits Emerson to such self-registration? (And does it require virtuosity? At the end of Emerson's magnificent "Experience," he calls for patience, and again patience.[2]) I understand him to be responding to his sense that "Every word they say chagrins us"—not chagrins him alone, which would make him a crank, but those he calls "all and sundry" (Nietzsche will say, everyone and no one), who seek to say what they have it at heart to say. Now this struggle for a language which, let us say, promises honesty (expresses, hence scrutinizes, our desires, so far as we are able to read our desires) is relentless and endless for one who aspires to write philosophy. If Socrates (along with a line of others extending at least to Wittgenstein in *Philosophical Investigations*) is right, and philosophy knows only what anyone knows or could know by bethinking themselves of what they say and do, then it manifests itself in writing—or thinking—that can be said either to be without authority (that shuns authorization) or, put otherwise, that authorizes only itself by continuing to question itself, to bethink itself, after all the others who claim philosophy's attention (in Plato's image at the close of his *Symposium*) have fallen asleep.

For an American, the discovery of such a language, one allowing the continuous registration of the self's motion, presents a double task, since America, as Emerson was beginning to write, had as yet to inherit effectively a patrimony in European philosophy; no one had proven that the encounter of America with philosophy (beyond its occurrence in certain political doctrines) was feasible, hence had shown what it might sound like. To express America's difference (one could say, to justify its existence, its independence) was for Emerson's generation most pressing in its call for a mode of literature that expressed the American experience. Emerson, in effect, established both modes of expression, suggesting that, for America, philosophy and literature would bear a relation to each other not envisioned in the given, outstanding traditions of philosophy in England and in Germany. Or, if it were said that this relation was in fact precisely envisioned in the movement called romanticism, both in England (in Coleridge and Wordsworth), and, more fervently and permanently, in Germany (in the Schlegels and Tieck, and in Novalis and in Hölderlin, affecting the future direction of German philosophy, in Hegel and his aftermath), it would have to be added that in both standing traditions the development of literary practice unfolded in the presence of, in a process of withstanding, established philosophy.

It is not for me to say whether the present book, collecting all the writing I have published that is mainly and explicitly devoted to Emerson, satisfies any reasonable image others may have of a book about Emerson. What I wish to say is that if I were to write a book about Emerson, who for a quarter of a century has affected my thoughts—I might say, my aspirations for thinking—as decisively as any other writer, then this (or some further version of it) is that book, the only one, or kind, it is given to me to write about Emerson's work. I cannot justify the selection of topics out of Emerson's work that have seemed to me to warrant a response out of mine. I would feel justified if, in each case, I have shown sufficiently why I have been stopped by a passage in Emerson and continued its thought far enough to convey my impression that he proposes in his essays a genre of writing that shows a finite prose text to contemplate an infinite response. The virtue I claim for my procedure is that it leaves open the possibility that one may plausibly and profitably be stopped for thought at almost any word in Emerson's work. His prose is not poetry (he could be said to write poetry in order to demonstrate this fact of his prose), but his sentences aspire to, let's say, the self-containment of poetry. I have elsewhere expressed something of this sense by saying that any sentence of an Emerson paragraph, or essay, may be taken to be the topic sentence. There are, of course, other ways to respond to an Emerson text. I cannot say why those ways are not mine, but I would hate to believe that they are generally incompatible with mine.

This unpredictable relation to Emerson, in which a response from me rarely even seems to take on a complete (so to speak) essay of Emerson, is expressed, it seems to me, in the fact that more often than not, in the essays that follow, I place Emerson's writing in conjunction with the writing of other writers. I imagine such conjunctions express my relation to an Emerson text less as an object of interpretation than as a means of interpretation, as I have sometimes put the matter, and the one because of the other. I suppose this is one way of taking a serious writer seriously.

I have sometimes been told, by prominent readers of Emerson whom I respect and have learned from, that the Emerson portrayed in the way I write about him cannot be the drastically famous man who is read and treasured, or deplored, so variously, by generations of Americans. In no case that I am aware of has this charge been accompanied by claiming to find that something I have said is false to Emerson's words. The matter is worse than that. The idea is, rather (as was at least once, in public discussion, made explicit to me), that if what I say about Emerson is true of him, almost no one could, or could seem to, understand him—at least without doing little else in any given day except read him.

I am grateful for discussions of such a response with two colleagues of mine celebrated for their work on the high tradition of American intellectuality and literary ambition. In a graduate seminar I offered jointly with Sacvan Bercovitch on Emerson some years ago, issues of the tension between the historical and the philosophical Emerson kept arising, mostly at our invitation but sometimes to our dismay. Illuminating as these issues promised to be, and much as we sought resolutions, we kept discovering the historical and the philosophical registers to outstrip each other, to assert one interest at the expense of the other. Then, recently, an extended exchange with Lawrence Buell about the chapter on Emerson's philosophizing in Buell's important recent book *Emerson*, which situates Emerson in the many roles he plays in American cultural life and in the wider contexts in which he places that life, has forcibly reminded me of how little unequivocal progress I have made in finding my way in the various conflicting contexts in which Emerson functioned. I have not given up on myself here, although it may be that I am hampered by too unyielding, or too small, a circle of ideas here, taking it that Emerson's lasting historical importance, even the waxing and waning of his fame, would not exist without the power of his thinking; and at the same time that that fame, in his own country (where alone he has achieved lasting fame, something beyond the testimony of individual great admirers elsewhere), is granted at the expense of stinting the acknowledgment of that power. Something unnerving to me about the condescension characteristically shown Emerson, understood as the expression of a doubt of America (voiced not alone by Emerson) about the promised originality of its culture, is the sense that this disappointment is in league with America's terrible arrogance, as though it senses its aspirations to democracy are fated to be less appreciated than its failures of it.

It may be that what incites the exasperated response to my reading of Emerson's texts is a certain idea or picture of what kind of difficulty Emerson causes, perhaps an idea that something complicated should be figured out and made plain. I myself do not find that such a task is more frequently posed in Emerson than in the prose of any other serious writer. What seems to me signature in Emerson is the weight he puts on the obvious, where the difficulty is taking him at his word. A favorite instance of mine is his liking for the connection between something happening casually and something creating a casualty. He is, in effect, calling attention to a point that language is making for us on its surface, namely, that what we do casually, every day, unthinkingly, distractedly—the hierarchies we assume, the slights we deliver and suffer, our adaptations (Emerson calls it our conformity) to the unconscionable—are as permanent in their effects, as much matters of life and death, as are catastrophes.

The matter is not how much time you spend with an Emerson text but—given for some reason, some odd day, a stunning encounter with a moment of such a text—what it is you expect of it. It is true that Emerson, in expecting to be understood, and misunderstood, gives plenty of satisfactions for unsublime, even routine expectations. But this is an obligation of any writer who takes on, perhaps beyond her or his will, certain, let's call them scriptural tasks. I might describe writing of this kind as struggling to keep its moral urgency, in principle evident in every word, fit for polite company, say tactful, recognizing that the urgencies of life, of sanity and derangement, are shared by all but are not open to discussion at announced or predictable times, that philosophy is not for every mood, that our separateness, our lack of synchrony in our concerns, is to be accepted, not just accepted but honored. This is as true, however different in appearance and knack, of Wittgenstein's *Philosophical Investigations* as it is of Emerson's most inexhaustible essays. A tendency (if that is what it is) of my writing on Emerson's texts—about which I remain unapologetic—is that of judging the reach of a difficult reading, resisting the flow of the writing, by testing it against what I make of what Thoreau and Nietzsche have made of Emerson's achievement, oftener, I guess, than I show. One effect, or intention, of this tendency is to underscore the mysteriousness of Emerson's knack in making his manner available to public occasion.

A fixed picture of Emerson's difficulty helps settle for, I would say, a more settled Emerson (who claims for himself that he would unsettle all things, meaning first, all settlers) than I perceive to be necessary. My sense, further, is that this fixed view is sustained by framing Emerson as essentially a forerunner of pragmatism. No one can sensibly deny that Emerson was a muse of pragmatism. But to my mind the assimilation of Emerson to pragmatism unfailingly blunts the particularity, the achievement, of Emerson's language, in this sense precisely shuns the struggle for philosophy—for, I might say, the right to philosophize, to reconceive reason—that Emerson sought to bequeath. Old and new friends have recently been urging upon me that their interest in the relation between Emerson and, say, Dewey, is not to assert Emerson as a "proto"-pragmatist but in effect to rediscover Dewey's textual debt to Emerson's, let's say, transcendentalism. This strikes me as an unequivocally interesting and promising turn of events.

It is internal to what Emerson is and remarkably remains for American culture that someone, unknown to me, has undertaken to distribute each day by e-mail, to anyone asking to be kept on his/her list, a citation from Emerson's *Journals*. I find it an agreeable way to relate to that monumental achievement. (I may be affected here by how much I enjoy being read to, or played music for, which is a reason I like listening to music on a decent concert or jazz radio station rather than, except as it were for business, choosing and playing recordings to myself.) The other day the citation was the following, from the journal entry for August 18, 1831 (still early in the game): "The sun shines and warms and lights us and we have no curiosity to know why this is so; but we ask the reason of all evil, of pain, and hunger, and musquitoes and silly people." I do not imagine that this observation will ever become a favorite touchstone of mine, but, though early, it is recognizably Emerson, and seeing it I at once had the thought: "Does this sound like pragmatism? It negates pragmatism." On second thought, it might be pragmatist to consider that what philosophy and theology have hitherto called "the problem of evil" and taken to be a metaphysical question concerning the nature of God should be put aside in favor of taking measures to discern the causes of human misery and putting this exercise of intelligence into the service of eradicating or mitigating

them. Is there a third thought, something like the question "What problem does the shining and warming and lighting of the sun pose that intelligence should solve?" The suggestion that this is a serious question again
would negate pragmatism. Or are these words of Emerson's merely a fancy
way of saying that our capacities for complaint outstrip our talent for
praise—a certain indication of the justice in the familiar charge against
Emerson that he lacks a tragic sense of life?

But suppose that Emerson's phrase "curiosity to know," in this context, is an ironic dig at philosophy's idea of knowledge, in the line of romanticism's questioning of the idea, though now questioning it from
within philosophy. In the many times I have heard cited the tag "Philosophy begins in wonder," the wonder in question, it is implied, is a state to
be satisfied by an explanation, one necessarily subject to confirmation by
the agreement of others, as if wonder were inherently (what we call) scientific, as it seems to be in Bacon's speaking of wonder as "the seed of knowledge." But Emerson's proposal to know why the sun shines and warms and
lights takes wonder, of the kind that will call for philosophy, precisely not
as curiosity but as, let's say, admiration—perhaps you could think of it as a
meta-curiosity. Wittgenstein registers this in one of the famous late lines
from his *Tractatus*: "Not *how* the world is, but *that* it is, is the mystical."
Why the sun rises has a scientific answer; part of the answer might be that
it does not rise. Why it rises (or the earth turns) every day is not a further
scientific question. But that for us the sun rises every day has been a source
not only of philosophical myth (as in Plato) or of epistemological puzzle
(as in Hume) but of something we might call philosophical wonder.

Thoreau was interested that dawn does not, or should not, wake us
just as it wakes birds; that what is early and what is late, what is appropri-
ate for night and what for day, origins and ends, are for us to measure;
that, perhaps one could say, the natural history of the human essentially
contains the unnatural, contests itself. Emerson records this one way in
saying that "The virtue in most request is conformity. Self-reliance is its
aversion." Since Emerson also speaks of our living always with an unattained but attainable self, I understand him to mean that to have a self is
always to be averse to one's attained self (in one's so far attained society);
put otherwise, to conform to the self is to relinquish it. Here, as is not un-
usual with me, an old and continuing respect for John Dewey prompts me
to ask how Emerson's "intellect," an essential predicate of which is that it
"dissolves," compares with Dewey's "intelligence," which is said to solve

problems arising in situations of decision, where a characteristically Deweyan criterion of intelligence is to demand an Aristotelian/Hegelian moment of choosing between extremes, say between hesitancy and precipitancy, between becoming an aesthete and becoming unfeeling, between whim and over-intellectuality, between conformity and eccentricity, between subservience and violence, an intellectual gesture that came to leave me feeling empty-handed, abstracted from thinking, however much I was being promised concreteness.

I can imagine that someone will suggest that Emerson's idea of dissolving also means capturing the need for a middle way. Emerson characterizes thinking as requiring (in a pair of his main predicates of human thinking in "The American Scholar"), conversion or transfiguration (the other main predicate is partialness). There is no middle way between, say, self-reliance and self- (or other-) conformity. What calls for thinking in Emerson occurs before—or as—our life of perplexities and aspirations and depressions and desperations and manifestations of destiny resolve themselves into practical problems. Singled out by a choice between subservience and violence (as, to take a high instance, in the face of the passage of the Fugitive Slave Law), one finds Emerson proposing, or provoking us to, a task of tracing and transfiguring, reconceiving, the everyday threads that have unnoticeably wound together our present forms of subservience and of violence.

The new emphasis I mentioned manifested in recent efforts to trace Emerson's textual influence on Dewey should serve as a welcome corrective to my earlier impatient and repeated claim that although Dewey admired and praised Emerson, he could make no use of him textually, that is, in the actual detailed work of philosophizing. If I regret the still prevalent attempted assimilations of transcendentalism into pragmatism, and do what I can to maintain their differences, it is not with the aim of choosing between them. What good, or wisdom, would prompt me to choose between serving the unconscionable and serving the impractical and the unintelligent?

Thinking of Emerson

For a program arranged by the Division on Philosophical Approaches to Literature at the annual convention of the Modern Language Association in New York, December 1978, Professor Leo Marx organized and chaired a meeting on Emerson whose panelists were asked to respond to the following passage from my book The Senses of Walden*:*

Study of *Walden* would perhaps not have become such an obsession with me had it not presented itself as a response to questions with which I was already obsessed: Why has America never expressed itself philosophically? Or has it—in the metaphysical riot of its greatest literature? Has the impulse to philosophical speculation been absorbed, or exhausted, by speculation in territory, as in such thoughts as Manifest Destiny? Or are such questions not really intelligible? They are, at any rate, disturbingly like the questions that were asked about American literature before it established itself. In rereading *Walden*, twenty years after first reading it, I seemed to find a book of sufficient intellectual scope and consistency to have established or inspired a tradition of thinking.[1]

My response was the following essay, not quite all of which was read at the meeting. I am grateful to Leo Marx for prompting me to go further with these thoughts and to Jay Cantor for reading the original draft and pressing me for certain clarifications. A conversation with John McNees was decisive for me in arriving at certain formulations about philosophical prose in relation to the idea of dialogue and hence to an idea of thinking. I should in this regard also like to refer to an essay by Morse Peckham which appears as the introduction to a facsimile edition of the first printing of Emerson's Essays *and* Essays: Second Series.² *I dedicate the present essay to the members, in the fall of 1978, of a graduate seminar at Harvard on the later writings of Heidegger.*

Thinking of Emerson, I can understand my book on *Walden* as something of an embarrassment, but something of an encouragement as well, since if what it suggests about the lack of a tradition of thinking in America is right—for example, about how Emerson and Thoreau deaden one another's words—then my concentration on understanding Thoreau was bound to leave Emerson out. He kept sounding to me like second-hand Thoreau.

The most significant shortcoming among the places my book mentions Emerson is its accusing him of "misconceiving" Kant's critical enterprise, comparing Emerson unfavorably in this regard with Thoreau. I had been impressed by Thoreau's sentence running "The universe constantly and obediently answers to our conceptions" as being in effect an elegant summary of the *Critique of Pure Reason.* When I requote that sentence later in the book, I take it beyond its Kantian precincts, adding that the universe answers whether our conceptions are mean or magnanimous, scientific or magical, faithful or treacherous, thus suggesting that there are more ways of making a habitable world or more layers to it than Kant's twelve concepts of the understanding accommodate. But I make no effort to justify this idea of a "world" beyond claiming implicitly that as I used the word I was making sense. The idea is roughly that moods must be taken as having at least as sound a role in advising us of reality as sense experience has; that, for example, coloring the world, attributing to it the qualities "mean" or "magnanimous," may be no less objective or subjective than coloring an apple, attributing to it the colors red or green. Or perhaps we should say: sense experience is to objects what moods are to the world. The only philosopher I knew who had made an effort to formulate a kind of epistemology of moods, to find their revelations of what we call "the world" as sure as the revelations of what we call "understanding," was the Heidegger of *Being and Time.* But it was hard to claim support there without committing oneself to more machinery than one had any business for.

Now I see that I might, even ought to, have seen Emerson ahead of me, since, for example, his essay "Experience" is about the epistemology, or say the logic, of moods. I understand the moral of that essay as being contained in its late, prayerful remark, "But far be from me the despair which prejudges the law by a paltry empiricism." That is, what is wrong with empiricism is not its reliance on experience but its paltry idea of experience. (This is the kind of criticism of classical empiricism leveled by John Dewey—for example, in "An Empirical Survey of Empiricisms"—who praised Emerson but so far as I know never took him up philosophically.) But I hear Kant working throughout Emerson's essay "Experience," with his formulation of the question "Is metaphysics possible?" and his line of answer: Genuine knowledge of (what we call) the world is for us, but it cannot extend beyond (what we call) experience. To which I take Emerson to be replying: Well and good, but then you had better be very careful what it is you understand by experience, for that might be limited in advance by the conceptual limitations you impose upon it, limited by what we know of human existence, that is, by our limited experience of it. When, for example, you get around to telling us what we may hope for, I must know that you have experienced hope, or else I will surmise that you have not, which is to say precisely that your experience is of despair.

Emerson's "Experience" even contains a little argument, a little more explicitly with Kant, about the nature of experience in relation to, or revelation of, the natural world. "The secret of the illusoriness [of life] is in the necessity of a succession of moods or objects. Gladly we would anchor, but the anchorage is quicksand. This onward trick of nature is too strong for us: *Pero si muove.*"[3] In the section of the *Critique of Pure Reason* entitled "Analogies of Experience," one of the last before turning to an investigation of transcendental illusion, Kant is at pains to distinguish within experience the "*subjective succession* of apprehension from the *objective succession* of appearances." The anchor he uses to keep subjectivity and objectivity from sinking one another is, as you would expect, gripped in transcendental ground, which is always, for Kant, a question of locating necessity properly, in this case the necessity, or rules, of succession in experience. (It is curious, speaking of anchoring, that one of Kant's two examples in this specific regard is that of seeing a ship move downstream.) The acceptance of Galileo's—and Western science's—chilling crisis with the Church over the motion of the earth recalls Kant's claim to have accomplished a Copernican Revolution in metaphysics; that is, understanding the configurations of the world as a function of the configurations or conditions of our own nature. Now I construe Emerson's implicit argument in the passage cited as follows. The succession of moods is not tractable by the distinction between subjectivity and objectivity Kant proposes for experience. *This* onward trick of nature is too much for us; the given bases of the self are quicksand. The fact that we are taken over by this succession, this onward-ness, means that you can think of it as at once a succession of moods (in-ner matters) and a succession of objects (outer matters). This very evanes-cence of the world proves its existence to me; it *is* what vanishes from me. I guess this is not realism exactly; but it is not solipsism either.

I believe Emerson may encourage the idea of himself as a solipsist or subjectivist, for example, in such a remark, late in the same essay, as "Thus inevitably does the universe wear our color." But whether you take this to be subjective or objective depends upon whether you take the successive colors or moods of the universe to be subjective or objective. My claim is that Emerson is out to destroy the ground on which such a problem takes itself seriously, I mean interprets itself as a metaphysical fixture. The uni-verse is as separate from me, but as intimately part of me, as one on whose behalf I contest, and who therefore bears the color I wear. We are in a state of "romance" with the universe (to use a word from the last sentence of the essay); we do not possess it, but our life is to return to it, to respond to its contesting for my attention, in ever-widening circles, "onward and on-ward," but with as directed a goal as any quest can have; in the present case, until "the soul attains her due sphericity." Until then, encircled, strait-ened, you can say the soul is solipsistic; surely it is, to use another critical term of Emerson's, partial. This no doubt implies that we do not have a universe as it is in itself. But this implication is nothing: we do not have selves in themselves either. The universe *is* what constantly and obediently answers to our conceptions. It is what *can* be all the ways we know it to be, which is to say, all the ways we can be. In "Circles" we are told: "Whilst the eternal generation of circles proceeds, the eternal generator abides. That central life . . . contains all its circles." The universe contains all the colors it wears. That it can wear no more than I can give is a fact of what Emer-son calls my poverty.

The Kantian ring of the idea of the universe as inevitably wearing our color implies that the way specifically Kant understands the generation of the universe keeps it solipsistic, still something partial, something of our, of my, making. Emerson's most explicit reversal of Kant lies in his picturing the intellectual hemisphere of knowledge as passive or receptive and the in-tuitive or instinctual hemisphere as active or spontaneous. Whereas for Kant the basis of the *Critique of Pure Reason* is that "concepts are based on the spontaneity of thought, sensible intuitions on the receptivity of impres-sions." Briefly, there is no intellectual intuition. I will come back to this.

But immediately, to imagine that Emerson could challenge the basis of the argument of the *Critique of Pure Reason*, I would have to imagine him to be a philosopher—would I not? I would have, that is to say, to imagine his writing—to take it—in such a way that it does not misconceive Kant but undertakes to engage him in dispute. I like what Matthew Arnold has to say about Emerson, but we ought no longer to be as sure as Arnold was that the great philosophical writer is one who builds a system; hence that Emerson is not such a writer on the ground that he was not such a builder. We are by now too aware of the philosophical *attacks* on system or theory to place the emphasis in defining philosophy on a product of philosophy rather than on the process of philosophizing. We are more prepared to understand as philosophy a mode of thought that undertakes to bring philosophy to an end, as, say, Nietzsche and Wittgenstein attempt to do, not to mention, in their various ways, Bacon, Montaigne, Descartes, Pascal, Marx, Kierkegaard, Carnap, Heidegger, or Austin, and in certain respects Kant and Hegel. Ending philosophy looks to be a commitment of each of the major modern philosophers, so it is hardly to be wondered at that some of them do not quite know whether what they are writing is philosophy. Wittgenstein said that what he did replaced philosophy. Heidegger said in his later period that what he was doing was thinking, or learning thinking, and that philosophy is the greatest enemy of true thinking. But to understand the attack on philosophy as itself philosophy, or undertaken in the name, or rather in the place, of philosophy, we must of course understand the attack as nevertheless internal to the act of philosophizing, accepting that autonomy. Church and State and the Academy and Poetry and the City may each suppress philosophy, but they cannot, without its complicity, replace it.

Can Emerson be understood as wishing to replace philosophy? But isn't that wish really what accounts for the poignancy, or dialectic, of Emerson's call, the year Thoreau graduated from college, not for a thinker but for Man Thinking? The American Scholar is to think no longer partially, as a man following a task delegated by a society of which he is a victim, but as leading a life in which thinking is of the essence, as a man whose wholeness, say whose autonomy, is in command of the autonomy of thinking. The hitch of course is that there is no such human being. "Man in history, men in the world today are bugs, spawn." But the catch is that we aspire to this man, to the metamorphosis, to the human—hence that we can be guided and raised by the cheer of thinking. In claiming the office of the scholar "to cheer, to raise, and to guide men" as well as demanding that "whatsoever new verdict Reason from her inviolable seat pronounces on the passing men and events of today,—this [the scholar] shall hear and promulgate," Emerson evidently requires the replacing of theology as well as of philosophy in his kind of building, his edification. We might think of this as internalizing the unending quarrel between philosophy and theology.

Whatever ways I go on to develop such thoughts are bound to be affected by the coincidence that during the months in which I was trying to get Emerson's tune into my ear, free of Thoreau's, I was also beginning to study the writing of the later Heidegger. This study was precipitated at last by a footnote of the editor of a collection of Heidegger essays, in which *The Senses of Walden* is described as in part forming an explication of Heidegger's notion of poetic dwelling.[4] Having now read such an essay of Heidegger's as "Building Dwelling Thinking," I am sufficiently startled by the similarities to find the differences of interest and to start wondering about an account of both. I am thinking not so much of my similarities with Heidegger (I had, after all, profited from *Being and Time*, and it may be that that book leads more naturally to Heidegger's later work than is, I gather, sometimes supposed) but of Heidegger's with Thoreau, at least with my picture of Thoreau. The relation to Emerson was still unexpected, and hence even more startling. The title of the Heidegger collection I referred to is from a sentence of his that says: "For questioning is the piety of thinking." In the right mood, if you lay beside this a sentence of Emerson's from "Intellect" that says "Always our thinking is a pious reception,"[5] you might well pause a moment. And if one starts digging to test how deep the connection might run, I find that one can become quite alarmed.

The principal text of Heidegger's to test here is translated as *What Is Called Thinking?* Here is a work that can be said to internalize the quarrel between philosophy and theology, that calls for a new existence from the human in relation to Being in order that its task of thinking be accomplished, a work based on the poignancy, or dialectic, of thinking about our having not yet learned true thinking, thinking as the receiving or letting be of something, as opposed to the positing or putting together of something, as this is pictured most systematically in Kant's ideas of representation and synthesis and most radically in Nietzsche's will to power, that attempts to stay clear of Kant's subjectivity and of the revenge upon time that Nietzsche understood us as taking. A climactic moment in Heidegger's descent into the origins of words is his understanding of the etymological entwining of thinking with the word for thanking, leading, for example, to an unfolding of ideas in which a certain progress of thinking is understood as a form of thanking, and originally a thanking for the gift of thinking, which means for the reception of being human. Here, if one can consider this to be something like philosophy, is something like a philosophical site within which to explore the crux in our relation to Emerson of his power of affirmation, or of his weakness for it.

We have surely known, at least since Newton Arvin collected the chorus of charges against Emerson to the effect that he lacked a knowledge of evil or of the sense of the tragic, that this missed Emerson's drift, that his task was elsewhere. Arvin insists, appropriately, that what Emerson gives us, what inspires us in him, "when we have cleared our minds of the cant of pessimism, is perhaps the fullest and most authentic expression in modern literature of the more-than-tragic emotion of thankfulness."[6] But we might have surmised from Nietzsche's love of Emerson that no sane or mere man could have convincingly conceived "all things [to be] friendly and sacred, all events holy, all men divine" who was not aware that we may be undone by the pain of the world we make and may not make again. The more recent cant of pleasure or playfulness is no less hard to put up with. Yet a more-than-tragic emotion of thankfulness is still not the drift, or not the point. The point is the achievement not of affirmation but of what Emerson calls "the sacred affirmative," the thing Nietzsche calls "the sacred Yes,"[7] the heart for a new creation. This is not an effort to move beyond tragedy but to move beyond nihilism, or beyond the curse of the charge of human depravity and its consequent condemnation of us to despair; a charge which is itself, Emerson in effect declares, the only depravity.

(I may interject here that the idea of thinking as reception, which began this path of reasoning, seems to me to be a sound intuition, specifically, to forward the correct answer to skepticism [which Emerson meant it to do]. The answer does not consist in denying the conclusion of skepticism but in reconceiving its truth. It is true that we do not know the existence of the world with certainty; our relation to its existence is deeper— one in which it is accepted, that is to say, received. My favorite way of putting this is to say that existence is to be acknowledged.[8])

So the similarity of Emerson to Heidegger can be seen as mediated by Nietzsche, and this will raise more questions than it can answer. As to the question of what may look like the direction of influence, I am not claiming that Heidegger authenticates the thinking of Emerson and

Thoreau; the contrary is, for me, fully as true, that Emerson and Thoreau may authorize our interest in Heidegger. Then further questions will concern the relation of the thinking of each of these writers to their respective traditions of poetry. To the figure of Hölderlin, Heidegger is indebted not only for lessons of thought but for lessons in reading, and I suppose for the lesson that these are not different, or rather that there is ground upon which thinking and reading and philosophy and poetry meet and part. Emerson's implication in the history of the major line of American poetry is something that Harold Bloom has most concretely and I dare say most unforgettably given to us to think through. Emerson's and Thoreau's relation to poetry is inherently their interest in their own writing; they are their own Hölderlins. I do not mean their interest in what we may call their poems, but their interest in the fact that what they are building is writing, that their writing is, as it realizes itself daily under their hands, sentence by shunning sentence, the accomplishment of inhabitation, the making of it happen, the poetry of it. Their prose is a battle, using a remark of Nietzsche's, not to become poetry—a battle specifically to remain in conversation with itself, answerable to itself. (So they do write dialogues, and not monologues, after all.)

Such writing takes the same mode of relating to itself as reading and thinking do, the mode of the self's relation to itself, call it self-reliance. Then whatever is required in possessing a self will be required in thinking and reading and writing. This possessing is not—it is the reverse of—possessive; I have implied that in being an act of creation, it is the exercise not of power but of reception. Then the question is: On what terms is the self received?

The answer I give for Emerson here is a theme of his thinking that further aligns it with the later Heidegger's, the thing Emerson calls "onward thinking," the thing Heidegger means in taking thinking to be a matter essentially of getting ourselves "on the way."

At the beginning of "Circles" Emerson tells us he means (having already deduced one moral in considering the circular or compensatory character of every human action) to trace a further analogy (or read a further sense, or deduce a further moral) from the emblem of the form of a circle. Since the time of "The American Scholar" he has told us that "science is nothing but the finding of analogy," and this seems a fair enough idea of thinking. In "Circles" he invites us to think about the fact, or what the fact symbolizes, that every action admits of being outdone, that around every circle another circle can take its place. I should like to extend the invitation to think about how he pictures us as moving from one circle to another, something he sometimes thinks of as expanding, sometimes as rising. I note that there is an ambiguity in his thoughts here between what he calls the *generating* and what he calls the *drawing* of the new circle, an ambiguity between the picturing of new circles as forming continuously or discontinuously. I will not try to resolve this ambiguity now, but I will take it that the essential way of envisioning our growth, from the inside, is discontinuous.

Then my questions are: How does Emerson picture us as crossing, or rather leaping, the span from one circumference to another? What is the motive, the means of motion, of this movement? How do we go on? (In Wittgenstein's *Philosophical Investigations*, knowing how to go on, as well as knowing when to stop, is exactly the measure of our knowing, or learning, in certain of its main regions or modes—for example, in the knowledge we have of our words. Onward thinking,[9] on the way, knowing how to go on,[10] are of course inflections or images of the religious idea of The Way, inflections which specifically deny that there is a place at which our ways end. Were philosophy to concede such a place, one knowable in advance of its setting out, philosophy would cede its own autonomy.)

You may imagine the answer to the question of how we move as having to do with power. But power seems to be the result of rising, not its cause. ("Every new prospect is power.") I take Emerson's answer to be what he means by abandonment. The idea of abandonment contains what the preacher in Emerson calls enthusiasm, or the New Englander in him calls forgetting ourselves, together with what he calls leaving or relief or quitting or release or shunning or allowing or deliverance, which is freedom as in "Leave your theory as Joseph his coat in the hand of the harlot, and flee"), together further with something he means by trusting or suffering (as in the image of the traveler—the conscious intellect, the intellect alone—"who has lost his way, [throwing] his reins on the horse's neck, and [trusting] to the instinct of the animal to find his road"). (Perhaps it helps if you think, as he goes on to say, that what carries us through this world is a divine animal. To spell it out, the human is the rational divine animal. It's a thought—one, by the way, which Heidegger would deny.)

This idea of abandonment gives us a way to grasp the act Emerson pictures as "[writing] on the lintels of the door-post, *Whim.*" He says he would do this after he has said that he shuns father and mother and wife and brother when his genius calls him, and he follows it by expressing the hope that it is somewhat better than whim at last.[11] (Something has happened; it is up to us to name it, or not to. Something is wrestling us for our blessing.) Whether his writing on the lintels of the door-post—his writing as such, I gather—is thought of as having the constancy of the contents of a mezuzah or the emergency of the Passover blood, either way he is taking upon himself the mark of God, and of departure. His perception of the moment is taken in hope, as something to be proven only on the way, *by* the way. This departure, such setting out, is, in our poverty, what hope consists in, all there is to hope for; it is the abandoning of despair, which is otherwise our condition. (Quiet desperation, Thoreau will call it; Emerson had said, silent melancholy.[12]) Hence he may speak of perception as "not Whimsical, but fatal," preeminently, here, the perception of what we may call whim. Our fatality, the determination of our fate, of whether we may hope, goes by our marking the path of whim. We hope it is better than whim at last, as we hope we may at last seem something better than blasphemers; but it is our poverty not to be final but always to be leaving (abandoning whatever we have and have known): to be initial, medial, American. What the ground of the fixated conflict between solipsism and realism should give way to—or between subjectivity and objectivity, or the private and the public, or the inner and the outer—is the task of onwardness. In Heidegger: "The *thanc* means man's inmost mind, the heart, the heart's core, that innermost essence of man which reaches outward most fully and to the outermost limits."[13] In Emerson: "To believe your own thought, to believe that what is true for you in your private heart, is true for all men,—that is genius. Speak your latent conviction, and it shall be the universal sense; for always the inmost becomes the outmost."[14] The substantive disagreement with Heidegger, shared by Emerson and Thoreau, is that the achievement of the human requires not inhabitation and settlement but abandonment, leaving. Then everything depends upon your realization of abandonment. For the significance of leaving lies in its discovery that you have settled something, that you have felt enthusiastically what there is to abandon yourself to, that you can treat the others there are as those to whom the inhabitation of the world can now be left.

2

An Emerson Mood

Accepting an honor, a happy public assessment of one's work, grants one a particular opportunity for self-assessment, a moment of perspective from within which to judge not so much the worth of the work as the direction of it, whether it is on the track. In seeking this perspective, in the course of thinking how I might respond in this Scholar's Day address to the honor of the invitation to deliver it, I found myself recurring to the most famous address, and I suppose the best, ever given by an American thinker on a scholar's day, I mean Emerson's "The American Scholar," delivered at Harvard the year Thoreau graduated there, a hundred and forty-two summers ago. Apparently I would like to assess my direction from those high thoughts. Surely this is reasonable, since Emerson and Thoreau may be taken to be philosophers of direction, orienters, tirelessly prompting us to be on our way, endlessly asking us where we stand, what it is we face. Two passages from Emerson especially came to my mind in terms of which, it seemed to me, I might look at all the writing and the teaching I have done until now. The first is from "The American Scholar" (1837):

I ask not for the great, the remote, the romantic; what is doing in Italy or Arabia; what is Greek art, or Provencal minstrelsy; I embrace the common, I explore and sit at the feet of the familiar, the low. Give me insight into today, and you may have the antique and future worlds. What would we really know the meaning of? The meal in the firkin; the milk in the pan; the ballad in the street; the news of the boat; the glance of the eye; the form and the gait of the body; show me the ultimate reason of these matters; show me the sublime presence of the highest spiritual cause lurking, as always it does lurk, in these suburbs and extremities of nature; . . . —and the world lies no longer a dull miscellany and lumber-room, but has form and order; there is no trifle, there is no puzzle, but one design unites and animates the farthest pinnacle and the lowest trench.

The second is from the book that began his reputation, *Nature*, published the year before:

Give me health and a day, and I will make the pomp of emperors ridiculous. The dawn is my Assyria; the sunset and moonrise my Paphos, and unimaginable realms of faerie; broad noon shall be my England of the senses and the understanding; the night shall be my Germany of mystic philosophy and dreams.

Something Emerson means by the common, the familiar, and the low is something I have meant, from the beginning to the end of the work I have so far accomplished, in my various defenses of proceeding in philosophy from ordinary language, from words of everyday life. In practice this has often meant, especially in the first decade of my writing, defending the procedures and certain of the views—even, I think, certain of the instincts—in the works of J. L. Austin of Oxford and in Wittgenstein's *Philosophical Investigations*, which really means attempting to inherit those writings.[1] They remain for me the guiding sources of, at a minimum, what is still known as ordinary language philosophy.

Along with any such inheritance one is likely to inherit intellectual competitors, together with a few guiding obsessions, or investments. I suppose the dominant obsession shared by Austin and Wittgenstein was to provide an answer to skepticism, both with respect to whether we can know that a world of things exists at all and whether we can know that there are other minds, creatures who share our capacities of consciousness, who are aware of us as we are of them. I had, it is true, already inherited this obsession from the teaching of C. I. Lewis at Harvard and, if I may say so, from Kant (from whom Lewis, and, indirectly, Wittgenstein, had themselves inherited it). But I suppose one inherits in philosophy only what one must recognize as one's own.

Austin's habit of answer was to show, in untiring detail, and in case after case, that philosophers who say things such as that "We do not know with certainty that there are things like tables and chairs because we do not really or literally see them but only see appearances or parts of them" are *not* properly using the words *parts* or *appearances* or *only* or *see* or *literally* or *things* or *know* or *certainty* or *really*. If "not properly using" means "not using these words in their ordinary contexts," Austin is perfectly right, and he achieved some dazzling and permanent results in his way of detailing what the ordinary contexts of words are, and systematizing these into several new subjects (e.g., those of speech acts and of excuses). This achievement should make us wonder why this detailing of our lives is something we have to be *made* to do, why it is hard to do.

But as a set of criticisms of philosophy, Austin's results are left quite up in the air; it is not clear that they need matter to a differently inspired philosopher. When Descartes, in his second *Meditation*, takes his famous bit of wax as an example of our knowledge of bodies, one of the results or morals of his investigation is the warning that "words impede me, and I am nearly deceived by the terms of ordinary language. For we say we see the same wax if it is present," whereas Descartes takes himself to have just now proven that we do not. And Descartes can be as convincing as Austin can be. Wittgenstein, satisfyingly, is at pains to work below this impasse. But his writing is sometimes obscure, and he has left his critics—yet so has Austin, who is clearer—with the impression that he writes in support of our ordinary beliefs about the world, our common sense of the world, and hence that he is anti-intellectual, or anyway anti-scientific. What is true is that Wittgenstein is opposed to the effort to make philosophy into science, or into anything else; he insists on the autonomy of philosophy, while at the same time he seeks, as he puts it, to replace philosophy.

As to the prior idea, that of Wittgenstein's defending ordinary beliefs, while this is a significantly wrong idea, it is hard to say what is wrong with it. I think it takes Wittgenstein's whole philosophy, at least, to say what is wrong with it, which really amounts to presenting the right alternative. Even if an ordinary language philosopher could convince a differently inspired philosopher, or an ordinary human being, that it is not quite right to say that we *believe* the world exists (though certainly we should not conclude that we do *not* believe this, that we *fail* to believe that it exists), and wrong even to say we *know* it exists (while of course it is equally wrong to say we fail to know this), he or she would have a hard time saying what it is right to say here, what truly expresses our convictions in the matter. I think this is a genuine, a fruitful, perplexity. What the ordinary language philosopher is feeling—but I mean to speak just for myself in this—is that our relation to the world's existence is somehow closer than the ideas of believing and knowing are made to convey. If a philosopher says, rather than speaking of our beliefs, that he is examining the meaning or the uses of our words, or investigating our concepts, these descriptions are none too clear themselves, and not clearly more accurate. What still wants expression is a sense that my relation to the existence of the world, or to my existence in the world, is not given in words but in silence. (This would not be a matter of keeping your mouth shut but of understanding when, and how, not to yield to the temptation to say what you do not or cannot exactly mean.)

While I find that this sense of intimacy with existence, or intimacy lost, is fundamental to the experience of what I understand ordinary language philosophy to be, I am for myself convinced that the thinkers who convey this experience best, most directly, and most practically are not such as Austin and Wittgenstein but such as Emerson and Thoreau. This sense of my natural relation to existence is what Thoreau means by our being *next* to the laws of nature, by our *neighboring* the world, by our being *beside* ourselves. Emerson's idea of the *near* is one of the inflections he gives to the common, the low.[2]

An emphasis on the ordinariness of human speech, as opposed to technicalities, whether of science or of logic or of any system of metaphysics, is a recurrent one in philosophy. It is something to see in Socrates, at the beginning of philosophy, and in the Northern reformers and the Renaissance Italian Humanists, and in the crises of philosophy throughout the present century. The confrontation of skepticism provides a way of grasping why this emphasis on the ordinary keeps on recurring. Speaking of ordinary or everyday language as *natural* language expresses something we would like to understand as, I might say, a natural relation to nature. It is this relation from which the skeptic's doubts distance us, so that his dissatisfaction in replacing this natural relation with a construction of certainty after the fact is so far a correct dissatisfaction. The recurrent appeal to ordinary or natural language in the history of philosophy is the sign that there is some inner wish of philosophy to escape as well as to recover the natural. I have put this elsewhere by saying that the appeal to ordinary language is an attempt to return the human being to the language of philosophy, as though philosophy were recurrently in danger of banishing it. But I have then gone on to acknowledge that the denial of the human, the wish to escape the conditions of humanity, call them conditions of finitude, is itself only human.[3]

By "embracing the common," by "sitting at the feet of the low," Emerson surely takes his stand on the side of what philosophers such as Berke-

ley and Hume would have called the vulgar. Unlike a certain line of
thinkers from Plato through Nietzsche to Heidegger, for whom real thinking requires spiritual aristocracy, those English writers will not depart from
and disdain the life of the vulgar altogether. It is internal to their philosophical ambitions to reconcile their philosophical discoveries with the
views of the vulgar, as Berkeley does when, for example, he says that his denial of the real existence of bodies, or corporeal substance, does not deny
the existence and reality of timber, stone, mountains, rivers, when taken *in
the vulgar sense* or *in the vulgar acceptation,* phrases he italicizes. His direct
opponent is rather, as Hume's is, the reputedly sophisticated philosopher.
Like Descartes they appeal to uncorrupted human understanding over the
head of established philosophy.

But Emerson goes rather beyond these reconciliations and alliances.
By "sitting at the feet" of the familiar and the low, this student of Eastern
philosophy must mean that he takes the familiar and the low to be his
study, his guide, his guru: as much his point of arrival as of departure. In
this he joins his thinking with the new poetry and art of his times, whose
topics he characterizes as "the literature of the poor, the feelings of the
child, the philosophy of the street, the meaning of household life." He calls
this "a great stride," a sign of new vigor. I note that when he describes himself as asking "not for the great, the remote, the romantic," he is apparently
not considering that the emphasis on the low and the near is exactly the
opposite face of the romantic, the continued search for a new intimacy in
the self's relation to its world.

In speaking of the near and praising it as "richer than all foreign
parts," this American scholar is also calling upon American scholars to give
over their imitations of Europe, to stop turning away from their own inspiration, something which for Emerson is the same matter of our salvation
in the intellectual life as it is in the religious life. It is hard to imagine anything more offensive to our pride of intellectual cosmopolitanism than
such a call to nativism, or ethnocentrism. One cause of this offense, I
should guess, is that it says again that philosophy is not science, which is
the cosmopolitan, anyway international, means of communication. But a
complimentary cause is that it asks us to consider what it is native to us to
do, and what is native to philosophy, to thinking. When I ask whether we
may not understand Emerson and Thoreau as part of our inheritance as
philosophers, I am suggesting that our foreignness as philosophers to these
writers (and it is hard to imagine any writers more foreign to our currently

established philosophical sensibility) may itself be a sign of an impover-
ished idea of philosophy, of a remoteness from philosophy's origins, from
what is native to it, as if a certain constitution of the cosmopolitan might
merely consist in a kind of universal provincialism, a worldwide shrinking
of the spirit.

In the passage we have taken from "The American Scholar," Emerson says, "Give me insight into today, and you may have the antique and
future worlds." In *Nature* he had said, "Give me health and a day, and I
will make the pomp of emperors ridiculous." When I first read the ensuing
summary of how Emerson proposed (as Thoreau will put it in *Walden*) to
"make a day of it,"[4] that is, of his sum of days, how he determined what his
dawn and sunset and moonrise will constitute, but especially his saying
"broad noon shall be my England of the senses and the understanding; the
night shall be my Germany of mystic philosophy and dreams," I felt I had
at once a determination of the goal of my private life, the putting together
of day and night, of body and soul; and a determination of a task of philosophy, the placing in the same daily cycle of England and of Germany, a
task I felt the perspective of America made both possible and necessary.
Something like the healing of the rift between the English and the German
traditions of philosophy—or failing that, the witnessing of it—has also
been a motive of my writing from its earliest to its latest installments.
Then a question for me becomes why it took me so long to get my bearings in Emerson.

Before considering that question I remark a feature of Emerson's
writing that associates it in my mind with my involvement in the study of
film. His list in "The American Scholar" of the matters whose "ultimate
reason" he demands students to know—"The meal in the firkin; the milk
in the pan; the ballad in the street; the news of the boat; the glance of the
eye; the form and the gait of the body"—is a list epitomizing what we may
call the physiognomy of the ordinary, a form of what Kierkegaard calls the
perception of the sublime in the everyday. It is a list, made three or four
years before Daguerre would exhibit his copper plates in Paris, that epitomizes the obsessions of photography. I once remarked that Baudelaire, in
his praise of a painter of modern life, had a kind of premonition of film.[5]
Here I should like to add that without the mode of perception inspired in
Emerson (and Thoreau) by the everyday, the near, the low, the familiar,
one is bound to be blind to the poetry of film, to the sublimity of it. Naturally I should like to say that this would at the same time insure deafness

to some of the best poetry of philosophy—not its mythological flights, nor its beauty or purity of argumentation, but its power of exemplification, the world in a piece of wax. If I say that film has become my sunset and moonrise, "my Paphos, and unimaginable realms of faerie," then I must add that Thoreau had become, or returned, my dawn.

Then why did it take me from the time I first remember knowing of Emerson's yoking of day and night and of my sense of implication in his words until just over a year ago, some two decades later, to begin to looking actively at his work, to demand explicitly my inheritance of him? This is to ask how it happened that I came to feel ready to listen to him. My answer on the present occasion will be to speak less of myself than of Emerson's voice, and first of the voices of philosophy.

Philosophical thinking is not something that a normal human being can submit to all the time, or at any time he or she may choose. Philosophical questions—say as to whether we can know that God or the world or others exist, or why it is that something exists rather than nothing, or whether we can know that we are not now asleep and dreaming that we are awake, or whether ethical or aesthetic values have an objective basis, or whether mind and body are one thing or two things, or whether men and women are the same or different—are not questions that are alive for one at just any time. And as if in consequence, when they come alive they cannot be put aside as normal questions can be. They drift between the boring and the urgent, or between the remote and the immediate. One image of the unpredictability of the appearance of philosophy is that of Socrates on his way to the symposium, turned aside from normal human intercourse, entranced by the call of his genius to contemplation. Another image of the exclusiveness and the exhaustiveness of the attention philosophy requires is given in the second paragraph of Descartes's *Meditations*, where he speaks of having freed his mind of all kinds of cares: "I feel myself, fortunately, disturbed by no passions; and I have found a serene retreat in peaceful solitude." I should like to speak in this connection of the *mood* of philosophy, a frame of mind in which it is sought, or sought further.

Emerson may be said to be a philosopher of moods, and it is one wise with moods who observes that "Our moods do not believe in each other." Neither do our philosophies, or visions, which is why the ideal of a pluralism in philosophy, however well meant, is so often an empty hope, and neither do our nonphilosophical and our philosophical moods believe in each other. The images I have cited of the philosophical mood in

Socrates and in Descartes are images of isolation, of singling oneself, or being singled, out. And we know there is also such a thing as philosophical
dialogue. But then isn't *lecturing* about philosophy an extraordinary, even
bizarre, activity, neither a time of a solitude nor of conversation? If we agree
that it is bizarre, then do we know how *writing* philosophy is any the less
bizarre? These doubts may usefully raise the question of the audience of
philosophy, perhaps in the form of asking how philosophizing is to sound.

The idea of a mood to which philosophical thinking must bring us is
still not quite enough to describe my inability for so long to get on with
Emerson. His words did not merely strike me as partaking of a mood to
which they could not draw me, and hence remained empty to me. They
seemed to me repellent, quite as if presenting me with something for
which I could not acknowledge my craving. His difference from other
philosophical writing is, I think, that it asks the philosophical mood so
purely, so incessantly, giving one little other intellectual amusement or eloquence or information, little other argument or narrative, and no other
source of companionship or importance, either political or religious or
moral, save the importance of philosophy, of thinking itself.

I must take up again a favorite passage of mine from "Self-Reliance,"
composed a year or two later than "The American Scholar," which I take
to be a parable of his writing and hence of what he wants of his readers.
My earlier remarks about the passage have not, I have reason to believe,
been successful in conveying the sense that Emerson's writing will, from
the outside, seem vague and inflated, but from inside will acquire a terrible
exactness. The passage runs as follows:

The doctrine of hatred must be preached, as the counteraction of the doctrine of
love, when that pules and whines. I shun father and mother and wife and brother,
when my genius calls me. I would write on the lintels of the door-post, *Whim.* I
hope it is somewhat better than whim at last, but we cannot spend the day in explanation. Expect me not to show cause why I seek or why I exclude company.
Then again, do not tell me, as a good man did today, of my obligation to put all
poor men in good situations. Are they *my* poor? I tell thee, thou foolish philanthropist, that I grudge the dollar, the dime, the cent I give to such men as do not
belong to me and to whom I do not belong.

The general background of substitution could hardly be clearer.
What Jesus required of one who would follow him Emerson requires of
himself in following his genius: to hate his father, and mother, and wife,
and children, and brethren, and sisters, yea, and his own life;[6] to recognize

that the promise of the kingdom of heaven is not an unconditional promise of peace but a fair warning that the time for decision and division will
come. This substitution of self for Jesus, or rather of the self's genius, was
not without precedent in this former preacher and author of the Divinity
School Address (1838), with his denunciation of an emphasis on the person
of Jesus and on some past, historical revelation. The economy of the passage is also of this background. He would not give money to the poor, who
are not *his* poor, for the reason that Jesus will not give words but in parables, because to those who have ears to hear and hear not, and do not understand, it is not given to know the mysteries of the kingdom of heaven;[7]
because "for whosoever hath not, from him shall be taken away even that
he hath."[8] Hard sayings; but no harder than the fact that he is the one he
is and that each of us is the one each of us is.

But it is the foreground of the passage that I wish to focus on, its setting of a certain scene of writing. I understand the writer to be accounting
both for the fact of his writing and for what he writes. When his genius
calls him and he divides himself from society he does not write on the lintels of the door-post "my genius calls me." Or does he? Does he write
"Whim"? He says he *would*. Why would he? Because, I gather, that is all
this scrupulous epistemologist of moods would claim to know. The call of
one's genius presents itself with no deeper authority than whim. And what
presents itself in the form of whim is bound sometimes to be exactly whim
and nothing more. (Or worse. In the paragraph preceding this one, Emerson had remembered, when young, being cautioned by a valued advisor
that his inner impulses may be from below, not from above, and remembered being prompted to reply: "They do not seem to me to be such; but if
I am the Devil's child, I will live then from the Devil.") He hopes it is
somewhat better than whim at last—for as with prophecy you can only
know the true from the false by its fruits. When later in the essay he says
that "perception is not whimsical, but fatal" (where perception is the organ
to which whim occurs) he is saying that something which is of the least importance, which has no importance whatever but for the fact that it is mine,
that it has occurred to me, becomes by that fact alone of the last importance; it constitutes my fate; it is a matter of my life and death. If we could
know in advance of departure after whim that it will truly prove to have
been our genius that has called us, then the gate to salvation would not be
strait; there would be little need for faith, and little to write about. But why
does he mark whim on the lintels of his door-post? Why mark anything?

We may understand this marking to invoke the Passover blood and accordingly again see writing as creating a division—between people we may call Egyptians and those we may call Jews—which is a matter of life and death, of the life and death of one's first-born.

Literal writing on the door-posts of one's house is more directly a description of the mezuzah (a small piece of parchment inscribed with two passages from Deuteronomy and marked with a name of God, which may be carried as an amulet but which is more commonly seen slanted on the door-post of a dwelling as a sign that a Jewish family lives within). (The spiritual danger in putting "Whim" in place of the name of God will seem a small thing to one convinced that the name of God is mostly taken in the place of whim.) Accordingly we should consider that the writing contained in the mezuzah explains why the mezuzah is there, why God has commanded that it be there. We are told in each of the passages it contains to obey God's commandments, particularly in view of the land we are to possess, of milk and honey. "Therefore shall ye lay up these my words in your heart and in your soul, and bind them for a sign upon your hand, that they may be as frontlets between your eyes. And ye shall teach them your children, speaking of them when thou sittest in thine house, and when thou walkest by the way, and when thou liest down, and when thou risest up. And thou shalt write them upon the door-posts of thine house."[9] Accordingly it is in obedience to Emerson's genius that he speaks of it wherever he is, showing that it speaks everywhere to him; not to acknowledge it would be not to keep faith with it. As if his essays were so many mezuzahs, declarations of his faith, and his part in attempting to keep this land of milk and honey from perishing.

(Here I must pause for the pleasure of identifying the title of one of the recent films I care most about as occurring in the mezuzah, *Days of Heaven.* "As the days of heaven upon the earth" is the phrase used in the King James version to describe our stay "in the land which the Lord sware unto your fathers to give them"—*if,* that is to say, we keep faith with the word of the covenant.[10] Several reviewers of this film have felt that it has something to do with the story of America. The source of its title specifies the phase of the story as one in which this promised land, in forgetting its faith and serving foreign gods, lies under a threat. It has been sent the plague of locusts; it has been warned; and this film, in the prophetic tradition of American literature, takes up the warning. As the land was given, on condition, so it can be taken away.)

To speak of Emerson's essays as the contents of new mezuzahs is to imply that he has written on his door-posts both "Whim" and the knowledge that his genius has called him, for the essays are the fruits by which his prophetic whim is to be known. Thus have I given something of the explanation he claimed we cannot spend the day in. Considering what he means by a day in our opening two texts, that it is the measure of our lives, he is saying that to begin to explain would be to spend his life in explanation. But then this is my occasion, not his, which was to verify what I named his epistemology of the call of his genius. There are always good reasons not to obey this call, not to verify it. From its beginning, from its presenting itself as whim, it follows that there must be obligations which it prompts you to leap over; there is always something to do first, something to say first before preaching the kingdom of heaven; for example, there are those at your house to whom to bid farewell, or there may be dead to bury.[11] And as for the poor, it took a brave man then, and a braver one now, if he is righteous, to imply that he has the poor with him always, but the call of his genius he has not always.[12]

Will this priority of a certain whim (to departure) over a certain obligation (to remain) not make a person rootless, and nowadays for nothing more than selfish reasons, which you may call religious but which religion is not likely to teach? And isn't there something especially troubling here for an American? True, this was to be the land where the individual could grow freely, wildly if he or she wished; but it was also a place to which strangers could come to put down roots, the place to which pilgrims and immigrants come home. Whereas when Emerson seems to say that he is responsible only for what he calls *his* poor, for such as belong to him and to whom he belongs, he suggests that responsibility is his to pick up or to put down. As if sinking roots is not a matter of finding out where you want to live but finding out what wants to live in you. As if your roots—that is, your origins—are matters not of the past but precisely of the present, always, fatally. As if America could banish history, could make of the condition of immigrancy not something to escape from but something to aspire to, as to the native human condition.

I am not unaware that this may sound like one of those transcendentalist sublimities which I confessed a while ago has seemed repellent to me, no doubt significantly because they may seem so easy for someone to voice who has Emerson's connections. But whatever needs rebuke and explanation here, this is not my present mood, or I will not, if I can help it, call upon this mood. I am at present surprised to find two other questions coming to mind: first whether that remark about immigrancy as the native human condition is something my immigrant father, dead three years this January, could have ever understood; and second whether the note of finding what is native to you, where this turns out to mean shunning the cosmopolitan and embracing the immigrant in yourself, is one a professor should strike. These are matters about which one cannot claim expertise, nothing for which a degree is a credential. Evidently the joining of these questions of what my father would be in a position to understand and of what I find myself in a position to say to students is meant to join a question as to the authority of one's address.

But the authority of making one's mark is just the question Emerson, for all his connections, is raising in his parable of writing "Whim" on his door-posts. It is written in a certain hope and in posing the issue of what he is to own, dividing those who belong to him and to whom he belongs from all others, asking who his poor are and hence who his rich are, and so who his honorable and dishonorable are, and who his beautiful and his ugly, his inspirers and his dispiriters. . . . It is agreeing to make a day not of explanation but of judgment. How can this be easier or harder for him than for any man or woman? It is frightening to be called upon to do, to further "the conversion of the world." And yet Emerson clearly regards himself as exercising the duties of the American scholar, that is, of Man Thinking, which he finds to be comprised in self-trust, soon to be renamed by him self-reliance. Along with guiding men, the office of the scholar is to cheer and to raise them. How can you cheer and raise them by frightening them?

Let us recall that Emerson depicts his immediate and constant audience as the young scholar or student (which, as he and Thoreau never tire of saying, is a capacity residing in each human being, the best part, even the essential, of the human being), and in particular depicts them, in "The American Scholar," as disgusted by the principles on which the world is managed, or ready to die of disgust, and in "Self-Reliance" as losing heart. Presumably our students have lost heart in failing, in another phrase of "Self-Reliance," to obey their heart; and presumably they would not have failed in this obedience unless it were frightening. Not difficult to do, but difficult to let yourself do. Once you do it it is easy; but everything conspires against it. It is a matter of taking back to yourself an authority for yourself you have been compelled to invest elsewhere. So the matter of authority is as much one of hearing as it is one of uttering—as Emerson's parable shows to have been his case as well. It is not up to him to create your whim for you, nor to create your mood of philosophy. His experience tells him—the thing that expertise can never know—that the whim and the mood are bound to occur. (Thoreau will call such things "opportunities" and say of them that there never is more than one of a kind.) His record is there, his prose in conversation with itself, dutifully watching for our participation, or our refusal of it. It does not require us. That is itself its guidance. We are at liberty to discover whether he belongs to us and we to him. We, who have already failed to obey the heart; and he, who has already succeeded, are to meet at a common origin. To say "Follow me and you will be saved," you must be sure you are of God. But to say "Follow in yourself what I follow in mine and you will be saved," you merely have to be sure you are following yourself.[13] This frightens and cheers me.

3

The Philosopher in American Life
(toward Thoreau and Emerson)

When in accepting the invitation to deliver a set of Beckman Lectures I asked what expectations are placed on such occasions, and I was assured by my hosts that they would be interested in whatever I wanted to talk about, I wasn't certain whether I was being answered or humored. It is true that since the time I was an undergraduate at Berkeley in the forties, and an assistant professor here (and movie-goer) in the fifties and early sixties, there have been at this university more members of its faculty from whom I have learned more about more things—from the art of music to Shakespeare and from skepticism to transcendentalism—than have been together at any other place. So I have the uncanny feeling that I could say anything here and be understood completely. But I will try not to press my luck.

I will not even explore the urgency of the wish to be understood completely, for example, trace the source of the wish in my intermittent sense that no utterance of mine could be acceptable simultaneously to all those by whom I desire understanding, say by the primarily philosophical and by the primarily literary. Some may accuse me of trying to reconcile my father and my mother. But if these terms (I mean philosophy and literature) name halves of my own mind, it is perhaps all the more immediately urgent for me to see that they keep in touch.

What I have done for these lectures, wishing to take the occasion of old memories and aspirations to form some measure of my progress, is to propose as their primary business the reading of a set of texts that represent the oldest and the newest of my interests, placing them in a loosely woven net of concepts. The point of the loose weave is to register that I am as interested in the weaving together of these texts as I am in their individual textures, and that I wish to leave open, or keep open usefully, how it is one gets from one to another of them.

One set of these connections forms perhaps the most pervasive, yet all but inexplicit, thought in these lectures: that the sense of the ordinary that my work derives from the practice of the later Wittgenstein and from J. L. Austin, in their attention to the language of ordinary or everyday life, is underwritten by Emerson and Thoreau in their devotion to the thing they call the common, the familiar, the near, the low. The connection means that I see both developments—ordinary language philosophy and American Transcendentalism—as responses to skepticism, to the anxiety about our human capacities as knowers that can be taken to open modern philosophy in Descartes, interpreted by that philosophy as our human subjection to doubt. My route to the connection lay in my tracing the ordinary language philosophers as well as the American transcendentalists to the Kantian insight that Reason dictates what we mean by a world, as well as in my feeling that the ordinariness in question speaks of an intimacy with existence, and of an intimacy lost, that matches skepticism's despair of the world. These routes from, say, Emerson to Wittgenstein are anticipated in a thought I have put many ways over the years, never effectively enough—the thought that ordinary language philosophy is not a defense of what may present itself as certain fundamental, cherished beliefs we hold about the world and the creatures in it but, among other things, a contesting of that presentation for, as it were, the prize of the ordinary. So that epistemologists who think to refute skepticism by undertaking a defense of ordinary beliefs, perhaps suggesting that there is a sense in which they are certain, or sufficiently probable for human purposes, have already given in to skepticism, they are living it.

But this thought of mine virtually says of itself that it must be ineffective, as well as abusive. Think of it this way. What it comes to is the claim that such an expression as "The world exists and I and others in it" does not express a belief about the world; in other words, the claim that belief is not the name of my relation to the existence of the world and I and others in it and that to insist otherwise is at variance with our ordinary word *belief*. But if that is so, one who has arrived at the surmise that perhaps the world and I and others do not exist, or anyway that we cannot know with certainty that they do, must simply feel; so much the worse for our ordinary words and for whatever you imagine that other relation to the world might have been.

After enough repetitions of and variations on this pattern of inconsequence or irresolution—or, put otherwise, after some five hundred pages of a belated doctoral dissertation on the subject—I concluded that the argument between the skeptic and the antiskeptic had no fixed conclusion, or that I would search for none. This left me at a place I called Nowhere, or, more specifically, it left me disappointed. I mean that, as I began to think and to write my way out of my nowhere, what I found I was writing about was disappointment, the life-consuming disappointments in Shakespearean tragedy, but also the philosophy-consuming disappointments with knowledge as expressed in Wittgenstein's *Philosophical Investigations*. It was in following out these paths, with some reason to believe that their crossings were definitive for my philosophical direction, that I came to the idea that philosophy's task was not so much to defeat the skeptical argument as to preserve it, as though the philosophical profit of the argument would be to show not how it might end but why it must begin and why it must have no end, at least none within philosophy, or what we think of as philosophy.

Here my thought was that skepticism is a place, perhaps the central secular place, in which the human wish to deny the unsettled condition of human existence is expressed, and so long as the denial is essential to what we think of as the human, skepticism cannot, or must not, be denied. This makes skepticism an argument internal to the individual, or separate, human creature, as it were an argument of the self with itself (over its finitude). That this is expressed as a kind of argument of language with itself (over its essence) is how it came to look to me as I worked out the thought that Wittgenstein's *Investigations* is not written—as it had in my experience uniformly been taken to be—as a refutation of skepticism (as if the problem of skepticism were expressed by a thesis), but as a response to what I have come to call the truth of skepticism (as if the problem of skepticism is expressed by its threat, or temptation, by our sense of groundlessness). The way I work this out in relation to the *Investigations* starts from the thought that we share criteria by means of which we regulate our application of concepts to things, means by which, in conjunction with what Wittgenstein calls "grammar," we set up the shifting conditions for conversation; in particular, from the thought that the explanatory power of Wittgenstein's idea depends on recognizing that criteria, for all their necessity, are open to our repudiation or dissatisfaction (hence they lead to, as well as lead from, skepticism), that our capacity for disappointment by them is essential to the way we possess language, in perhaps the way that Descartes found our capacity for error to be essential to our possession of the freedom of the will. (If we could not repudiate them they would not be *ours*, in the way we discover them to be; they would not be our responsibility.) The record of this work is given in the first and especially in the fourth and last part of *The Claim of Reason*, the middle two parts of which consist essentially of the dissertation that some twenty years earlier had led to my nowhere.

The lead I wish to follow in these lectures is something that kept pressing for attention in the fourth part of that book, the outcropping of moments and lines of romanticism. While I tried at each of these outbreaks to give expression to this pressure (for future reference, so to speak) I felt it was threatening the end of my story, if for no other reason than that I did not know enough, or how, to accept it. But my ignorance has become a luxury I can no longer afford to excuse, because the pressures to make a beginning, consecutive to the book, at uncovering the connection with romanticism have become irresistible. A signal of these pressures is my having marked my sense of the underwriting of ordinary language philosophy in the work of Emerson and Thoreau by speaking of an intimacy with existence, or intimacy lost—a signal recognizing the claim that the transcendentalism established in their pages is what became of romanticism in America.

Accordingly, given my interest in putting Wittgenstein's and Austin's preoccupation with the ordinary and the everyday together with Emerson's and Thoreau's emphasis on the common, the near, and the low, it is understandable that I would eventually want to understand more about Wordsworth's notorious dedication of his poetic powers, in the preface to *Lyrical Ballads*, to "[making] the incidents of common life interesting" and his choosing for that purpose "low and rustic life," together with the language of such men as lead that life, which he calls "a far more philosophical language than that which is frequently substituted for it by Poets." My concern with Coleridge more or less follows, but it has special features which will come forward when I read him in a certain detail in succeeding lectures. What I mean by romantic is meant to find its evidence—beyond the writing of Emerson and Thoreau—in the texts of Wordsworth and Coleridge that I explicitly consider. If what I say about romanticism is false to these texts, then for my purposes here it is false of romanticism, period. If what I say is true but confined to just the texts I consider, I shall be surprised but not abashed; I know very well that there is in any case work ahead of me. I have chosen to talk about warhorses not only because I want my evidence, if narrow, to be as widely shared as possible, but also because I am not concerned here with subtleties of definition or with history. What I say about romantic exemplifications can only be useful if it is obvious—as obvious as the other examples philosophers use. (Here I am siding with philosophers for whom the obvious is the subject of philosophy: for example, Wittgenstein and, partially, Heidegger.)

But look for a moment, before coming back to America, at the magnitude of the claim in wishing to make the incidents of common life interesting. Beyond the word *common* take the words *make* and *interesting*. Wordsworth's modest statement first of all carries on its face its competition with other conceptions of poetry, since the verb *to make* is forever being cited as what the word *poetry* declares itself to take on. Presumably this is meant to call attention to the fact that poems are made, invented, that they are created, hence by creators; this would be confirmed in such a remark as Auden's, that "poetry makes nothing happen." What the words "make interesting" say is that poetry is to make something happen—in a certain way—to the one to whom it speaks; something inside, if you like. That what is to happen to that one is that he or she become interested in something aligns the goal with what I have taken to be the explicit presiding ambition of *Walden* and with the enterprises of such philosophers as Wittgenstein and Austin. They perceive us to be uninterested, in a condition of boredom, which they regard as, among other things, a sign of intellectual suicide. (So metaphysics would be seen as one more of the false or fantastic excitements that boredom craves. So *may* be the activities appealed to in refuting or replacing metaphysics: for example, appeals to logic or to play.) This is what Wittgenstein has against metaphysics, not just that it produces meaningless propositions. Even in the sense in which that is true, it would be only a derivative of its trouble. His diagnosis of it is, rather, that it is empty—empty of interest, as though philosophy were motivated by a will to emptiness. When Austin says of philosophical examples that they are "jejune,"[1] he is using a common-room word to name, with all due differences of sensibility, the Nietzschean void. What worse term of criticism does he have? (As if J. P. Morgan were to say of a business's collateral that it is jejune.)

I realize that connections of the kind I am proposing here are not exactly native to professional philosophy, that reading texts of Wordsworth and Coleridge, for example, as though they are responding to the same problems philosophers have, even responding in something like the same way (a way that cannot be dissociated from thinking), is not how you would expect a philosopher from our English-speaking tradition and profession of philosophy to proceed. The interest for me in mentioning this is that my connections and procedures here are not exactly foreign to that profession either, that they represent, to my mind, rather a quarrel with it, which hence acknowledges a kinship with it. But then I had better get on soon with the main burden of this first or introductory lecture, to say something about a way I see the differences of my connections and procedures from those of that profession, which will mean saying something about philosophy as a profession, something that for me will mean saying something about why Emerson and Thoreau are not regarded as belonging to it.

Another word or two before that, by way of indicating my path from *The Claim of Reason* to the lead of romanticism.

That book is heavily indebted to an idea I call acknowledgment, which forms a key to the way I see both the problematic of skepticism and that of tragedy. This idea has been criticized on the ground, roughly, that in offering an alternative to the human goal of knowing either it gives up the claim of philosophy to reason or else it is subject to the same doubts that knowing itself is. Perhaps this takes my idea as offering something like a mode of feeling to replace knowing, and it may be that moves of this sort have been made in theology and in moral philosophy when proofs of God's existence were repudiated and the rational ground of moral judgment became incredible. These results can seem the wish of a sentimental romanticism; if they were ones I had been moved to, I would surely feel that I owed a better understanding of feeling or sentiment than any I have had from such philosophies. Or perhaps the criticism of acknowledgment takes my idea as offering an alternative to knowing in a different direction, say as embodied in Santayana's title *Skepticism and Animal Faith*. But Santayana's notions of skepticism and of faith refer to a realm of things (namely, essence), which he defines as fixed beyond knowledge, an impulse just about perfectly hostile to the way I think. However the word *animal* is supposed to modify the word *faith* in Santayana's title, it puts faith out of the reach of our ordinary word. I put the suggestion, when it came up for me in my dissertation, as the concluding question of its pages on skepticism, declaring my nowhere: "How is that faith achieved [the supposed faith that the things of our world exist], how expressed, how deepened, how threatened, how lost?"[2]

I do not propose the idea of acknowledging as an alternative to knowing, but rather as an interpretation of it, as I take the word *acknowledge*, containing *knowledge*, itself to suggest (or perhaps it suggests that knowing is an interpretation of acknowledging). In an essay on the tragedy of *King Lear* I say, "For the point of forgoing knowledge is, of course, to know,"[3] as if what stands in the way of further knowledge is knowledge itself, as it stands, as it conceives of itself—something not unfamiliar in the history of knowledge, as expressed in the history of science. Otherwise the concept of acknowledgment would not have its role in the progress of tragedy and comedy.

But it is not in this direction that my concept of acknowledgment has mainly caused suspicion, not in the claim that tragedy is the working out of skepticism—but in the reverse direction, as I might put it, that skepticism is the playing out of a tragedy, that accordingly our ordinary lives partake of tragedy in partaking of skepticism (Chekhov calls these lives comedies, no doubt as a concession to our constricted circumstances). This means that an irreducible region of our unhappiness is natural to us but at the same time unnatural. So that the skepticism is as live in us as, let me say, the child.

Thoreau calls this everyday condition quiet desperation; Emerson says secret melancholy; Coleridge and Wordsworth are apt to say despondency or dejection; Heidegger speaks of it as our bedimmed averageness; Wittgenstein as our bewitchment; Austin both as a drunken profundity (which he knew more about than he cared to let on) and as a lack of seriousness. To find what degrees of freedom we have in this condition, to show that it is at once needless yet somehow, because of that, all but necessary, inescapable, to subject its presentation of necessity to diagnosis, in order to find truer necessities, is the romantic quest I am happy to join. In writing about Samuel Beckett's *Endgame*, I express this perception of the everyday as of "the extraordinary of the ordinary,"[4] a perception of the weirdness, or surrealism, of what we call, accept, adapt to, as the usual, the real—a vision captured in the opening pages of *Walden* when its writer speaks of his townsmen as appearing to be absorbed in fantastic rituals of penance, a perception of arbitrariness in what they call necessities. In this *Walden* links with those works of our culture specifically devoted to an attack on false necessities, say to Plato's vision of us as staring at a wall in a cave, or Luther's idea of us as captives, or Rousseau's or Thoreau's sense of us as chained, or the perception of our self-subjugation in the case histories of Marx and Freud.

It is this history of devotion to the discovery of false necessity that brought me to the ambiguity of the title I give to these lectures, *In Quest of the Ordinary*; to the sense that the ordinary is subject at once to autopsy and to augury, facing at once its end and its anticipation. The everyday is ordinary because, after all, it is our habit, or habitat; but since that very inhabitation is from time to time perceptible to us—we who have constructed it—as extraordinary, we conceive that some place elsewhere, or this place otherwise constructed, must be what is ordinary to us, must be what romantics—of course including both E. T. and Nicholas Nickelby's alter ego Smike—call "home."

Probably the most famous text adducible on the topic of the professionalizing of philosophy is Thoreau's, in the early paragraphs of *Walden*: "There are nowadays professors of philosophy, but not philosophers." In my hearing this sentiment is invoked always as a crack at academics, and of course in part it surely is that. But to suppose that is the exhaustive, or primary, target of the sentiment is to underrate Thoreau's complexity, let alone the extent of his hopes and his disappointments; and it is to overrate the attention he is giving to what we call professors of philosophy. The thing he is saying about "nowadays"—its loss of philosophy—is not something that a particular group of people, call them professors of philosophy, either have caused or could reverse. It will help even the balance if we quote the much less famous sentence following the one just quoted: "Yet it [i.e., philosophy] is admirable to profess because it was once admirable to live." But since Thoreau will say later on in this first chapter that by philosophy he means an economy of living, and since "an economy of living" is a perfectly accurate brief description of *Walden* as a whole, it should follow that *Walden* is meant to establish his claim to be a philosopher. Then why does he say there are nowadays no philosophers?

I think of a number of reasons. First, the very openness of his avowal to the aspiration of philosophy makes him, literally, a professor of philosophy, one who acknowledges it, and if that is something other than a philosopher, then he is not a philosopher. Second, if being admirable is essential to the living of philosophy, then again he is not a philosopher because his life neither is found admirable (rather, he depicts its effects on others as being questionable) nor ought to be found so (it ought, if it attracts you, to be lived). Third, when this writer uses a word like *nowadays* we should be alert to the ways in which time is one of his favorite playthings: he will, in the third chapter, identify himself with "the oldest Egyptian or Hindoo philosopher [when they] raised the veil from the statue of the divinity," saying that "no time has elapsed"—"it was I in him that was then so bold and it is he in me that now reviews the vision"; and in the second chapter he describes a spot he has sat down in as one he has lived in ("What is a house but a *sedes*, a seat?—better if a country seat. I discovered many a site for a house. . . . There I might live, I said; and there I did live, for an hour, a summer and a winter life"). Accordingly he might mean *nowadays* to cover the entire period of philosophy since Plato, or the pre-Socratics, that is, since what we call the establishment of philosophy; or he might well mean precisely that *now*, since he is writing his book, he is professing and not living philosophy, and that this is admirable (only) because that former life, which his writing depicts, was admirable. However, fourth, since I also take him to claim that his writing is *part* of his living, an instance of the life of philosophy, I take him to be saying, or implying, that the reader could not understand his claim to be a philosopher until he or she understands what it is to be his reader, what he asks of understanding. *Nowadays* inscribes the fact that the reader comes to his words after the writer has left them, hence—this is a central claim of my book on *Walden*—he makes good on his identification of his book as a testament, a promise, as Luther puts it, in view of the testator's death, so that the life depicted in Thoreau's book is declared over by the time you come to its page. There is, accordingly, no philosopher there nowadays, unless you are one, that is, unless you accept the promise as yours, which would mean to identify yourself as one who "reviews its vision."

As noted at the opening of Chapter 1, in writing *The Senses of Walden*, I found myself asking: "Why has America never expressed itself philosophically? Or has it . . . ?"[5]—a form of question that implies that if we have expressed ourselves philosophically we may not recognize that we have, as if we continued to lack the authority to take authority over our minds. And the context of the question implied that I was taking the question of American philosophical expression to be tied up with the question whether Thoreau (and Emerson) are to be recognized as philosophers. It isn't as if I did not know in 1970 that America was pretty well assuming the leadership of what is called Anglo-American analytical philosophy, which is half of what the Western world calls philosophy. Nor is it that I felt this half to be foreign to the American genius, as if it were still trading on importations from the Vienna and the Berlin of the 1930s. Logical positivism found genuine intellectual comradeship with, for example, strains in American pragmatism. It was and is just as much a question for me whether pragmatism, often cited as the American contribution to world philosophy, was expressive of American thought—in the way I felt that thought could be or had been expressed. Is this a reasonable question?

Something I had in mind can be seen by recalling Max Weber's celebrated address "Science as a Vocation," delivered in 1918, about half way between this lecture and the year Thoreau finished *Walden*. The term *science* here would include philosophy as a separate discipline. Weber begins by "practically and essentially" identifying the question as to the material conditions of science as a vocation with the question: "What are the prospects of a graduate student who is resolved to dedicate himself professionally to science in university life?" In America at any rate, practically speaking this identification still holds, that the conditions for devoting oneself to philosophy are essentially the prospects of holding a position in the philosophy department of a university. Yet we should find an uneasiness in granting this that Weber could scarcely have known. He had a pair of assurances that I take us to lack. He was assured simultaneously that in his culture authoritative philosophy could be achieved by professors of philosophy (it can be taken as the mission of Kant and Hegel to have demonstrated this, somewhat to our confusion); and he was assured that this achievement was a part of the common literary inheritance that had, for example, produced and profited from him. Whereas American intellectuals can be said to hold nothing in common, nothing, that is, of high culture. (Perhaps it follows from this that no American philosophy *could*, of itself, give expression to America.)

I can imagine a number of responses to what may appear as my wish for the participation of philosophy and literature in one another, some ruder than others. One response would be that it is exactly the nature of professional philosophy—whether of Anglo-American analysis or of Continental systematizing—to give up, even to escape, the pleasures and the seductions of literature. And isn't this faithful to philosophy's origins in Plato, who ruled most of poetry out of his philosophical republic? But this is hardly an answer until we know why he ruled it out, and we cannot, I think, know why until we know what it means for philosophy to be in *competition* with poetry, as for the same prize. Besides, something Plato ruled *in* to his philosophy is what we might call the obligation of therapy, and professional philosophy does not on the whole follow Plato slavishly in this. Philosophy was seen, like poetry, to possess the power to change people, to free the soul from bondage. In the past couple of millennia other contestants have presented themselves, in addition to philosophy and poetry, on the field of therapy; religion has, and, most recently, psychotherapy (though here we need a separate term to cover the direct assault on the mind by practitioners from Mesmer to Freud). Certainly there are good grounds for rejoicing that philosophy has escaped the business of therapy; I dare say they are roughly the same grounds for rejoicing that philosophy has become professional. It is my impression that those professionals who take Wittgenstein with limited seriousness as a philosopher do not take at all seriously his likening of philosophical procedures to therapies. Certainly I do not wish to see philosophy, as a profession, get back into the business of therapy, anyway not as philosophy stands, and not into what we are likely to think of as therapy; but I confess that the idea is more painfully ludicrous than I wish it were, because I am of the view that philosophy is, or ought to be, haunted by the success of its escape from this obligation. I might express my outlook by saying that if you conceive philosophy and poetry and therapy in ways that prevent you from so much as seeing their competition with one another then you have given up something I take to be part of the philosophical adventure, I mean a part of its intellectual adventure.

That nothing of high culture is common to us means that for us no text is sacred, no work of this ambition is to be preserved at all costs. But then this is a conclusion, or rather a premise, Emerson and Thoreau want us to arrive at, that, as Emerson puts it, "around every circle another can be drawn," that "all that we reckoned settled shakes and rattles; and literatures, cities, climates, religions, leave their foundations and dance before our eyes." All this has its ecstasies of expectation and equality, which is so far to the good. But think what it means about our everyday intellectual life. If Emerson and Thoreau are the founding thinkers of American culture, but the knowledge of them, though possessed by shifting bands of individuals, is not possessed in common by that culture, then what way have we of coming to terms on the issues that matter most to us, as say the fundamental issues of philosophy and of art can matter to us?

So extraordinary a cultural amnesia must have many sources. As food for thought I cite three sentences from Bruce Kuklick's book entitled *The Rise of American Philosophy: Cambridge, Massachusetts, 1860–1930*. It presents the story of American philosophy proper as beginning with the conflict engendered by Transcendentalism's attack on Unitarianism, the Christianity of the Boston gentry. Kuklick describes the situation this way: "When Transcendentalism attacked the foundation of accepted faith, Unitarian laymen looked to philosophy [specifically to the philosophers at Harvard] to buttress the established religion. The laity were not disappointed. . . . Adept and knowledgeable in argument, the Harvard thinkers consistently outmaneuvered the Transcendentalists philosophically. Although Emerson and his well-known circle won over a band of converts, the philosophical bases of Unitarianism remained unshaken."[6] Kuklick, I gather, takes this as rather a grand day for American philosophy; but without disputing this as the beginning of American philosophy as a discipline, nor directly contesting a positive evaluation of it, consider how extraordinary a beginning it is, extraordinary even that it should be plausible as such a beginning. The period in question is the middle of the nineteenth century, a time at which Marx could announce (in the introduction of his proposed book on Hegel's *Philosophy of Right*) that "the criticism of religion is in the main complete." While thinkers like Nietzsche and Heidegger will come to show how far from complete that criticism was, Marx's remark calls to mind the centuries in which European philosophy was establishing its modern basis by quarreling with religion, posing a threat to religion whether it appeared to attack it (say as in Hume) or to defend it (say, as in Kant), because the price religion pays for philosophy's defense is a further dependence on philosophy's terms; and the philosophical is as jealous of its autonomy (call this "Reason") as the religious is (call this "Faith").

Even if one accordingly interpreted the Harvard philosophers' defenses of an established religion in the middle of the nineteenth century not as the beginning of the story of the American discipline of philosophy but as a sign that this discipline had not yet begun independently, the moral to draw may be only that American intellectual development is not in phase with European developments, something we perhaps already knew. But the other half of the story Kuklick tells is that the philosophical defense was precisely taken against Emerson and Transcendentalism, and here the defense seems to have been much more lasting. There has been no serious move, as far as I know, within the ensuing discipline of American philosophy to take up Emerson philosophically. The moral to draw here may of course be the one Kuklick draws, that Emerson and Thoreau are to be comprehended as philosophical amateurs, toward whom, it would be implied, there is no professional obligation. But suppose the better moral is that Emerson and Thoreau are as much threats, or say embarrassments, to what we have learned to call philosophy as they are to what we call religion, as though philosophy had, and has, an interest on its own behalf in looking upon them as amateurs, an interest, I think I may say, in repressing them. This would imply that they propose, and embody, a mode of thinking, a mode of conceptual accuracy, as thorough as anything imagined within established philosophy, but invisible to that philosophy because based on an idea of rigor foreign to its establishment.

Before giving a name to this foreign rigor I have at least to indicate some way to avoid, or postpone, a standing and decisive consideration that professional philosophers will have for refusing to hear out an articulation of the intuition that Emerson and Thoreau warrant the name of philosophy—the consideration that no matter what one may mean by, say, conceptual accuracy, a work like *Walden* has nothing in it to call *arguments*. And while someone may rest undisturbed at the prospect of philosophy forgoing its therapeutic dimension, no one should rest easy at the idea of philosophy abandoning the business of argument. But suppose that what is meant by argumentation in philosophy is one way of accepting full responsibility for one's own discourse. Then the hearing I require depends upon the thought that there is another way, another philosophical way (for poetry will have its way, and therapy will have its way) of accepting that responsibility.

This other philosophical way I am going to call reading; others may call it philosophical interpretation. This associates Emerson and Thoreau with the Continental tradition of philosophizing and at once dissociates them from it. It associates them according to the thought, as I express it at the opening of *The Claim of Reason*, that philosophy may be inherited either as a set of problems to be solved (as Anglo-American analysts do) or else as a set of texts to be read (as Europe does—except of course where it has accepted, or reaccepted, analysis). You can sense how different imperatives for training, different standards for criticism and conversation, different genres of composition, different personas of authorship, will arise from this difference in modes of inheritance.

This sense is enforced by seeing how the devotion to reading at the same time dissociates Emerson and Thoreau from the Continental tradition. To say how, I must first describe what I have sometimes called the "two myths of philosophizing," or myths of the role of reading in philosophical writing.

In the one myth the philosopher proceeds from having read everything, in the other from having read nothing.[7] Perhaps this duality is prefigured in the division between Plato's writing and Socrates' talking, but it is purely enough illustrated in this century by contrasting Heidegger's work, which assumes the march of the great names in the whole history of Western philosophy, with that of Wittgenstein, who may get around to mentioning half-a-dozen names, but then only to identify a remark which he happens to have come across and which seems to get its philosophical importance only from the fact that he finds himself thinking about it. Common to the two myths is an idea that philosophy begins only when there are no further texts to read, when the truth you seek has already been missed, as if it lies behind you. In the myth of totality, philosophy has still not found itself, at least until it has found you; in the myth of emptiness, philosophy has lost itself in its first utterances.

Now I can put my idea about a difference between the transcendentalists and the Continentals, within the affinity between them, this way: while Emerson and Thoreau proceed with the tasks of philosophy—for example, with the task of endless responsibility for one's own discourse—by something they portray as reading, and not as argumentation, they are nevertheless not interested in what we are likely to call philosophical texts more than in others, and indeed nothing is more constant in their philosophical mission than to warn the student against much book reading altogether. It is no wonder if they are an embarrassment to a university curriculum.

Then what, or how, do they recommend reading? I will begin an answer to this by spending the rest of this lecture reading a few further sentences from *Walden* on the subject, and then from Emerson's "Self-Reliance."

Having praised the written beyond the spoken word and finding that the "heroic books . . . will always be in a language dead to degenerate times," the writer of *Walden* interprets "the noblest written words" by a startling identification: "*There* are the stars, and they who can may read them."[8] This is an interpretation of nature as a text, of course, but it is one of Thoreau's clearest interpretations of what reading itself is. It interprets reading (dangerously invoking, to revise, the idea of the astrological) as a process of *being read*, as finding your fate in your capacity for interpretation of yourself. "Will you be a reader, a student merely, or a seer? Read your fate, see what is before you, and walk on into futurity."[9] What is before you is precisely not, if you catch Thoreau's tune, something in the future; what is before you, if you are, for example, reading, is a text. He asks his reader to see it, to become a seer with it. Only then can you walk beyond where you are. In the course of *Walden* he depicts himself reading in two or three specific books, and each time he is interrupted. One time, at the beginning of "Brute Neighbors," the interruption is openly allegorized as the personification of the Poet inviting the personification of the Hermit to leave off his meditation on some sentences of Confucius and to come fishing. The Hermit stalls for a moment, but then accedes to this other pleasure and need. Since Thoreau typically uses openness to conceal something, one may take this personified exchange as being with himself, hence to betoken that his own wish to write (to fish with the poet in him) interrupts his wish to read, which would, according to his way of thinking, mean that his writing is continuously a matter of interrupting writing, genuine writing being a matter of breaking in upon something, call this meditation, or silence, or call it language, or the present. (If "the present" here may be figured as metaphysical "presence," and this, further, as narcissistic "self"-presence, then writing in this allegory occurs as the expression or creation of desire, something beyond, something wanted, lacking, "breaking in." Then writing figures the reception of language, of others, as such. When Thoreau insists on writing alone, writing only, as opposed to speaking ["the labor of my hands only," as in his opening paragraph—here, not a labor of my mouth; but this will come forth against the dedication of his mouth to God's words], he is withdrawing his investment in others, taking his voice back to itself, enacting a "return" to the presocial [it would take an "advance" to the postsocial]. And then his writing figures, as it were, the states before writing, before its contrast with voicing, before its breaking in. [Thoreau will call this "running amok against him."[10]] This suggests the level at which what Thoreau calls "disobedience," refusing to listen, makes his neighbors anxious: as if, if society persists in the error of its ways, there is no assurance that society will in the future be able to break into metaphysical solitude, that is, that it will be *wanted*, and *consented* to.)

In the introduction to *The Senses of Walden* in 1972, in response to an earlier query whether I had been reading Derrida and Lévi-Strauss, and as a way of explaining, not without a certain worry even then, why I thought my ignorance of other work would not compromise the specific effort of mine, I said, "My remarks about writing as such are not meant as generalities concerning all of literature but as specific acknowledgments of the intention of the writer in this book, in particular two phases of this intention: to rest his achievement of the condition of writing as such specifically upon his achievement of a genuine Scripture; and to alarm his culture by refusing it his voice, i.e., by withholding his consent." This response has, I believe, been taken by some readers of *The Senses of Walden* to mean that my book is without theoretical ambition. What the response meant was that no theory I was aware of had the power to account for *Walden*'s practice and the theory of writing that is part of that practice; and that it itself, on the understanding I had reached of it, contained a theory of itself, hence of any text—to the extent that another text's relation to it, call this its difference, is specifically measured. It is, I trust, somewhat understandable why, revising the present chapter in 1987, I added this statement and the parenthetical observation at the end of the preceding paragraph. I do not wish to seem unteachable, or unresponsive to the demand to relate what I do to the practice and theory of deconstruction. But those who wish me well, and I hope some others, will appreciate that 1972 (and the years preceding, during which the work that goes into *The Senses of Walden* was in preparation) is as yet an immeasurable distance in American time. Naturally I am aware of the possibility that intellectual events of the past two decades may have preempted the fields I find myself in; but it is my fortune, good or bad, to imagine otherwise. I was early enough so that a different start was quickly too late for me. If this were a race, I would bet on the hare every time. But if it is not, if there is not just one course, and if indeed we are not on the ground but at sea, the turtle may make sense.

Another interruption of reading, in "Sounds," goes this way. The writer describes himself as "look[ing] up from my book" upon hearing a train pass, and it takes a moment to realize that what he calls "my book" is the one he is now writing. And when he looks up at the train here is what happens. "This carload of torn sails is more legible and interesting now than if they should be wrought into paper and printed books. Who can write so graphically the history of the storms they have weathered as these rents have done?"[11] What happened when he looked up from his book is that he went on reading (and writing). He went on seeing what was before him; he found the train legible; hence he walked on into futurity, for example, into his book. So his reading and writing were not interrupted after all. That reading is a way, or a goal, of seeing is something attested—as I found in *The Claim of Reason*—by the history of the word *reading* in a word for advising, which in turn contains a word for seeing. Now here in his book *Walden* what its writer was reading then is now before us, and not only in a narrative of it as, say, a newspaper might have it, but in an account of it (an account is Thoreau's habitual economic term for what his writing is), which means a calculation of its value. He has wrought (written, and, since they already contained writing, he has translated) the torn sails into a book of printed pages, and in this transaction it is still by the rents of these sheets, evidence of what has happened to them, by the distress that caused them and the distress and the satisfaction they will cause, that they still write the history of the storms they have weathered. The transaction of sails into pages reduces their interest, he says; so apparently writing is for him a capital expenditure. And in his translation, those "rents" also go to make good his claims as an economist, or accountant, and become the payments he gives in return for his weathering of his history.

These two sentences of Thoreau's about the legible train prompt me to add up what he means by reading along the following lines. Reading is a variation of writing, where they meet in meditation and achieve accounts of their opportunities; and writing is a variation of reading, since to write is to cast words together that you did not make, so as to give or take readings. Since these accounts are of what Thoreau calls economy, which is his philosophical life, it follows that his economics, resulting from the interplay of writing and reading, is what he claims as philosophy. An implication of this line of interpretation is that while philosophizing is a product of reading, the reading in question is not especially of books, especially not of what we think of as books of philosophy. The reading is of whatever is before you. Where this happens to be a verbal matter, what you read are words and sentences, at most pages. Whole books are not read, any more than they are written, at a sitting; not exactly or simply because they are too long but because they would dictate the length of a session of reading, whereas meditation is either to be broken off or to bring itself to an end. (The theme here is of the ending of philosophy as one of philosophy's unshaken tasks.) Books of philosophy would especially not be read, I imagine for two reasons: (1) Philosophical books are forever postponing their conclusions. (This is roughly the criticism made of Hegel by Kierkegaard.) Being outwardly systematic, everything is made to depend on how it works out; that is, it is a narrative—a narrative of concepts, it so happens—hence based on suspense. In this respect books of philosophy are of no more philosophical use than novels are. A book of philosophy suitable to what Thoreau envisions as "students" would be written with next to no forward motion, one that culminates in each sentence. This sounds like a prescription for a new music, say a new discourse, and hence like a negation of poetry as well as of narrative, since it implicitly denies, in a work of literary originality, the role of the line; the sentence is everything. Naturally I hope it also sounds like a description of *Walden*. (2) Americans are not, anyway not yet, what might be called professors of philosophy, obliged to read any and every text that gives itself out as philosophy and to find a place for it in our thoughts. We are possessed of no standing discourse within which to fit anything and everything philosophers have said. We are either philosophers or nothing; we have nothing to profess. Either we are able to rethink a thought that comes our way, to own and assess it as it occurs, or we must let it pass, it is not ours.

The discourse Thoreau invents for this assessment, his economics, proceeds, in the absence of a philosophical vocabulary, by taking us, as suggested, over the fantastically elaborated network of terms of assessment— terms of economy—our language naturally possesses, assessing words as they are employed, which often and critically comes to turning the face of a word to a value of it we would ordinarily not notice as economic—for example, faces of the words *account, settle, redemption, living, interest, terms*. Whether you accept Thoreau as a philosopher depends on whether you accept his invention of a discourse, along with his other beginnings, as a beginning of a philosophical discourse. The implication of this invention may seem the biggest of the brags in this book of brags. The writer is claiming to be writing the *first* book of philosophy.

—But *is* this really so exceptional a brag? It is a claim of authority, that he has a right to his words; in his terms, that they are earned, a labor of his hands only. But he does not say that he is the *only* such writer or earner. He emphatically does not think he comes to his work earlier than the "oldest" (Egyptian or Hindu) philosophers we hear him invoking, merely coevally with them: there is no philosophy present until the philosopher is *being* read (at least, necessarily by himself, by herself.) Nor does he claim that he is unique *nowadays*; he emphatically denies this. The uncomfortable implication is rather that philosophical authority is non-transferable, that each claim to speak for philosophy has to earn the authority for itself, say account for it.

I spoke earlier of philosophy as a bequeathing; now I am speaking of it as an inheriting. Anxious not to be misunderstood in emphasizing the nationality of philosophy, the demand a philosophy places upon its nation, forcing it to put its philosophy on trial, to repress it, so that it can return ("It is true, I might have . . . run 'amok' against society; but I preferred that society should run 'amok' against me, it being the desperate party"[12]), I do not wish to leave the impression that Thoreau is shunning the influence of foreign philosophy. His invocation of the oldest Egyptian and Hindu philosophers should itself secure that fact, along with its implication that America must inherit philosophy not—or not alone, not primarily?—from Europe, but also from where Europe inherited it, from wherever Plato inherited it (which only philosophy will know). Here is just another version of *Walden*'s mythical brag to philosophy, specifically announcing, in all modesty, that to inherit philosophy you have already to be in the way of philosophy.

Walden, as said, opens with its writer declaring that when he wrote his pages he earned his living "by the labor of [his] hands only," and whatever debt or guilt he is there disclaiming, he goes on to work out a chain of economic terms to figure his debt to philosophy. *The Senses of Walden* more or less says of itself that it may be derived from two axioms: that the house being built in *Walden* is *Walden* (which also means America, the spiritual construction, or discovery, or constitution, of, Thoreau tells us, Walled-In, which may image imprisonment, but which is what Paradise says), and that accordingly every act of its writer is an allegory, or staging, of its writing. So that when in the chapter falling first he says, "It is difficult to begin without borrowing," and reports that on the day he went down to the woods he borrowed an axe, adding that "I returned it sharper than I received it," he is to be understood as describing his literary-philosophical borrowing, which entails his competing with it. Such confession is reinforced by claims like "Nothing was given me of which I have not rendered some account," which suggests (not that it follows) that his account is of nothing other than what was given him. Perhaps most unmistakably, or summarily, there is the scene in which he "takes down" a shanty for which he had bargained and which he bought for boards for his envisioned house, where the picture of dismantling and removal to a new site, and the figuration of buying as believing and of bargaining as coming to terms all figure in his account of his account.[13]

To say that Emerson and Thoreau "found" philosophy for America is to say, among other things, that, in teaching the nation that it is, and how it is, to be born into thought, they demonstrate how thinking (from Europe, from the past, from where it finds philosophy) is to be brought to these shores, which in Thoreau's book means turned to account.[14]

I have emphasized that the writing and the reading or seeing that Thoreau exemplifies are not about something *else*, something past or future, to be called his living; they are themselves either exemplifications, modes, of philosophical life or they are philosophically worthless. To say that the central narrative of *Walden* is the building of home is to say that the book is about what you might call edification. Edification might also be a reasonable term for what we were calling therapy. It is, under this description, exactly the thing that good professionals, like Hegel, are at pains to deny to philosophy. I do not assert that Thoreau would mean by edification what Hegel means by it. The issue is alive in works like *Being and Time* and in *Philosophical Investigations*, where one feels that some spiritual claim (call it) is leveled at the reader and that this claim cannot, or must not, be interpreted as some specifically moral claim. It may be the case that in a given age the edification to which philosophy may aspire can only happen when philosophy is professional, or in touch with the professional. Ours is perhaps such an age. Edification of any kind may be taken as what Max Weber deplores in the university classroom; he describes the wish he deplores, making science into something it cannot be, as a wish for a substitute redemption. (I see on late night television that a professor of philosophy and theology, arguing against a secular humanist, so he called him, appeals to science to prove that the universe is caused, hence has a source in some intelligence. I take it Weber would not approve. Neither did the secular humanist. Such also is our age.)

And Thoreau's case is worse, from a professional point of view, than has so far come out, for he will accept no substitute for redemption. One of his most innocuous, hence most suspicious, sentences goes this way: ".You only need sit still long enough in some attractive spot in the woods that all its inhabitants may exhibit themselves to you by turns."[15] All of *Walden* is condensed in these few drops. Grant for now that this attitude of sitting allegorizes the reading and writing we have noted. I will also just assert that, among many other things, "by turns" means by verses and by conversions. (You may imagine that it also means "by tropes." But this would only be the case where Thoreau's figures [stressed by his numbers in his "account"] are taken as figurations of, or refigurings, recountings of, figuration, according to which "by turns" would have to mean "by turning around the idea of trope itself.") Then what he is saying is that he—that is, his book—has a power of stillness, say silence, that is sufficiently attractive to be looked to as redemptive. This should be put together with *Walden*'s interpretation of being seated that we cited earlier, the one that identifies a house as a seat, hence being seated anywhere as a way and a time you might be living, spending your life, in a word, taking up residence. The context of that remark is one in which Thoreau goes to extravagant lengths—that is, his usual lengths—to show that this being seated or residence is part, as the word says, of possessing the landscape that radiated from him, and the farms and the trees and, in short, everything within the dozen miles on every side of where, sitting, he is living; the country is taking its origin in him.[16] Why the equation of the postures of writing and reading and those of owning should be noted in this way is something we will have occasion to speculate about.

I would like to take the claim of Thoreau's sentence that concerns (and shows) the writer sitting still long enough (in attraction) as fulfilling one of what I had meant by the tasks or predicates of philosophy—here the task of inviting questions by its silence, or of confronting by not speaking the first word. (Socrates is overtaken in the public street; Wittgenstein's *Investigations* opens with a quotation, the words of someone else; so does Heidegger's *Being and Time*; the writer of *Walden* begins, after a brief paragraph introducing himself, by saying that he is answering some very particular inquiries made by his townsmen concerning his mode of life.) But the use of a seductive or attractive silence to elicit another's revelation of himself, herself suggests procedures and powers which, even if they are well thought of as teaching, universities have no credentials for.

In turning to Emerson for his testimony about reading, I note that the story of his and Thoreau's cultural neglect needs complication. Emerson's story has to include an account of the tremendous fame attaching to him in his lifetime, which persisted for some decades after his death and which, after further decades in which he seemed unreadable, there have been recurrent efforts to revive, themselves invariably producing counterefforts to destroy it again. How one understands these twists of his reputation generally seems tied up with what one takes his writing to be, as if the writing and the reputation formed one case for us, and the case is always undecided, as if we do not yet know what this man is and what he wants.

A way of considering what it is about his writing that produces this wavering toward it, this not knowing how it is to be taken, is to consider that Emerson makes the question of how to take it (how seriously, I would like to say, *he* takes it, the question of authenticating its own seriousness), a guiding question he asks for himself, of himself.

I have more than once cited the following passage from "Self-Reliance" as one in which he is dramatizing his mission as a writer, presenting the credentials of his vocation: "I shun father and mother and wife and brother when my genius calls me. I would write on the lintels of the doorpost, *Whim*. I hope it is better than whim at last, but we cannot spend the day in explanation." I will not recall again the biblical contexts which show Emerson there to be specifying the call to write as following the new promise of redemption, and specifying the act of writing as marking his old dwelling as with a mezuzah, or with blood, as on Passover. The question is pushed at us: How seriously does he mean these specifications? Is there any philosophical point to them beyond the literary, whatever that may be?

I go on here to note that the entire essay "Self-Reliance," for all its fame as preaching individualism (which is not wrong certainly, but certainly not clear), is a study of writing, as if one's wish to write simply *Whim* already took upon oneself the full-blown burden of writing. The writer writes *Whim* in the place others place the word of God, as if to mock the commoner habit of taking God's name in the place of Whim. As if there were no greater standing authority for using the word *Whim*—or any other word, however small—than for using the word *God*; no justification for language apart from language.

That "Self-Reliance" is a study of (philosophical) writing (hence of reading and of thinking) is insistently established in the essay by Emerson's draw upon the reach of the words *expression* and *character* and *communication*, using them throughout to call attention at once to the externals of writing and to the internals of the one doing the writing, backing it, fronting it, hence to assert that both writing and writer are to be read, which is about to say, both are texts, perhaps testing, contesting, one another. (It is from that essay that I will go on to take my quotations from Emerson here, unless I specify otherwise.) He says, for example, that "A character is like an acrostic or Alexandrian stanza—read it forward, backward, or across, it still spells the same thing." And after warning near the beginning "we but half express ourselves" and claiming in the middle that while we "may err in the expression" of our intuitions we know that they are so (they are *so, this* way) and are "not to be disputed," he speaks near the end of the wise man as "[making] men sensible [of something] by the expression of his countenance." What the wise man is making us sensible of, says Emerson in this instance, is that the soul stays home, that even when he is called from his house he is still, whatever others say, at home. But since being called, for a wise man, is evidently being called by his genius, and since for Emerson that is to write, Emerson is submitting his writing to the condition of acquiring whatever authority and conviction is due to it by looking at its countenance, or surface.

Our philosophical habits will prompt us to interpret the surface of writing as its manner, its style, its rhetoric, an ornament of what is said rather than its substance, but Emerson's implied claim is that this is as much a philosophical prejudice as the other conformities his essay decries, that, so to speak, words are no more ornaments of thought than tears are ornaments of sadness or joy. Of course, they may be seen so, and they may in a given case amount to no more; but this just means that expressions are the last things to take at face value.

What countenance will count as the writing of the wise? Emerson finds in the communication of those who "conform to usages," who, that is, are without self-reliance, that "every word they say chagrins us and we do not know where to begin to set them right." If every one of our words is implicated in the conformity to usage, then evidently no word assures a safe beginning; whether a given word will do must accordingly depend upon how it allows itself to be said, the countenance in which it puts its utterer, whether it can be uttered so as not to chagrin us, which is to say sadden us, but rather, to use a favorite Emersonian phrase, to raise and cheer us. As if these were the fixed alternatives for the practice of philosophy.

Here we come upon the most familiar of all the complaints leveled at Emerson, the complaint that more than any other has clouded his reputation among intellectuals in this century: that he is recklessly affirmative, that he lacks the sense of tragedy. Whatever this means, and however often it has ineffectually been denied, a prior question is bound to rise to the lips of a philosopher: simply the question what difference it makes, what philosophical difference, whether the countenance of speech saddens or cheers us. These are merely psychological matters of the *effects* of words, whereas what matters philosophically is whether what is said is true. But then it is up to us at least to get the psychology straight. Emerson says in a companion essay ("Circles"), "The simplest words,—we do not know what they mean except when we love and aspire." Whatever states these words are meant to name, this remark says, not that the states are the effects of words, but rather that they are their causes, or conditions of understanding words. While it may not be unprecedented for a philosopher to tell us that the words we use every day are imprecise or prompt illusions, it is not usual, even not normal in philosophy, to say that the way to their meaning lies through a change of heart.

Whatever this itself means will presumably depend on how accurately it describes Emerson's own practice of writing and thinking, that is, on his particular countenancing of words. Let us look, finally, at two further sentences exemplifying his practice of describing his practice. When he says, "Who has more obedience than I masters me," this is to be taken in connection with his speaking of writing as something to which one is called, something to which one is harkening, showing obedience. Then to "master" him is not exactly to overcome him, as if he were an unruly impulse or an insubordinate slave, but to have command of him as of a difficult text or of language. And however difficult the text may be that concerns the subject of being called, I find it no harder to command, and more serviceable, than any number of texts that less affirmative aestheticians have produced concerning the subject of intention.

Both the idea of grasping the intention of a text and the idea of sharing or hearing what has called it are interpretations of reading, of following a text. But the idea of being intended can close out what the idea of being called and of obedience, of listening, brings into investigation: namely, how it is that one writes better than one knows (as well as worse) and that one may be understood better by someone other than oneself (as well as understood worse). These are matters worth looking into. Emerson is looking into them when he remarks: "Character teaches above our wills. Men imagine that they communicate their virtue or vice only by overt actions, and do not see that virtue or vice emit a breath every moment." I find this a frightening notation of an anxiety in writing; an acknowledgment that one must give over control of one's appropriations, as if to learn what they are.

To write knowing that your words emit a breath of virtue or vice every moment, that they communicate the means by which you are expressing your desires, know them or not, is to leave your character unguarded. To leave what I say unguarded has been a point of honor with me, even though I know that some risks are not worth taking. If one could not write better than one is, and understand a writer better than they may understand themselves, if we were not capable of better obedience than we have shown, obedience to something better, then the case of writing would be more pitiable than it is, because then it could propose no measures for putting itself aside, no relief for writer or reader. It follows that I am at any time subject to indictment by what I set down, or else it goes for nothing.

I have not wished to disguise a certain pathos in my sense of struggle for the writing of philosophy, in the position and the place I find myself in, I mean, for example, as a Professor of Philosophy in America, and elsewhere. At the same time I have not wished to make the struggle unduly personal, because the struggles it joins are nothing if not common—those between philosophy and poetry, between writer and reader, between writer or reader and language, between language and itself, between the American edifice of fantasy and the European edifice of philosophy, between the hope and the despair of writing and reading redemptively.

But how about the very pathos in posing these issues as struggles? Isn't that to romanticize what are merely intellectual problems? Is philosophy as such—nowadays? still?—to be cloaked as a romantic undertaking? I suppose my finding Emerson and Thoreau to underwrite Wittgenstein and Austin suggests a certain romantic taint in what I regard as some of the most advanced thought of our time, and Heidegger's relation to romantic literature, especially, of course, to Hölderlin, suggests that it is a taint he takes on willingly. It may be that the claim upon the reader I have pointed to in Heidegger's and Wittgenstein's work, the claim I said is not to be captured exactly as moral, may be thought of as a romantic demand for, or promise of, redemption, say self-recovery. But in all philosophical seriousness, a recovery from what? Philosophy cannot say sin. Let us speak of a recovery from skepticism. This means, as said, from a drive to the inhuman.[17] Then why does this present itself as a recovery of the self? Why, more particularly, as the recovery of the (of my) (ordinary) (human) voice? What is romantic about the recovery of, the quest for, the ordinary or everyday? What business is it of philosophy?

4

Emerson, Coleridge, Kant
(Terms as Conditions)

In this lecture I follow out certain intuitions of the one preceding: that philosophy's essential business has become the response to skepticism, as if philosophy's business has essentially become the question of its own existence; that the recovery of the (my) ordinary (voice) from skepticism, since it is itself a task dictated by skepticism, requires the contesting of skepticism's picturing of the task; that in philosophy the task is associated with the overcoming, or say critique, of metaphysics, and in literature with the domestication of the fantastic and the transcendentalizing of the domestic, call these movements the internalization, or subjectivizing, or democratizing, of philosophy; and that this communication between philosophy and literature, or the refusal of communication, is something that causes romanticism, causes at any rate my present experiments with romantic texts, experiments caused by the discovery of these texts among the effects of *The Claim of Reason.*

Working within an aspiration of philosophy that feeds, and is fed by, a desire to inherit Emerson and Thoreau as thinkers, I take it for granted that their thinking is unknown to the culture whose thinking they worked to found (I mean culturally unpossessed, unassumable among those who care for books, however possessed by shifting bands of individuals), in a way it would not be thinkable for Kant and Schiller and Goethe to be unknown to the culture of Germany, or Descartes and Rousseau to France, or Locke and Hume and John Stuart Mill to England. While I have been variously questioned about what this means, and what it betokens, I am not yet prepared to describe the mechanisms that have made it possible and necessary. But since I rather imply that the repression of Emerson and Thoreau as thinkers is linked with their authority as founders, I should at least note the preparation of their repression by their self-repressions.

Founders generally sacrifice something (call this Isaac, or call it Dido) and teach us to sacrifice or repress something. And they may themselves be victimized by what they originate. I take such matters to be in play in the way Emerson and Thoreau write in and from obscurity, as if to obscure themselves is the way to gain the kind of standing they require of their fellow citizens. As if to demonstrate their self-repression, hence their powers to undo this repression, were to educate us in self-liberation, and first of all to teach us that self-liberation is what we require of ourselves. That this is within our (American) grasp means that to achieve it we have above all to desire it sufficiently. This achievement of desire is equally an intellectual and a spiritual or, say, passionate, exercise. In "Thinking of Emerson," I characterize the thinking that Emerson preaches and practices in terms of abandonment, abandonment of something, by something, and to something.[1] Those who stay with the entering gentilities of Emerson's prose will naturally take his reputed optimism as a sign of his superficiality and accommodation; it is an understandable stance, because to follow his affirmations to their exits of desire is to be exposed to the intransigent demands they place upon his reader, his society. (As an exercise in these demands, in obscurities amounting to self-repression, in the incessant implication that the language does not exist in which to stake claims quite philosophically, or say nationally, you may assign yourself a meditation on the opening question of Emerson's great essay "Experience": "Where do we find ourselves?" Hint [as they used to say after posing a tricky problem in American high school math textbooks]: Take the question as one staked for American thinkers by the thinking and practice of Columbus [say by the fact that Native Americans are called Indians], as if the very direction to America, the brute place of it, and that we call it "discovered," say "found," threaten the assured edifice of metaphysics. And then take Emerson's question of where we find ourselves as asking how we are founding ourselves, since there is no one voyage to America. As if Emerson's self-repression is to enact the wish to found a tradition of thinking without founders, without foundation; as if we are perhaps to ratify ourselves with Foundling Fathers.)[2]

Heidegger's idea that thinking is something to which we stand to be attracted is exactly not an idea he expects to attract his fellow citizens, but at best is to single out rare, further, thinkers. A thinker is one drawn, you might say seduced, by the authority of thinking, that is, drawn to the origin of thinking (say in Parmenides) that philosophy has obscured, or repressed in establishing itself, or say founding itself. But as I conceive of Emerson and of Thoreau, they play Parmenides to their own Plato, Dido to their own Aeneas, Hölderlin to their own Heidegger. (I am not here speaking of comparative quality but of comparative structure, although without my conviction in the soundness of the Americans' quality, I do not know that I would be interested in their structure.) Even in the absence of an understanding of how it is that the repressed performs its own repression, one may surmise that a thinker would wish to acquire the authority of thinking in this way in order to teach the authority whose acquisition consists in its relinquishment. I think of this as philosophical authority. If something like this is an intelligible and practical background to bring to Emerson and Thoreau, the advantage, to it and to them, is that it can be investigated with, as it were, one's own hands, and in open air, as if the origins of philosophy on these shores were hardly different in age from the origins of movies. Someone my age will have had a teacher whose teacher could have heard Emerson. So that the philosophical waltz of obviousness and obscurity is—most obviously, if *therefore* most obscurely—of one's own calling.

It is habitually said, I suppose correctly, that what we think of as romanticism is a function of (whatever else) how we conceive the philosophical settlement proposed in the achievement of Kant. Since what we think about any view of the relation of the mental and the material, so to speak, is bound to be some such function (that is, since Kant's achievement is part of how we think) this is not a very specific claim. In this essay I specify what I understand a certain force of the Kantian function to be. That I confine myself to working this out only relative to a reading of one essay of Emerson's—"Fate," from *The Conduct of Life*—and a few passages from Coleridge's autobiographical prose will naturally require various justifications, not to say excuses. The fact that these texts do not undertake to quote and refute particular passages from Kant's writing would not for me be enough to show that, in a reasonable view of argument, they are not in argument with his philosophy. This too depends on what you understand Kant to have accomplished (what you think the name *Kant* means) and on what you understand to be the cause of the kind of writing in which romantics have expressed themselves. That it is not what we may expect of philosophical prose would hardly take such writers by surprise, as if they wrote as they did inadvertently, or in ignorance of the sound of philosophy. Consider that they were attacking philosophy in the name of redeeming it. Should professional philosophers, now or ever, care about that? It is true that philosophy habitually presents itself as redeeming itself, hence struggling for its name, famously in the modern period, since Bacon, Locke, and Descartes. But can philosophy be redeemed *this way*, this romantic way? To consider further what this way is is a motive for taking up the texts in question here.

To prepare for them I had better set out some version of what can be said to be Kant's accomplishment. Or let Kant say it for us, in two summary paragraphs from his *Prolegomena to Any Future Metaphysics*.

Since the oldest days of philosophy inquirers into pure reason have conceived, besides the things of sense, or appearances (phenomena), which make up the sensible world, certain creations of the understanding, called noumena, which should constitute an intelligible world. And as appearances and illusion were by those men identified (a thing which we may well excuse in an undeveloped epoch), actuality was only conceded to the creations of thought.

And we indeed, rightly considering objects of sense as mere appearances, confess thereby that they are based upon a thing in itself, though we know not this thing in its internal constitution, but only know its appearances, viz., the way in which our senses are affected by this unknown something. The understanding therefore, by assuming appearances, grants the existence of things in themselves also, and so far we may say, that the representation of such things as form the basis of phenomena, consequently of mere creations of the understanding, is not only admissible, but unavoidable.[3]

You can take these paragraphs as constituting the whole argument of the *Critique of Pure Reason*, in four or five lines. (1) Experience is constituted by appearances. (2) Appearances are of something else, which accordingly cannot itself appear. (3) All and only functions of experience can be known; these are our categories of the understanding. (4) It follows that the something else—that of which appearances are appearances, whose existence we must grant—cannot be known. In discovering this limitation of reason, reason proves its power to itself, over itself. (5) Moreover, since it is unavoidable for our reason to be drawn to think about this unknowable ground of appearance, reason reveals itself to itself in this necessity also.

Then why do we need the rest of the eight-hundred-plus pages of the *Critique of Pure Reason*? They can be said to be divided between those that set up or fill in the pictures or structures necessary to get this argument compellingly clear (clear, you might say, of the trucks that are invited to drive through it), and those pages that set out the implications of the argument for human nature, hence for our moral and aesthetic and scientific and religious aspirations. I am prepared to call all of these pages pages of philosophy. What I claim is that if you are not at some stage gripped by a little argument very like the one I just drew out, your interest in those eight-hundred-plus pages will be, let me say, literary. The question would still remain whether you are seriously interested in that argument—interested more than, let me say, academically—if you are not interested in those eight hundred pages. A good answer, I think, and sufficient for my purposes, is yes and no. I am going to focus here on the yes side.

What would the argument, supposing it is convincing, accomplish? Kant had described his philosophical settlement as limiting knowledge in order to make room for faith. This is a somewhat one-sided way of describing his effort concerning knowledge, since what he meant by "limiting" it was something that also secured it, against the threat of skepticism and powers of dogmatism. It can accordingly be seen as one in the ancient and mighty line of the philosophical efforts to strike a bargain between the respective claims upon human nature of knowledge or science and of morality and religion. Kant's seems to be the most stable philosophical settlement in the modern period; subsequent settlements have not displaced it, or rather they have only displaced it. I take this stability, for the purposes of the story I have to tell, as a function of the balance Kant gives to the claims of knowledge of the world to be what you may call subjective and objective, or, say, to the claims of knowledge to be dependent on or independent of the specific endowments—sensual and intellectual—of the human being. The texts I am using as examples of romanticism I understand to be monitoring the stability of this settlement—both our satisfaction in the justice of it and our dissatisfaction with this justice.

The dissatisfaction with such a settlement as Kant's is relatively easy to state. To settle with skepticism (and dogmatism, or fanaticism, but I won't try to keep including that in the balance), to assure us that we do know the existence of the world or, rather, that what we understand as knowledge is *of* the world, the price Kant asks us to pay is to cede any claim to know the thing in itself, to grant that human knowledge is not of things as they are in themselves (things as things, Heidegger will come to say). You don't—do you?—have to be a romantic to feel sometimes about that settlement: Thanks for nothing.

The companion satisfaction with the settlement is harder to state. It is expressed in Kant's portrait of the human being as living in two worlds, in one of them determined, in the other free, one of which is necessary to the satisfaction of human Understanding, the other to the satisfaction of human Reason. One romantic use for this idea of two worlds lies in its accounting for the human being's dissatisfaction with, as it were, itself. It appreciates the ambivalence in Kant's central idea of limitation, that we simultaneously crave its comfort and crave escape from its comfort, that we want unappeasably to be lawfully wedded to the world and at the same time illicitly intimate with it, as if the one stance produced the wish for the other, as if the best proof of human existence were its power to yearn, as if for its better, or other, existence. Another romantic use for this idea of our two worlds is its offer of a formulation of our ambivalence toward Kant's ambivalent settlement, or a further insight into whatever that settlement was a settlement of—an insight that the human being now lives in *neither* world, that we are, as it is said, between worlds.

Emerson and Thoreau joke about this from time to time. "Our moods do not believe in each other," Emerson says in "Circles"; "I am God in nature; I am a weed by the wall." And Thoreau identifies his readers as, for example, those "who are said to *live* in New England."[4] That Wittgenstein and Heidegger can be understood to share this romantic perception of human doubleness I dare say helps account for my finding its problematic unavoidable—Wittgenstein perceiving our craving to *escape* our commonness with others, even when we recognize the commonness of the craving; Heidegger perceiving our pull to *remain* absorbed in the common, perhaps in the very way we push to escape it.

About our worldlessness or homelessness, the deadness to us of worlds we still see but, as it were, do not recollect (as if we cannot quite place the world)—about this Wordsworth and Coleridge do not joke (though they can be funny), as though they hadn't quite the American confidence that world-changing change would come, or that they could help it happen. When Wordsworth dedicated his poetry, in his preface to *Lyrical Ballads*, to arousing men in a particular way from a "torpor," the way he sought was "to make the incidents of common life interesting," as if he saw us as having withdrawn our interest, or investment, from whatever worlds we have in common, say this one or the next. This seems to me a reasonable description at once of skepticism and of melancholia, as if the human race had suffered some calamity and were now entering, at best, a period of convalescence. The most familiar interpretation of this calamity has seen it as the aftermath of the French Revolution; Nietzsche will say the death of God. However this calamitous break with the past is envisioned, its cure will require a revolution of the spirit, or, as Emerson puts it at the close of "The American Scholar," the conversion of the world. Wittgenstein accounted for his appearance by saying that history has a kink in it. I am not interested here in comparing romantic writers in terms of whether they saw redemptive possibilities in politics, or in religion, or in poetry. My subject is rather how such an idea may pressure philosophy to think about its own redemption.

Since those who are said to live in New England, or for that matter in England, are after all alive, a vision such as that expressed in *The Ancient Mariner* has recourse to the idea of the living dead, or rather of death-in-life, for example, of reanimated bodies. Here the relation to Kant's worlds is, as I read it, all but explicit, as is the idea that the place we inhabit, in which we are neither free nor natural, is itself a world, as it were a Third World of the spirit, so that our consciousness is not double, but triple.

Of course all such notions of worlds, and being between them and dead to them and living in them, seeing them but not knowing them, as if no longer knowing them, as it were not remembering them, haunted by them, are at most a sheaf of pictures. How seriously one takes them is a matter of how impressed one is by the precision and comprehension of their expression. To test this is a purpose of the texts under discussion here.

Emerson's fluctuating reputation is a gaudy expression of the tendency of romantic writing to go dead for one periodically, perhaps permanently, as if in obedience to its perception both of our capacity to reabsorb our investment in the world, and of our capacity, or nerve, to ask, and sometimes to get, a melodramatic exaggeration of one's life in response to its investment. I have had occasion to say how long it took me to forgive Emerson, so to speak, for his nerve, and to follow my sense of his precision and depth.[5] The essay "Fate" is especially useful here because of its pretty explicit association with Kantian perplexities. "The bulk of mankind believe in two gods," it declares, having established the two gods, or poles of the essay, as Freedom and Fate (or, say, determinism, or nature). It would be Emerson's reputation as much as his sound that makes it hard for one to credit him with the philosophical stamina to take on Kant and his worlds, and I pause before that essay in part to make that reputation one more feature of the problem Emerson presents to one who acknowledges him as a thinker.

Of all the moments in the history of what I am calling the repression of Emerson in American philosophy, none seems to me more decisive, apart from the professionalization of philosophy itself, than Santayana's marking of him as a pillar of the Genteel Tradition. (This moment of the professionalization of philosophy is gone into at somewhat greater length in my essay entitled "Politics as Opposed to What?"[6]) It is hard for me, coming from the Harvard Philosophy Department to lecture at Berkeley on subjects in romanticism and skepticism, to put aside a discussion of Santayana's fantastically influential essay named, and naming, "The Genteel Tradition in American Philosophy," delivered at Berkeley a little over seventy years ago, written by a man who was living in Boston during the last ten years of Emerson's life, and who at Harvard had been the most glamorous teacher of one who would be my glamorous teacher of *Walden* when I was an undergraduate at Berkeley halfway back those seventy-odd years.[7] Particularly hard since Santayana remains, I believe, the figure most likely to occur to an American intellectual who hears that someone is proposing, or remembering, some confrontation of philosophy and poetry by one another. For some, Santayana will represent the last serious writer in America in whose work such a confrontation was undertaken, for others, a warning that such an undertaking is doomed to posturing: if infectious for a while, in the end ineffectual. I hope that both representations are wrong, but I will not argue against them now. What interests me here is that when, in "The Genteel Tradition," Santayana describes Emerson as "a cheery, childlike soul, impervious to the evidence of evil" he does not show (there or anywhere else I know that he mentions Emerson) any better understanding of Emerson's so-called optimism than, say, his contemporary H. L. Mencken shows of Nietzsche's so-called pessimism—he merely retails, beautifully, of course, but essentially without refinement, the most wholesale view there is of him.

In recent years this charge of cheeriness has been under attack by, among others, Stephen Whicher and Harold Bloom,[8] and a more sophisticated picture has emerged according to which Emerson's early optimism is tempered by a mature or more realistic acceptance of life's limits and ravages, signaled most perfectly in "Fate," the opening essay of *The Conduct of Life*, published two decades after his first volume of essays. But in what is the new maturity in "Fate" supposed to reside? It strikes me that people who talk about Emerson on the whole quote him (if they do—Santayana, so far as I know, harps on him without quoting one line of his prose) as they would quote a writer of incessant public celebrations, as though he wears all he means that way. Whereas an essay such as "Fate" seems to me excruciatingly difficult to come to terms with, presenting writing that is as indirect and devious as, say, Thoreau's is, but more treacherous because of its care to maintain a more genteel surface.

I guess the new maturity is supposed to be announced in sentences like the following:

The book of Nature is the book of Fate. . . . Nature is what you may do. There is much you may not. We have two things,—the circumstance, and the life. Once we thought positive power was all. Now we learn that negative power, or circumstance, is half. Nature is the tyrannous circumstance, the thick skull, the sheathed snake, the ponderous, rock-like jaw; necessitated activity; violent direction; the conditions of a tool, like the locomotive, strong enough on its track, but which can do nothing but mischief off of it.

Is the change in this marked by "Once we thought. . . . Now we learn"? But why take this to be sheer autobiography? It would be more like Emerson to be speaking of the human race, or human maturation, generally. As for himself personally, he says somewhere, I seem to remember, that he was born old.[9]

In any case, if this is the sort of thing that is supposed to show a new maturity, our new respect for it is bound in turn to fade. In 1930 the historian James Truslow Adams published in the *Atlantic Monthly* a piece called "Emerson Reread" (Stephen Whicher cites it as perhaps one of the two most intelligent anti-Emerson statements), in which Adams finds Emerson, who had been for him, as he was for so many others, an inspiration when he was a youth, no longer able to sustain the man of fifty. Adams has the grace to ask whether this is his or Emerson's fault; but not for long; he knows the answer. Emerson fails because he does not know about evil— about war, disease, misfortunes of every kind. As far as I can tell, these evils are the very sort of circumstances Emerson is summarizing when he says, halfway through "Fate," drawing a breath for a new response, "No picture of life can have any veracity that does not admit the odious facts." He had listed some facts earlier in the essay in a well-remembered pair of sentences: "The way of Providence is a little rude. The habit of snake and spider, the snap of the tiger and other leapers and bloody jumpers, the crackle of the bones of his prey in the coil of the anaconda,—these are in the system, and our habits are like theirs." But these are lists of matters no less obvious than "the heart-ache and the thousand natural shocks / That flesh is heir to." What could it mean to suppose that Emerson, in his early writing, had not known of their existence? That he mostly does not mention them, early or late, is surely more plausibly to be attributed to his finding them too obvious to mention than too obscure to have noticed.

But I think I know by now what the man of fifty finds distasteful that made the boy of sixteen or seventeen ecstatic. It is an idea that Emerson and any romantic would be lost without, that the world could be—or could have been—so remade, or I in it, that I could wholly desire it, as it would be, or I in it. In time the idea is apt to become maddening if kept green (certainly it makes one's grown-up acquaintances impatient), a continuous rebuke to the way we live, compared to which, or in reaction to which, a settled despair of the world, or cynicism, is luxurious. This dual perspective, of hope and of despair, proves to be internal to the argument of the essay on Fate, which I might summarize as the overcoming of Kant's two worlds by diagnosing them, or resolving them, as perspectives, as a function of what Emerson calls "polarity." It is as if Emerson's present essay is prophesying the fate of his reputation when it says, "In youth we clothe ourselves with rainbows and go as brave as the zodiac. In age we put out another perspiration—gout, fever, rheumatism, caprice, doubt, fretting and avarice."

Yet there is, I agree, a departure in the essay "Fate," a steady awareness that may present itself as a new maturity or realism. I find it contained in the statement "[In] the history of the individual is always an account of his condition, and he knows himself to be party to his present estate"—as if we are conspirators either for or against ourselves. The departure, or advance, shows in comparing this with a remark from "Self-Reliance": "Society everywhere is in conspiracy against the manhood of every one of its members." Now, in "Fate," it emerges that in, so to speak, taking our place in the world we are joining the conspiracy, and we may join it to our harm or to our benefit. "If Fate follows and limits Power [elsewhere called will], Power attends and antagonizes Fate. . . . [Man is] a stupendous antagonism, a dragging together of the poles of the Universe."

Living this antagonism (as relentless as electricity), we polar beings are either victims or victors of Fate (a remark about Fate as much as about us, the sort of thing Wittgenstein calls a grammatical remark); the remark above all means that Fate is not a foreign bondage, human life is not invaded, either by chance or by necessities not of its own making. "The secret of the world is the tie between person and event. . . . He thinks his fate alien, because the copula is hidden." Freud and Marx say no less. (I think here of a remark from the *Investigations*: "It is in language that an expectation and its fulfillment make contact."[10])

Of course this is all, if you like, mythology, and as such cannot philosophically constitute what Emerson claims for it: namely, "one key, one solution to the old knots of fate, freedom, and foreknowledge." But suppose I emphasize, on his behalf, that he is offering his solution *merely* as a key. And, as Pascal had put it, a key is not a hook—a key has just what Pascal calls the *aperitive* virtue, that is, it only opens, it does not further invite, or provide. Whether you find Emerson entitled to such a gloss will depend on who you think Emerson is, something I am trying to leave, or to get, open. It would be, to my mind, key enough if Emerson's thought here opens to us the thought, or opens us to the thought, that our past solutions to these mysteries, however philosophical in aspect, are themselves mythology, or, as we might more readily say today, products of our intuitions, and hence can progress no further until we have assessed which of our intuitions are satisfied, and which thwarted, by the various dramas of concepts or figures like fate, and freedom, and foreknowledge, and will. Disagreements over such matters do not arise (as they do not arise in skepticism) from one of us knowing facts another does not know, but, so Emerson is saying, from how it is one aligns the facts, facts any of us must have at our disposal, with ideas of victimization, together with whatever its opposites are. (One of Emerson's favorite words for its opposite is *Lordship*.) Something you might call philosophy would consist in tracing out the source of our sense of our lives as alien to us, for only then is there the *problem* of Fate. This looks vaguely like the project to trace out the source of our sense of the world as independent of us, for only then is skepticism a problem.

Even someone willing to suspend disbelief this far might insist that Emerson's writing maintains itself solely at the level of what I was calling mythology. So I must hope to indicate the level at which I understand the onset of philosophy to take place.

One key to Emerson's "Fate" is the phrase "the mysteries of human condition." I take the hint from the awkwardness of the phrase. I assume, that is, that it is not an error for "the mysteries of *the* human condition," as if Emerson were calling attention to mysteries of something which itself has well-known attributes. One attribute of what is called *the* human condition may be said to be that man must earn his bread by the sweat of his brow, another that the spirit is willing but the flesh is weak, another that we are subject to Fate. Such are not Emerson's bread, but his grist. The hint the phrase "the mysteries of human condition" calls attention to is that there is nothing Emerson will call the human condition, that there is something mysterious about condition as such in human life, something which leads us back to the idea that "in the history of the individual is always an account of his condition," and that this has to do with his "[knowing] himself to be a party to his present estate." "Condition" is a key word of Emerson's "Fate," as it is of the *Critique of Pure Reason*, as both texts are centrally about limitation. In the *Critique*: "Concepts of objects in general thus underlie all empirical knowledge as its a priori conditions."[11] I am taking it that Emerson is turning the *Critique* upon itself and asking: What are the conditions in human thinking underlying the concept of condition, the sense that our existence is, so to speak, had on condition? (Descartes pivotally interpreted an intuition of conditionality, or limitation, or finitude, as the dependence of human nature on the fact and on the idea of God, from which followed a proof of God's existence. Nietzsche reinterpreted such an interpretation of dependence as an excuse for our passiveness, or self-punishment, our fear of autonomy, hence as a cover for our vengefulness, from which follows the killing of God.)

It is as if in Emerson's writing (not in his alone, but in his first in America) Kant's pride in what he called his Copernican Revolution for philosophy, understanding the behavior of the world by understanding the behavior of our concepts of the world, is to be radicalized, so that not just twelve categories of the understanding are to be deduced, but every word in the language—not as a matter of psychological fact, but as a matter of, say, psychological necessity. Where Kant speaks of rules or laws brought to knowledge of the world by Reason, a philosopher like Wittgenstein speaks of bringing to light our criteria, our agreements (sometimes they will seem conspiracies). Starting out in philosophical life a quarter of a century ago, I claimed in "The Availability of Wittgenstein's Later Philosophy"[12] that what Wittgenstein means by "grammar" in his grammatical investigations—as revealed by our system of ordinary language—is an inheritor of what Kant means by "Transcendental Logic"; that, more particularly, when Wittgenstein says, "Our investigation . . . is directed not towards phenomena but, as one might say, towards the 'possibilities' of phenomena"[13] he is to be understood as citing the concept of possibility as Kant does in saying, "The term 'transcendental' . . . signifies [only] such knowledge as concerns the a priori possibility of knowledge, or its a priori employment."[14] Here I am, still at it.

Whatever the conditions are in human thinking controlling the concept of condition, they will be the conditions of "the old knots of fate, freedom, and foreknowledge," immediately because these words, like every other in the language, are knots of agreement (or conspiracy) which philosophy is to unravel, but more particularly because the idea of condition is internal to the idea of limitation, which is a principal expression of an intuition Emerson finds knotted in the concept of Fate. His first way of expressing Fate is to speak of "irresistible dictation"—we do with our lives what some power dominating our lives knows or reveals them to be, enacting old scripts. The problem has famously arisen with respect to God, and with God's or nature's laws. Emerson adds the new science of statistics to the sources of our sense of subjection to dictation, as if to read tables concerning tendencies of those like me in circumstances like mine— Emerson spoke of circumstances as "tyrannous"—were to read my future; as if the new science provides a new realization of the old idea that Fate is a book, a text, an idea Emerson repeatedly invokes.[15] Then further expressions of the concept of condition are traced by the rest of the budget of ways Emerson hits off shades of our intuition of Fate—for example as predetermination, providence, calculation, predisposition, fortune, laws of the world, necessity—and in the introductory poem to the essay he expresses it in notions of prevision, foresight, and omens.

Emerson's initial claim on the subject (and it may as well be his final) is this: "But if there be irresistible dictation, this dictation understands itself. If we must accept Fate, we are not less compelled to affirm liberty, the significance of the individual, the grandeur of duty, the power of character." This sounds like a nice little bale of genteel sentiments. Perhaps we can now begin to unpack it.

Dictation, like *condition,* has something to do with language—dictation with talking, especially with commanding or prescribing (which equally has to do with writing), condition with talking together, with the public, the objective. "Talking together" is what the word *condition,* or its derivation, says. Add to this that conditions are also terms, stipulations that define the nature and limits of an agreement, or the relations between parties, persons, or groups, and that the term *term* is another repetition in Emerson's essay. Then it sounds as though the irresistible dictation that constitutes Fate, that sets conditions on our knowledge and our conduct, is our language, every term we utter. Is this sound attributable to chance? I mean is the weaving of language here captured by (the conditions, or criteria of) our concept of chance?

"This dictation understands itself," Emerson says; but the essay sets this understanding as our task. And he says: "A man's fortunes are the fruit of his character." The genteel version of this familiarly runs, "Character is fate,"[16] and it familiarly proposes anything from a tragic to a rueful acquiescence in our frailties. But to speak of the fruit of one's character is to suggest that our character is under cultivation by us, and Emerson says of it (in line with a line of his from "Self-Reliance") that it constantly "emits" something, that it is "betrayed," betrays itself, to anyone who can "read [its] possibility." (In that earlier essay, which in "The Philosopher in American Life"[17] I claimed is about communication, and specifically writing, Emerson had said, unnervingly: "Character teaches above our wills. Men imagine that they communicate their virtue or vice only by overt actions, and do not see that virtue or vice emit a breath every moment.") He emphasizes that this reading is a trivial, daily matter: "The gross lines are legible to the dull." And now add that by "character," associated with ideas of being read, and with communicating itself, Emerson is again, as in "Self-Reliance," proposing us as texts; that what we are is written all over us, or branded; but here especially the other way around, that our language contains our character, that we brand the world, as, for example, with the concept of Fate; and then listen again to such an idea as that one's character is one's fate.

Now it says openly that language is our fate. It means, hence, that not exactly prediction, but diction, is what puts us in bonds, that with each word we utter we emit stipulations, agreements we do not know and do not want to know we have entered, agreements we were always in, that were in effect before our participation in them. Our relation to our language—to the fact that we are subject to expression and comprehension, victims of meaning—is accordingly a key to our sense of our distance from our lives, of our sense of the alien, of ourselves as alien to ourselves, thus alienated.

"Intellect annuls Fate. So far as a man thinks, he is free." This apparently genteel thought now turns out to mean that we have a say in what we mean, that our antagonism to fate, to which we are fated, and in which our freedom resides, is as a struggle with the language we emit, of our character with itself. By the way, *annul* here, I feel sure, alludes to the Hegelian term for upending antitheses (*aufheben*), or what Emerson calls our polarity, our aptness to think in opposites, say in pitting together Fate and Freedom. *Annul* also joins a circle of economic terms in Emerson's essay, for instance, *interest, fortunes, balances, belongings,* as well as *terms* and *conditions* themselves, and in its connection with legislation, in the idea of voiding a law, it relates to the theme of the essay that "We are as lawgivers." The terms of our language are economic and political powers. They are to be positioned in canceling the debts and convictions that are imposed upon us by ourselves, and first by antagonizing our conditions of polarity, of antagonism.

In putting aside Emerson's essay for a moment, I note that this last idea of us as lawgivers suggests that the essay is built on a kind of philosophical joke, a terrible one. Philosophy, as in Kant and as in Rousseau, has taken human freedom to be our capacity to give law to ourselves, to be autonomous. Emerson's essay shows that fate is the exercise of this same capacity, so that fate is at once the promise and the refusal of freedom. Then on what does a decision between them depend? I think this is bound up with another question that must occur to Emerson's readers: Why, if what has been said here is getting at what Emerson is driving at, does he write that way? That he shows himself undermining or undoing a dictation would clearly enough show that his writing is meant to enact its subject, that it is a struggle against itself, hence of language with itself, for its freedom. Thus is writing thinking, or abandonment. Still the question remains why it is a genteel surface that he works at once to provide and to crack.

I turn to Coleridge, the figure from whom the American transcendentalists would have learned to turn to Kant, and to German philosophy generally, and by whom Emerson would have been preceded in his emphasis on polarity in human thinking.

I had opened the *Biographia Literaria* many times, increasingly in the past few years, recognizing in its mode of obsession at once with the existence of the external world and with German philosophy a forerunning of my own excitements in linking Transcendentalism, both in Kant and later in Emerson and Thoreau, with ordinary language philosophy's confrontation of skepticism. But I had never been able to stay with it for longer than a chapter, and maybe half of the next, before closing the book with fear and frustration—both at the hopelessness in its ambitions for reconstituting the history of thought, by means, for example, of its elated obscurities as it translates Schelling on the task of something called uniting subject and object, and at its oscillation of astounding intelligence and generosity together with its dull and withholding treatment of Wordsworth's sense in claiming for poetry the language of the rustic and the low. I do not know that anything short of my growing sense of its pervasive bearings on the issues I have recently found myself involved with would have taken me all the way through it. The pain in it mounts, the more one feels the hatred in Coleridge's ambivalent address toward Wordsworth, praising his power and promise in terms reserved for the heroes of language, but cursing him, no doubt in the profoundly friendliest way, for not doing what it was given to him to do, for failing his power and breaking his promise.

I do not see how one can fail to sense projection in this, but of course the claim could still—could it not?—be true. Then, has it been considered that it may also be false, or worse, that whatever Coleridge had in mind in demanding of Wordsworth "the first genuine philosophic poem,"[18] it was something Wordsworth had already produced, and not just massively in *The Prelude* but fully in, for example, the Intimations Ode—that, so to speak, such achievements are all Coleridge could have meant in his prophecies? That it was critical for him to deny these achievements in this light, to project the achievements back into promises, is proven for me in the very incessance of his brilliance about them.

Since it was Coleridge who defined what many of us mean by literary criticism, he is, I assume, beyond praise in this regard. But what he actually says, in the *Biographia*, when at last he gets around to mentioning the intellectual drive of a work like the Intimations Ode, while it is as brilliant as his technical discussions of poems and of what poetry should be, is as dismissive and supercilious as anything he felt in the poisonous critics he so bravely and tirelessly defends his friends against. He dismisses thinking about what Wordsworth may have meant in invoking Plato's notion of Recollection, beyond saying that he cannot have meant it literally (then why insinuate that perhaps he did?), and he concludes that by describing the child as a philosopher Wordsworth can have meant nothing sensible whatever. It is this sudden: when Wordsworth flies his philosophical colors, then Coleridge's seemingly limitless capacity for sympathetic understanding toward other writers he thought genuine is stripped away, his tolerance for mysticism and his contempt for reductive empiricisms forgotten, and he starts firing at will. I do not deny that Wordsworth is in trouble when he talks philosophy. But we are speaking of what one is to expect of Coleridge.

I propose one day—even alerted to the folly in being, or remaining, promising—to write something about this book based on the assumption that it is composed essentially without digression. May I remind you how perverse a claim that must seem, as if contesting with the perverseness of the book itself, which cannot be foreign to its permanence. Its fourth chapter opens with the remark, "I have wandered far from the object in view," when he has described no such object; the tenth chapter explicitly summarizes itself in its headnote as "A chapter of digressions and anecdotes, as an interlude preceding that on the nature and genesis of the imagination," but the chapter it precedes—the eleventh—is not about imagination, but, as its headnote describes it, is "An affectionate exhortation to those who in early life feel themselves disposed to become authors," and that chapter opens with a sentence whose second clause is fully worthy to be considered the title of an essay of Montaigne's: "It was a favorite remark of Mr. Whitbread's, that no man does any thing from a single motive." The next chapter, twelve, describes itself as "A chapter of requests and premonitions concerning the perusal or omission of the chapter that follows," and what follows, chapter 13, which actually entitles itself "On the imagination," consists mostly in its absence; more specifically, it consists largely in the printing of a letter the author says he received—a letter in prose self-evidently identical with the prose which we have all along been treated to— which he says persuaded him not to print the chapter, on the ground that it really belongs with that major work he has been (and will be forever) promising. The last sentence of that chapter refers the reader, for further amplification, to an essay said to be prefixed to a new edition of *The Ancient Mariner*, an essay which turns out also to be nonexistent. Thus ends the first volume of the *Biographia Literaria*.

To say that the book is composed without digression means accordingly that if it has some end, the approach to it is followed in as straightforward a path as the terrain permits. This suggests that the end is, or requires, continuous self-interruption. But then this will be a way of drawing the consequence of philosophy's self-description as a discourse bearing endless responsibility for itself. And this could be further interpreted as a matter of endless responsiveness to itself—which might look to be exactly irresponsible.

The end is indicated by the surface of the book's concern to preserve or redeem genuine poetry from its detractors and its impersonations, in a world that, as he demonstrates, cannot read, and to demonstrate that this preservation is bound up with the preservation or redemption of genuine philosophy, where the preservation of poetry and philosophy by one another presents itself as the necessity of recovering or replacing religion. This contesting of philosophy and poetry and religion (and I guess of politics) with one another, for one another, together with the disreputable sense that the fate of the contest is bound up in one's own writing and, moreover, with the conviction that the autobiographical is a method of thought wherein such a contest can find a useful field and in which the stakes appear sometimes to be the loss or gain of our common human nature, sometimes to be the loss or gain of nature itself, as if the world were no more than one's own—some such statement represents the general idea I have of what constitutes serious romanticism's self-appointed mission, the idea with which I seek its figures. Our current humanist appeals to the interdisciplinary would be traces of such contests.

From where is such an intellectual ambition to gain backing? Having repudiated the English and the French philosophical traditions because of their basis in the occurrence to the mind of ideas construed as representations and subject to laws, Coleridge turns for inspiration—and teaches us to turn—to German philosophy, both to the religious and mystical Germans who preceded Kant and to the Idealists, preeminently Schelling, who thought to overcome Kant's limitations. And an essential preparation for the success of the ambition is the diagnosis of the fear and hatred of those who oppose such writing as he is undertaking and championing, as though an understanding of the hatred and the fear of poetry and of philosophy is internal to (grammatically related to) an understanding of what those aspirations are. No wonder Coleridge remarks, "Great indeed are the obstacles which an English metaphysician has to encounter."[19] I take it as to Coleridge's philosophical credit that he finds the initial obstacle—perhaps therefore the greatest, the image of all the rest— to be the finding of a place to begin, undigressively. Such is a cost of refusing to identify the vocation to philosophy with the vocation to science, enviable and glamorous as that may be.

The Kantian pressure upon the *Biographia* is conveniently measured in taking the book as the key to a Kantian reading of *The Ancient Mariner*. For this purpose we can expose the issue by breaking in on a moment of the *Biographia* in which Coleridge is struggling with two of his main obsessions: his particular, engulfing sense of indebtedness to the work of others, and his tendency to deal in shady regions of learning.

The moment is occupied by a pair of sentences in which he is expressing his gratitude, his debt, to the writings of mystics, the boon he has received from them in "[preventing my] mind from being imprisoned within the outline of any single dogmatic system. They contributed to keep alive the *heart* in the *head*; gave me an indistinct, yet stirring, and working presentiment, that all the products of the mere *reflective* faculty partook of DEATH."[20] It is they, he goes on to say, who "during my wanderings through the wilderness of doubt . . . enabled me to skirt, without crossing, the sandy deserts of unbelief." Now since it is of objects, or what he calls "objects as objects," that Coleridge otherwise speaks of as "dead, fixed" in contrast to the will or to imagination, and since he speaks of "the writings of the illustrious sage of Königsberg" as having "[taken] possession of me as with a giant's hand," I interpret the death, of which the reflective faculty partakes, to be that of the world made in our image, or rather through our categories, by Kant's faculty of the understanding, namely that very world which was meant to remove the skeptic's anxieties about the existence of objects outside us.

Here is extreme testimony that what both the world and the faculty of the world need redeeming from is felt to be at once skepticism and the answer to skepticism provided in the *Critique of Pure Reason*. And I think the feeling or intuition can be expressed by saying: since the categories of the understanding are ours, we can be understood to be carrying the death of the world in us, in our very requirement of creating it, as if it does not yet exist.

Naturally it may be imagined that someone will profess not to understand how the world could die. But then there will also be those who will profess not to understand how the existence of the world may be doubted. A difference between these cases is that a philosopher might undertake to provide you with skeptical considerations that lead you to the possibility he or she has in mind, whereas a romantic will want you to see that his vision expresses the way you are living now. Both may fail in their demands. No one wants to be a skeptic; to be gripped by its threat is to wish to overcome it. And for each one who wants to be a romantic, there is someone else who wishes him to outgrow it.

Against a vision of the death of the world, the romantic calling for poetry, or quest for it, the urgency of it, would be sensible; and the sense that the redemption of philosophy is bound up with the redemption of poetry would be understandable: the calling of poetry is to give the world back, to bring it back, as to life. Hence romantics seem to involve themselves in what look to us to be superstitious, discredited mysteries of animism, sometimes in the form of what is called the pathetic fallacy.

Now this quest of poetry for the recovery of the world (which I am interpreting as the recovery of, or from, the thing in itself), this way of joining or paralleling the philosophical effort to recover from skepticism, will look to poetry very like the quest for poetry, as if the cause of poetry has become its own survival. For what is poetry without a world—I mean, what is a fuller expression of the romantics' sense of the death of the world than a sense of the death of the poetry of the world? But then again, how can the loss of poetry be mourned *in poetry*? (If it is gone, it is gone.) Which I take as the twin of the question: How can philosophy be ended *in philosophy*? (If it is here, it is here.) Yet ending philosophy is something a creative philosophy seems habitually to undertake.

I recognize that certain of these recent formulations concerning romanticism are under the influence at once of a decisive indebtedness to what I have so far read on these subjects by M. H. Abrams, Harold Bloom, Geoffrey Hartman, and Paul de Man,[21] and at the same time of an uneasiness with those readings. For all their differences, they seem to share (in the writings in question) an assumption, as Bloom has expressed it in *Romanticism and Consciousness*, "that the central spiritual problem of Romanticism is the difficult relation between nature and consciousness." Of course, I do not think this assumption is wrong, and its receipts have been rich. But I find that I do not know how to assess the price of so fundamental a stake in the concept of consciousness. By its price I mean two matters primarily: that the concept takes in train a philosophical machinery of self-consciousness, subjectivity, and imagination, of post-Kantianism in general, that for me runs out of control; and that it closes out a possible question as to whether what is thought of as fundamental to romanticism, especially to what any of its critics will feel as its sense of estrangement, is first of all the relation of consciousness and nature, or first of all, say, the relation of knowledge and the world; and whether accordingly self-consciousness is the cause or the effect of skepticism, or whether they are simultaneous, or whether one or other of these possibilities leads from and to one or another version or notion of romanticism.

Provisionally taking skepticism to be fundamental, or anyway more under my control, I will propose *The Ancient Mariner* to be a study of the issue of Kant's two worlds, in the following way. I begin with the prose argument that prefaced its first printing in 1798, which was replaced, to be amplified, by the running marginal prose gloss in 1817, the year of the *Biographia*.

How a Ship having passed the line was driven by Storms to the cold Country towards the South Pole; . . . and of the strange things that befell; and in what manner the Ancient Mariner came back to his own Country.

(We are bound, I guess, to hear this as inviting us to pass, by warning us against passing, beyond and below the lines of poetry and prose. I am taking it as asking us to go beyond this way of taking it.) I note an implied image of a mental line to be crossed that is interpreted as a geographical or terrestrial border, in the following passage early in chapter 12 of the *Biographia*.

A [philosophical] system, the first principle of which is to render the mind intuitive of the *spiritual* in man (i.e., of that which lies *on the other side* of our natural consciousness) must needs have a greater obscurity for those who have never disciplined and strengthened this ulterior consciousness. It must in truth be a land of darkness, a perfect *Anti-Goshen*, for men to whom the noblest treasures of their own being are reported only through the imperfect translation of lifeless and sightless *notions*. . . . No wonder, then, that he remains incomprehensible to himself as well as to others. No wonder, that, in the fearful desert of his consciousness, he wearies himself out with empty words, to which no friendly echo answers.

Earlier in that paragraph Coleridge says of this "common consciousness" that it "will furnish proofs by its own direction, that it is connected with master-currents below the surface." I will relate this to the Mariner's returning "Slowly and smoothly/Moved onward from beneath" back toward the line, in particular moved onward by what the marginal gloss calls "The Polar Spirit."

Later in the *Biographia* chapter, as he is announcing his philosophical theses, Coleridge gives the geographical or civilian name of what the Mariner's glosses only call "the line," and places that feature of the earth at the center of thinking:

For it must be remembered, that all these Theses refer solely to one of the two Polar Sciences, namely, to that which commences with, and rigidly confines itself within, the subjective, leaving the objective (as far as it is exclusively objective) to natural philosophy, which is its opposite pole. . . . The result of both the sciences, or their equatorial point, would be the principle of a total and undivided philosophy.

That Coleridge is part of a tradition obsessed with the polarity of human thought needs no confirmation from me. (See, for instance, Thomas McFarland, "Coleridge's Doctrine of Polarity and Its European Contexts."[22]) In the passage just cited I understand the very impossibility of the idea of an "equatorial point," taken as an image or picture, to express his diagnosis of the Mariner's curse—that in being drawn toward one pole he is drawn away from the other, that is, that he is enchanted by a way of thinking, an isolated Polar Science, one in which, let me say, a diagram of the mind (as by a line below which knowledge cannot reach) is not an allegory but a representation, as of a matching substance. So the "Polar Spirit" with which the Mariner returns has yet to enter into the "two Polar Sciences" which in the vision of the *Biographia* will institute an undivided philosophy.

I end here with two remarks about this proposal for reading *The Ancient Mariner*.

1. By 1798 Coleridge knew something about Kant, but scholars agree that the giant's hand did not take hold of him until his return from Germany a few years later. Accordingly I am not saying that when he wrote his poem he meant it to exemplify Kant's *Critique of Pure Reason*, merely that it does so, and that there are passages in the *Biographia* where Coleridge is summarizing his hopes for philosophy in the form of post-Kantian Idealism, primarily in Schelling, in which he virtually states as much. Conviction in this idea obviously depends on how strongly or naturally one envisions the first *Critique* as projecting a *line* below which, or a circle outside which, experience, hence knowledge, cannot, and must not presume to, penetrate. Here I must appeal to the experience of those who have tried to explain Kant's work, if just to themselves, I mean to that moment at which, quite inevitably, one pictures its architectonic by actually drawing a line or circle, closing off the region of the thing in itself. I realize that I imply, in this appeal, not merely that such a gesture is not accidental, but that so apparently trivial a sketch can control, or express, one's thinking for a long lifetime, like a Fate. Then one profit in thinking through the Mariner's journey by means of the poem is to assess that Fate, to suggest, for example, that if the Mariner's experience *is* to be imagined or conceived as of the region below the line, showing that its structure can be mapped, then it is not an a priori limitation of reason that prohibits its penetration by knowledge, but some other power, less genteel: call it repression.

This cautions me to be explicit that the region of the thing in itself, below the line, underlies both the inner and the outer horizons of knowledge (using Kant's distinction), toward the self or mind as toward the world or nature. Here is a way I can understand something of Freud's contempt and fear of the standing of philosophy. One reason Freud gives for shunning philosophy is that it identifies the mental with consciousness, but this seems no truer of Kant than it does of Plato. Something like the reverse would be a cause to fear Kant. If Freud's unconscious is what is not available to knowledge (under, let us say, normal circumstances) then Kant's reason projects a whole realm of the self or mind which is even more strongly unavailable to knowledge; but, as part of reason, it is surely mental! What Freud must object to, however, is Kant's ground for excluding this realm from knowledge, namely, that this realm cannot be *experienced,* hence that there is something in the self that *logically* cannot be brought to knowledge. If this is the wisdom of reason, Freud *must* try to outdistance it, which is to say, to change the shape of reason. Here is a sense in which he was preceded by romanticism.

2. I do not take this projected reading of *The Ancient Mariner* to be in competition with the familiar reading of it as an allegory of the Fall. Rather, on the contrary, I take it to provide an explanation of why it fits the Fall, that is, of what the Fall is itself an allegory of. Accordingly, I take the story in the poem to allegorize any spiritual transgression in which the first step is casual, as if, to borrow a phrase, always already taken, and the downward half of the journey—to the cold country—is made "Driven by Storms," as if by natural, or conceivably logical, consequences. On this understanding the transgression fits what I understand the idea to come to of the craving to speak, in Wittgenstein's phrase, "outside language games." (It had better fit, since I take that idea to be itself an interpretation of the Kantian *Critique*.) For that description ("outside language games") from the *Philosophical Investigations* itself is hardly more than an allegory, or myth.[23] I use it in *The Claim of Reason* to record the pervasive thought of that book that a mark of the natural in natural language is its capacity to repudiate itself, to find arbitrary, or merely conventional, the lines laid down for its words by our agreement in criteria, our attunement with one another (which is to say, in my lingo, that the threat of skepticism is a natural or inevitable presentiment of the human mind), together with the discovery that what presents itself upon a skeptical repudiation of this attunement is another definite, as it were frozen, structure—one to which I habitually say (I now realize afresh) that we are "forced" or "driven."

But if the Fall is also to be read as an interpretation of this condition, it is no wonder that it seems a romantic's birthright, not to say obligation, at some point to undertake an interpretation of the story of Eden. A dominant interpretation of it, as in Hegel, if I understand, is that the birth of knowledge is the origin of consciousness, hence self-conscious-

ness, hence of guilt and shame, hence of human life as severed and es-
tranged, from nature, from others, from itself. Hence the task of human
life is of recovery, as of one's country, or health. I find myself winding up
somewhat differently.

The explicit temptation of Eden is to knowledge, which above all
means: to a denial that, as we stand, we know. There was hence from the
beginning no Eden, no place in which names are immune to skepticism. I
note that the story in the Bible as told does not equate the knowledge of
nakedness with being ashamed, or with self-consciousness (however con-
sequential such things will be), but with fear. "I was afraid, because I was
naked; and I hid myself," Adam says. And when God thereupon asks him,
"Who told thee that thou wast naked?" the very fantasticality of that question of course drives us to ask what nakedness is and what it is to learn it
of oneself. The feature of the situation I emphasize is that its sense of exposure upon the birth of knowledge pertains not only to one's vulnerability to knowledge, to being known, to the trauma of separation, but as well
to the vulnerability of knowledge itself, to the realization that Eden is not
the world, but that one had been living as within a circle or behind a
line—because when God "drove out the man," the man was not surprised
that there was an elsewhere.

5 ▓▓▓▓▓▓

Being Odd, Getting Even
(Descartes, Emerson, Poe)

In the lobby of William James Hall at Harvard, across the story-tall
expanse of concrete above the bank of elevators facing you as you enter,
brass letters spell out the following pair of sentences attributed by further
such letters to William James:

THE COMMUNITY STAGNATES WITHOUT THE IMPULSE

OF THE INDIVIDUAL

THE IMPULSE DIES AWAY WITHOUT THE SYMPATHY

OF THE COMMUNITY

The message may be taken as empirically directed to whoever stands beneath and reads it, and thence either as a warning, an exhortation, or a description of a state of current affairs—or else it may be taken as claiming a
transcendental relation among the concepts of community and individual
as they have so far shown themselves. Does this multiplicity produce what
certain literary theorists now speak of as the undecidable? Or is the brass
indifference of this writing on the wall an apt expression of our avoidance
of decision, a refusal to apply our words to ourselves, to take them on?

This lecture is a kind of progress report on my philosophical journey to locate an inheritance of Wittgenstein and Heidegger, and of Emerson and Thoreau before them, for all of whom there seems to be some question whether the individual or the community as yet, or any longer, exists. This question (or, you may say, this fantasy) gives ground equally for despair and for hope in the human as it now stands. It is also the question or fantasy in which I have been seeking instruction from certain Hollywood comedies of remarriage and, before them, from Shakespearean romance and tragedy. In this mood I do not wish to propose a solution to the riddle of whether society is the bane or the blessing of the individual, or to offer advice about whether a better state of the world must begin with a reformation of institutions or of persons, advice that would of course require me to define institutions and individuals and their modes of interpenetration. So I will pick up the twist in the story of the discovery of the individual where Descartes placed it in his *Meditations*—before, so to speak, either individual or institutional differences come into play. This twist is Descartes's discovery that my existence requires, hence permits, proof (you might say authentication)—more particularly, requires that if I am to exist I must name my existence, acknowledge it. This imperative entails that I am a thing with two foci, or in Emerson's image, two magnetic poles[1]—say a positive and a negative, or an active and a passive.

Such a depiction may not seem to you right off to capture Descartes's cogito argument. But that something like it does capture that argument is what I understand the drift of Emerson's perhaps inaudibly familiar words in "Self-Reliance" to claim. My first task here will be to establish this about Emerson's essay; my second will be to say why I think Emerson is right, as right in his interpretation and inheritance of Descartes as any other philosophical descendant I know of. Following that, as a third principal task, I will take up a pair of tales by Edgar Allan Poe, primarily "The Imp of the Perverse" and subordinately "The Black Cat." These stories, I find, engage with the same imperative of human existence: that it must prove or declare itself. And since Poe's "The Imp of the Perverse" alludes more than once to *Hamlet*, it will bring us to my title, the idea of thinking about individuality (or the loss of it) under the spell of revenge, of getting even for oddness.

Emerson's incorporation of Descartes into "Self-Reliance" is anything but veiled. At the center of the essay is a paragraph that begins: "Man is timid and apologetic; he is no longer upright; he dares not say 'I think,' 'I am,' but quotes some saint or sage." It is my impression that readers of Emerson have not been impressed by this allusion, or repetition, perhaps because they have fallen into an old habit of condescending to Emerson (as if to pay for a love of his writing by conceding that he was hardly capable of consecutive thought, let alone capable of taking on Descartes), perhaps because they remember or assume the cogito always to be expressed in words that translate as "I think, *therefore* I am." But in Descartes's Second Meditation, where I suppose it is most often actually encountered, the insight is expressed: "*I am, I exist*, is necessarily true every time that I pronounce it or conceive it in my mind." Emerson's emphasis on the *saying* of "I" is precisely faithful to this expression of Descartes's insight.

It is this feature of the cogito that is emphasized in some of the most productive thinking about Descartes in recent analytical philosophy, where the issue, associated with the names of Jaakko Hintikka and Bernard Williams, is phrased as the question whether the certainty of existence required and claimed by the cogito results from taking the claim "I think" as the basis (i.e., premise) for an inference, or as the expression of some kind of performance.[2] Williams does not quite rest with saying, with Hintikka, that the cogito just is not an inference, and just is a performance of some kind, but Williams does insist that it is not an ordinary, or syllogistic, inference, as he insists, at the end of his intricate discussion, that the performance in play is no less peculiar of its kind, demanding further reflection. The cogito's peculiarity can be summarized as follows, according to Williams. On the one hand, the force of the first person pronoun is that it cannot fail to refer to the one using it, hence one who says "I exist" must exist; or, put negatively, "I exist" is undeniable, which is to say, "I do not exist" cannot coherently be said. On the other hand, to be said sensibly, "I" must distinguish the one saying it, to whom it cannot fail to refer, from others to whom it does not, at that saying, refer. But Descartes's use of it arises exactly in a context in which there are no others to distinguish himself (so to speak) from. So the force of the pronoun is in apparent conflict with its sense.

Compared with such considerations, Emerson's remark about our not daring to say "I think," "I am," seems somewhat literary. But why? Emerson is picking up a question, or a side of the question, that succeeds the inferential or performance aspect of the cogito—namely, the question of what happens if I do *not* say (and of course do not say the negation of) "I am, I exist" or "conceive it in my mind." An analytical philosopher will hardly take much interest in this side of the question, since it will hardly seem worth arguing for or against the inference that if I do not say or perform the words "I am" or their equivalent (aloud or silently), therefore I perhaps do not exist. Surely the saying or thinking of some words may be taken to bear on whether the sayer or thinker of them exists at most in the sense of determining whether he or she *knows* of his or her existence, but surely not in the sense that the saying or thinking may create that existence.

But this assurance seems contrary to Descartes's findings. He speculates a few paragraphs after announcing the cogito: "I am, I exist—that is certain; but for how long do I exist? For as long as I think; for it might perhaps happen, if I totally ceased thinking, that I would at the same time completely cease to be." This does not quite say that my ceasing to think would cause, or would be, my ceasing to exist. It may amount to saying so if I must think of myself as having a creator (hence, according to Descartes, a preserver) and if all candidates for this role other than myself dropped out. These assumptions seem faithful to Descartes's text, so that I am prepared to take it that the cogito is only half the battle concerning the relation of my thinking to my existing, or perhaps "I think, therefore I am" expresses only half the battle of the cogito: Descartes establishes to his satisfaction that I exist only while, or if *and only if,* I think. It is this, it seems, that leads him to claim that the mind always thinks, an idea Nietzsche and Freud will put to further use.

Emerson goes the whole way with Descartes's insight—that I exist only if I think—but he thereupon denies that I (mostly) do think, that the "I" mostly gets into my thinking, as it were. From this it follows that the skeptical possibility is realized—that I do not exist, that I, as it were, haunt the world,[3] a realization perhaps expressed by saying that the life I live is the life of skepticism. Just before the end of the Second Meditation, Descartes observes that "if I judge that [anything, say the external world] exists because I see it, certainly it follows much more evidently that I exist myself because I see it." Since the existence of the world is more doubtful than my own existence, if I do not know that I exist, I so to speak even more evidently do not know that the things of the world exist. If, accordingly, Emerson is to be understood as describing the life left to me under skepticism—implying that I do not exist among the things of the world, that I haunt the world—and if for this reason he is to be called literary and not philosophical, we might well conclude, so much the worse for philosophy. Philosophy shrinks before a description of the very possibility it undertakes to refute, so it can never know of itself whether it has turned its nemesis aside.

But it seems to me that one can see how Emerson arrives at his conclusion by a continuing faithfulness to Descartes's own procedures, to the fact, as one might put it, that Descartes's procedures are themselves as essentially literary as they are philosophical and that it may even have become essential to philosophy to show as much. After arriving at the cogito, Descartes immediately raises the question of his metaphysical identity: "But I do not yet know sufficiently clearly what I am, I who am sure that I exist." He raises this question six or seven times over the ensuing seven or eight paragraphs, rejecting along the way such answers as that he is a rational animal, or that he is a body, or that his soul is "something very rarefied and subtle, such as a wind, a flame, or a very much expanded air . . . infused throughout my grosser components," before he settles on the answer that he is essentially a thing that thinks. There is nothing in these considerations to call argument or inference; indeed, the most obvious description of these passages is to say that they constitute an autobiographical narrative of some kind. If Descartes is philosophizing, and if these passages are essential to his philosophizing, it follows that philosophy is not exhausted in argumentation. And if the power of these passages is literary, then the literary is essential to the power of philosophy; at some stage the philosophical becomes, or turns into, the literary.

Now I think one can describe Emerson's progress as his having posed Descartes's question for himself and provided a fresh line of answer, one you might call a grammatical answer: I am a being who to exist must say I exist, or must acknowledge my existence—claim it, stake it, enact it.

The beauty of the answer lies in its weakness (you may say its emptiness)—indeed, in two weaknesses. First, it does not prejudge what the I or self or mind or soul may turn out to be, but only specifies a condition that whatever it is must meet. Second, the proof only works in the moment of its giving, for what I prove is the existence only of a creature who *can* enact its existence, as exemplified in actually giving the proof, not one who at all times does in fact enact it. The transience of the existence it proves and the transience of its manner of proof seem in the spirit of the *Meditations*, including Descartes's proofs for God; this transience would be the moral of Descartes's insistence on the presence of clear and distinct ideas as essential to, let me say, philosophical knowledge. Only in the vanishing presence of such ideas does proof take effect—as if there were nothing to rely on but reliance itself. This is perhaps why Emerson will say, "To talk of reliance is a poor external way of speaking."

That what I am is one who to exist enacts his existence is an answer Descartes might almost have given himself, since it is scarcely more than a literal transcript of what I set up as the further half of the cogito's battle. It is a way of envisioning roughly the view of so-called human existence taken by Heidegger in *Being and Time*: that Dasein's being is such that its being is an issue for it. But for Descartes to have given such an answer would have threatened the first declared purpose of his Meditations, which was to offer proof of God's existence. If I am one who can enact my existence, God's role in the enactment is compromised. Descartes's word for what I call "enacting"—or "claiming" or "staking" or "acknowledging"—is "authoring." In the Third Meditation:

I wish to pass on now to consider whether I myself, who have the idea of God, could exist if there had been no God. And I ask, from what source would I have derived my existence? Possibly from myself, or from my parents. . . . But if I were . . . the author of my own being, I would doubt nothing, I would experience no desires, and finally I would lack no perfection . . . I would be God (himself). . . . Even if I could suppose that possibly I have always been as I am now . . . it would not follow that no author of my existence need then be sought and I would still have to recognize that it is necessary that God is the author of my existence.

Apparently it is the very sense of my need for a human proof of my human existence—some authentication—that is the source of the idea that I need an author. ("Need for proof" will be what becomes of my intuition of my transience, or dependence, or incompleteness, or unfinishedness, or unsponsoredness—of the intuition that I am unauthorized.)

But surely the idea of self-authorizing is merely metaphorical, the merest exploitation of the coincidence that the Latin word for author is also the word for creating, nothing more than the by now fully discredited romantic picture of the author or artist as incomprehensibly original, as a world-creating and self-creating genius. It is true that the problematic of enacting one's existence skirts the edge of metaphysical nonsense. It asks us, in effect, to move from the consideration that we may sensibly disclaim certain actions as ours (ones done, as we may say, against our wills), and hence from the consideration that we may disclaim certain of our thoughts as ours (ones, it may be, we would not dream of acting on, though the terrain here gets philosophically and psychologically more dangerous), to the possibility that none of my actions and thoughts are mine—as if, if I am not a ghost, I am, I would like to say, *worked*, from inside or outside. This move to the metaphysical is like saying that since it makes sense to suppose that I might lack any or all of my limbs I might lack a body altogether, or that since I never see all of any object and hence may not know that a given object exists I may not know that the external world as such exists. Ordinary language philosophy, most notably in the teaching of Austin and of Wittgenstein, has discredited such moves to the metaphysical, as a way of discrediting the conclusions of skepticism. But in my interpretation of Wittgenstein, what is discredited is not the appeal or the threat of skepticism as such, but only skepticism's own pictures of its accomplishments. Similarly, what is discredited in the romantic's knowledge about self-authoring is only a partial picture of authoring and of creation, a picture of human creation as a literalized anthropomorphism of God's creation—as if to create myself I were required to begin with the dust of the ground and magic breath, rather than with, say, an uncreated human being and the power of thinking.

That human clay and the human capacity for thought are enough to inspire the authoring of myself is, at any rate, what I take Emerson's "Self-Reliance," as a reading of Descartes's cogito argument, to claim. I take his underlying turning of Descartes to be something like this: there is a sense of being the author of oneself that does not require me to imagine myself God (that may just be the name of the particular picture of the self as a self-present substance), a sense in which the absence of doubt and desire of which Descartes speaks in proving that God, not he, is the author of himself is a continuing task, not a property, a task in which the goal, or the product of the process, is not a state of being but a moment of change, say of becoming—a transience of being, a being of transience. (Emerson notes: "This one fact the world hates; that the soul *becomes*.") To make sense of this turn, Emerson needs a view of the world, a perspective on its fallenness, in which the *uncreatedness* of the individual manifests itself, in which human life appears as the individual's failure at self-creation, as a continuous loss of individual possibility in the face of some overpowering competitor. This is to say that, if my gloss of Emerson's reading of Descartes is right, the cogito's need arises at particular historical moments in the life of the individual and in the life of the culture.

Emerson calls the mode of uncreated life "conformity." But each of the modern prophets seems to have been driven to find some way of characterizing the threat to individual existence, to individuation, posed by the life to which their society is bringing itself. John Stuart Mill (in *On Liberty*) called it the despotism of opinion, and he characterized being human in his period in terms of deformity; he speaks of us as withered and starved, and as dwarfs. Nietzsche called the threat: the world of the last man, the world of the murderers of God. Marx thinks of it rather as the preexistence of the human. Freud's discovery of the uncomprehended meaningfulness of human expression belongs in the line of such prophecy. Emerson's philosophical distinction here lies in his diagnosis of this moment and in his recommended therapy.

It is as a diagnosis of this state of the world that Emerson announces that Descartes's proof of self-existence (the foundation, Descartes named it, of the edifice of his former opinions, the fixed and immovable fulcrum on which to reposition the earth) cannot, or can no longer, be given, thus asking us to conclude (such is the nature of this peculiar proof) that man, the human, does not, or does no longer, exist. Here is Emerson's sentence again, together with the sentence and a half following it: "Man is timid and apologetic; he is no longer upright; he dares not say 'I think,' 'I am,' but quotes some saint or sage. He is ashamed before the blade of grass or the blowing rose . . . they are for what they are; they exist with God today." We can locate Emerson's proposed therapy in this vision of so-called man's loss of existence if we take the successive notations of this vision as in apposition, as interpretations of one another: being apologetic; being no longer upright; daring not to say, but only quoting; being ashamed, as if for not existing today. There are, as Wittgenstein is once moved to express himself, a multitude of familiar paths leading off from these words in all directions.[4] Let us take, or at least point down, two or three such paths.

To begin with, the idea that something about our mode of existence removes us from nature, and that this has to do with being ashamed, of course alludes to the romantic problematic of self-consciousness (or the post-Kantian interpretation of that problematic), a particular interpretation of the Fall of Man. But put Emerson's invocation of shame in apposition to his invocation of our loss of uprightness, and he may be taken as challenging, not passing on, the romantic interpretation of the Fall as self-consciousness, refusing to regard our shame as a metaphysically irrecoverable loss of innocence but seeing it instead as an unnecessary acquiescence (or necessary only as history is necessary) in, let me say, poor posture, a posture he calls timidity and apologeticness. I will simply claim, without citing textual evidence (preeminently the contexts in which the word "shame" and its inflections are deployed throughout Emerson's essay), that the proposed therapy is to become ashamed of our shame, to find our ashamed posture more shameful than anything it could be reacting to. One might say that he calls for more, not less, self-consciousness; but it would be better to say that he shows self-consciousness not to be the issue it seems. It, or our view of it, is itself a function of poor posture.

But really everything so far said about existence, preexistence, and so forth may be some function of poor posture—including, of course, our view of what poor posture may be. Bad posture Emerson variously names, in one passage, as peeping or stealing or skulking up and down "with the air of a charity-boy, a bastard, or an interloper in the world which exists for him"; in another, he finds men behaving as if their acts were fines they paid "in expiation of daily non-appearance on parade," done "as an apology or extenuation of their living in the world—as invalids and the insane pay a high board. Their virtues are penances." This vision of human beings as in postures of perpetual penance or self-mortification will remind readers of *Walden* of that book's opening pages (not to mention Nietzsche's *Genealogy of Morals*).

Good posture has two principal names or modes in "Self-Reliance": standing and sitting. The idea behind both modes is that of finding and taking and staying in a place. What is good in these postures is whatever makes them necessary to the acknowledgment, or the assumption, of individual existence, to the capacity to say "I." That this takes daring is what standing (up) pictures; that it takes claiming what belongs to you and disclaiming what does not belong to you is what sitting pictures. Sitting is thus the posture of being at home in the world (not peeping, stealing, skulking, or, as he also says, leaning), of owning or taking possession. This portrayal of the posture of sitting is, again, drawn out in *Walden*, at the opening of the second chapter ("Where I Lived, and What I Lived for") where what Thoreau calls acquiring property is what most people would consider passing it by. Resisting the temptation to follow the turnings of these paths, I put them at once in apposition to the notation that in not daring to say something what we do instead is to quote.

There is a gag here that especially appeals to contemporary sensibilities. Emerson writes, "Man . . . dares not say . . . but quotes." But since at that moment he quotes Descartes, isn't he confessing that he too cannot say but can only quote? Then should we conclude that he is taking back or dismantling (or something) the entire guiding idea of "Self-Reliance"? Or is he rather suggesting that we are to overcome the binary opposition between saying and quoting, recognizing that each is always both, or that the difference is undecidable? That difference seems to me roughly the difference between what Thoreau calls the mother tongue and the father tongue,[5] hence perhaps makes the difference between language and literariness. And since I am taking the difference between saying and quoting as one of posture, the proposal of undecidability strikes me as the taking of a posture, and a poor one. I imagine being told that the difference in posture partakes of the same undecidability. My reply is that you can decide to say so. My decision is otherwise. (It is helped by my intuition that a guiding remark of Freud's is conceivable this way: Where thought takes place in me, there shall I take myself.)

Emerson's gag, suggesting that saying is quoting, condenses a number of ideas. First, language is an inheritance. Words are before I am; they are common. Second, the question whether I am saying them or quoting them—saying them firsthand or second hand, as it were—which means whether I am thinking or imitating, is the same as the question whether I do or do not exist as a human being and is a matter demanding proof. Third, the writing, of which the gag is part, is an expression of the proof of saying "I," hence of the claim that writing is a matter, say the decision, of life and death, and that what this comes to is the inheriting of language, an owning of words, which does not remove them from circulation but rather returns them, as to life.

That the claim to existence requires returning words to language, as if making them common to us, is suggested by the fourth sentence of "Self-Reliance": "To believe your own thought, to believe that what is true for you in your private heart is true for all men,—that is genius." (One path from these words leads to the transformation of the romantics' idea of genius: Genius is not a special endowment, like virtuosity, but a stance toward whatever endowment you discover is yours, as if life itself were a gift, and remarkable.) Genius is accordingly the name of the promise that the private and the social will be achieved together, hence of the perception that our lives now take place in the absence of either.

So Emerson is dedicating his writing to that promise when he says: "I shun father and mother and wife and brother when my genius calls me. I would write on the lintels of the door-post, *Whim*." (I will not repeat what I have said elsewhere concerning Emerson's marking of Whim in the place of God and thus staking his writing as a whole as having the power to turn aside the angel of death.) The point I emphasize here is only that the life-giving power of words, of saying "I," is your readiness to subject your desire to words (call it Whim), to become intelligible, with no assurance that you will be taken up. ("I hope it may be better than whim at last, but we cannot spend the day in explanation.") Emerson's dedication is a fantasy of finding your own voice, so that others, among them mothers and fathers, may shun you. This dedication enacts a posture toward, or response to, language as such, as if most men's words as a whole cried out for redemption: "Conformity makes them not false in a few particulars, authors of a few lies, but false in all particulars . . . so that every word they say chagrins us and we know not where to begin to set them right."

Citing authorship as the office of all users of language, a thing as commonly distributed as genius, is the plainest justification for seeing the enactment or acknowledgment of one's existence as the authoring of it and in particular for what we may take as Emerson's dominating claims for his writing: first, that it proves his human existence (i.e., establishes his right to say "I," to tell himself from and to others); second, that what he has proven on his behalf, others are capable of proving on theirs.

These claims come together in such a statement as "I will stand for humanity," which we will recognize as marking a number of paths: that Emerson's writing is in an upright posture; that what it says represents the human, meaning both that his portrait of himself is accurate only insofar as it portrays his fellows and that he is writing on their behalf (both as they stand, and as they stand for the eventual, what humanity may become); that he will for the time being stand humanity, bear it, as it is; and that he will stand up for it, protect it, guard it, presumably against itself. But to protect and guard someone by writing to and for that same one means to provide them instruction, or tuition.

The path I am not taking at this point leads from Emerson's speaking of "primary wisdom as Intuition," to which he adds, "All later teachings are Tuitions." I note this path to commemorate my annoyance at having to stand the repeated, conforming description of Emerson as a philosopher of intuition, a description that uniformly fails to add that he is simultaneously the teacher of tuition, as though his speaking of all later teachings as tuitions were a devaluing of the teachings rather than a direction for deriving their necessary value. Take the calling of his genius as a name for intuition. Marking *Whim* on his doorpost was intuition's tuition; an enactment of the obligation to remark the calling, or access, of genius; to run the risk (or, as Thoreau puts it, to sit the risk) of noting what happens to you, of making this happenstance notable, remarkable, think-able—of subjecting yourself, as said, to intelligibility.

How could we test the claim Emerson's writing makes to be such enactment, its claim to enact or acknowledge itself, to take on its existence, or, in Nietzsche's words, or rather Zarathustra's (which I imagine are more or less quoting Emerson's), to show that Emerson "does not say 'I' but performs 'I'"?[6] (The mere complication of self-reference, the stock-in-trade of certain modernizers, may amount to nothing more than the rumor of my existence.) How else but by letting the writing teach us how to test it, word by word?

"Self-Reliance" as a whole presents a theory—I wish we knew how to call it an aesthetics—of reading. Its opening words are "I read the other day," and four paragraphs before Emerson cites the cogito he remarks, "Our reading is mendicant and sycophantic," which is to say that he finds us reading the way he finds us doing everything else. How can we read his theory of reading in order to learn how to read him? We would already have to understand it in order to understand it. I have elsewhere called this the (apparent) paradox of reading;[7] it might just as well be called the para-dox of writing, since of writing meant with such ambitions we can say that only after it has done its work of creating a writer (which may amount to sloughing or shaking off voices) can one know what it is to write. But you never know. I mean, you never know when someone will learn the posture, as for themselves, that will make sense of a field of movement, it may be writing, or dancing, or passing a ball, or sitting at a keyboard, or free asso-ciating. So the sense of paradox expresses our not understanding how such learning happens. What we wish to learn here is nothing less than whether Emerson exists, hence could exist for us; whether, to begin with, his writ-ing performs the cogito he preaches.

He explicitly claims that it does, as he must. But before noting that, let me pause a little longer before this new major path, or branching of paths: the essay's theory of reading, hence of writing or speaking, hence of seeing and hearing. The theory, not surprisingly, is a theory of communi-cation, hence of expression, hence of character—character conceived, as Emerson always conceives it, as naming at once, as faces of one another, the human individual and human language. The writing side of the theory is epitomized in the remark: "Character teaches above our wills. Men imagine that they communicate their virtue or vice only by overt actions, and do not see that virtue or vice emit a breath every moment." The reading side of the theory is epitomized in: "To talk of reliance is a poor external way of speaking. Who has more obedience than I masters me, though he should not raise his finger."

On the reading side, the idea of mastering Emerson is not that of controlling him, exactly (though it will be related to monitoring him), but rather that of coming into command of him, as of a difficult text, or instrument, or practice. That this mastery happens by obedience, which is to say, by a mode of listening, relates the process to his dedicating of his writing as heeding the call of his genius, which to begin with he is able to note as Whim. It follows that mastering his text is a matter of discerning the whim from which at each word it follows. On the writing side, the idea of communicating as emitting a breath every moment (as if a natural risk of writing were transmitting disease) means that with every word you utter you say more than you know you say (here genteel Emerson's idea is that you cannot smell your own breath), which means in part that you do not know in the moment the extent to which your saying is quoting.

(Let me attract attention to another untaken path here, on which one becomes exquisitely sensible of the causes of Nietzsche's love of Emerson's writing. I am thinking now of Nietzsche's *Ecce Homo*, a book about writing that bears the subtitle *How One Becomes What One Is*. Its preface opens with the declaration that the author finds it indispensable to say who he is because in his conversations with the educated he becomes convinced that he is not alive; the preface continues by claiming or warning that to read him is to breathe a strong air. This book's opening part, "Why I Am So Wise," closes by saying that one of its author's traits that causes difficulty in his contacts with others is the uncanny sensitivity of his instinct for cleanliness: the innermost parts, the entrails, of every soul are *smelled* by him.)

So the question Emerson's theory of reading and writing is designed to answer is not "What does a text mean?" (and one may accordingly not wish to call it a theory of interpretation) but rather "How is it that a text we care about in a certain way (expressed perhaps as our being drawn to read it with the obedience that masters) invariably says more than its writer knows, so that writers and readers write and read beyond themselves?" This might be summarized as "What does a text know?" or, in Emerson's term, "What is the genius of the text?"

Here I note what strikes me as a congenial and fruitful conjunction with what I feel I have understood so far of the practices of Derrida and of

Lacan. Others may find my conjunction with these practices uncongenial if, for example, they take it to imply that what I termed the genius of the text, perhaps I should say its engendering, is fatal to or incompatible with the idea of an author and of an author's intention. This incompatibility ought to seem unlikely since both genius and intending have to do with inclination, hence with caring about something and with posture. Austin, in a seminar discussion at Harvard in 1955, once compared the role of intending with the role of headlights. (This material is published under the title "Three Ways of Spilling Ink.") An implication he may have had in mind is that driving somewhere (getting something done intentionally) does not on the whole happen by hanging a pair of headlights from your shoulders, sitting in an armchair, picking up an unattached steering wheel, and imagining a destination. (Though this is not unlike situations in which W. C. Fields has found himself.) Much else has to be in place—further mechanisms and systems (transmission, fuel, electrical), roads, the industries that produce and are produced by each, and so on—in order for headlights and a steering mechanism to do their work, even to be what they are. Even if some theorists speak as though intention were everything there is to meaning, is that a sensible reason for opposite theorists to assert that intention is nothing, counts for nothing in meaning? Is W. C. Fields our only alternative to Humpty Dumpty?

(In linking W. C. Fields's suffering of convention with Humpty Dumpty's claim to be master, by his very wishes, of what words shall mean (and thinking of his fate), I find I have not forgotten a passage during the discussions of "Must We Mean What We Say?" the day I delivered it in 1957 (at Stanford, it happens). Against a certain claim in my paper, one philosopher cited Humpty Dumpty's view of meaning (by name) as obviously, in all solemnity, the correct one. This was, I think, the first time I realized the possibility that parody is no longer a distinguishable intellectual tone since nothing can any longer be counted on to strike us in common as outrageous.)

But I was about to locate Emerson's explicit statement, or performance, of his cogito. In his eighth paragraph he writes: "Few and mean as my gifts may be, I actually am, and do not need for my own assurance or the assurance of my fellows any secondary testimony." Earlier in the paragraph he had said: "My life is for itself and not for a spectacle. . . . I ask primary evidence that you are a man, and refuse this appeal from the man to his actions." And two paragraphs later he will promise: "But do your work, and I shall know you."[8]

In refusing the evidence of actions, or say behavior, Emerson is refusing, as it were before the fact, the thrashing of empiricist philosophy to prove the existence of other minds by analogy with one's own case, which essentially involves an appeal to others' behavior (and its similarity to our own) as all we can know of them with certainty. But how does Emerson evade and counter the picture on which such a philosophical drift repeatedly comes to grief, namely, the picture according to which we cannot literally or directly have the experiences of others, cannot have what it is he apparently calls "primary evidence" of their existence? Emerson's counter is contained in the idea of what I called his promise: "But do your work, and I shall know you." Your work, what is yours to do, is exemplified, when you are confronted with Emerson's words, by reading those words—which means mastering them, obeying and hence following them, subjecting yourself to them as the writer has by undertaking to enact his existence in saying them. The test of following them is, according to Emerson's promise, that you will find yourself known by them, that you will take yourself on in them. It is what Thoreau calls conviction, being convicted by his words, read by them, sentenced. To acknowledge that I am known by what this text knows does not amount to agreeing with it, in the sense of believing it, as if it were a bunch of assertions or as if it contained a doctrine. To be known by it is to find thinking in it that confronts you. That would prove that a human existence is authored in it. But how will you prove thinking? How will you show your conviction?

One possibility Emerson presents as follows: "The virtue in most request is conformity. Self-reliance is its aversion." This almost says, and nearly means, that you find your existence in conversion, by converting to it, that thinking is a kind of turning oneself around. But what it directly says is that the world of conformity must turn from what Emerson says as he must turn from it and that since the process is never over while we live—since, that is, we are never finally free of one another—his reader's life with him will be a turning from, and returning from, his words, a moving on from them, by them. In "Fate," Emerson will call this aversion "antagonism": "Man is a stupendous antagonism," he says there. I can testify that when you stop struggling with Emerson's words they become insupportable.

But why does self-reliance insist that it will know its other, even create its other, meaning authorize the other's self-authorization, or auto-creation? Because it turns out that to gain the assurance, as Descartes had put it, that I am not alone in the world has turned out to require that I allow myself to be known. (I have called this requirement subjecting myself to intelligibility, or, say, legibility.) But doesn't this beg the question whether there *are* others there to do this knowing?

I would say rather that it orders the question. The fantasy of aloneness in the world may be read as saying that the step out of aloneness, or self-absorption, has to come without the assurance of others. (Not, perhaps, without their help.) "No one comes" is a tragedy for a child. For a grown-up it means the time has come to be the one who goes first (to offer oneself, allow oneself, to be, let us say, known). To this way of thinking, politics ought to have provided conditions for companionship, call it fraternity; but the price of companionship has been the suppression, not the affirmation, of otherness, that is to say, of difference and sameness, call these liberty and equality. A mission of Emerson's thinking is never to let politics forget this.

In declaring that his life is not for a spectacle but for itself, Emerson is not denying that it is a spectacle, and he thus inflects and recrosses his running themes of being seen, of shame, and of consciousness. A last citation on this subject will join "Self-Reliance" with Poe's "Imp of the Perverse."

In his fifth paragraph, Emerson says: "The man is as it were clapped into jail by his consciousness. As soon as he has once acted or spoken with *éclat* he is a committed person, watched by the sympathy or the hatred of hundreds, whose affections must now enter into his account. There is no Lethe for this." The idea is that we have become permanently and unforgettably visible to one another, in a state of perpetual theater. To turn aside consciousness, supposing that were possible, would accordingly only serve to distract us from this fact of our mutual confinement under one another's guard. The solution must then be to alter what it is we show, which requires turning even more watchfully to what it is we are conscious of and altering our posture toward it.

For example: "A man should learn to detect and watch that gleam of light which flashes across his mind from within, more than the lustre of the firmament of bards and sages. Yet he dismisses without notice his own thought, because it is his. In every work of genius we recognize our own rejected thoughts; they come back to us with a certain alienated majesty." Here I find a specification of finding myself known in this text; in it certain rejected thoughts of mine do seem to come back with what I am prepared to call alienated majesty (including the thought itself of my rejected thoughts). Then presumably this writer has managed not to dismiss his own thoughts but to call them together, to keep them on parade, at atten-tion. ("Tuition" speaks differently of being guarded; and unguarded.)

Yet he speaks from the condition of being a grown-up within the cir-cumstances of civil (or uncivil) obedience he describes, so he says all he says clapped into jail by his consciousness—a decade before Thoreau was clapped into jail, and for the same reason, for obeying rejected things. How is he released? If, going on with Emerson's words, there were Lethe for our bondage to the attention of others, to their sympathy or hatred, we would utter opinions that would be "seen to be not private but necessary, would sink like darts into the ear of men and put them in fear"—that is, my vis-ibility would then frighten my watchers, not the other way around, and my privacy would no longer present confinement but instead the conditions necessary for freedom. But as long as these conditions are not known to be achieved, the writer cannot know that I am known in his utterances, hence that he and I have each assumed our separate existences. So he cannot know but that in taking assurance from the promise of knowing my exis-tence he is only assuming my existence and his role in its affirmation, hence perhaps shifting the burden of proof from himself and still awaiting me to release him from his jail of consciousness, the consciousness of the consciousness of others. When is writing *done*?

That "Self-Reliance" may accordingly be understood to show writing as a message from prison forms its inner connection with Poe's "The Imp of the Perverse." (The thought of such a message, of course, forms other connections as well—for example, with Rousseau's *Social Contract*, whose early line, "Man is born free and everywhere he is in chains," names a con-dition from which the writer cannot be exempting his writing, especially if his interpretation of his writing's enchainment is to afford a step toward the freedom it is compelled, by its intuition of chains, to imagine.) I can hardly do more here than give some directions for how I think Poe's tale should, or anyway can, be read. This is just as well, because the validation of the reading requires from first to last that one take the time to try the claims on oneself. The claims have generally to do with the sound of Poe's prose, with what Emerson and Nietzsche would call its air or its smell. Poe's tale is essentially about the breath it gives off.

The sound of Poe's prose, of its incessant and perverse brilliance, is uncannily like the sound of philosophy as established in Descartes, as if Poe's prose were a parody of philosophy's. It strikes me that in Poe's tales the thought is being worked out that, now anyway, philosophy exists only as a parody of philosophy, or rather as something indistinguishable from the perversion of philosophy, as if to overthrow the reign of reason, the reason that philosophy was born to establish, is not alone the task of, let us say, poetry, but is now openly the genius or mission of philosophy itself. As if the task of disestablishing reason were the task of reconceiving it, of exacting a transformation or reversal of what we think of as thinking and so of what we think of as establishing the reign of thinking. A natural effect of reading such writing is to be unsure whether the writer is perfectly serious. I dare say that the writer may himself or herself be unsure, and that this may be a good sign that the writing is doing its work, taking its course. Then Poe's peculiar brilliance is to have discovered a sound, or the condition, of intelligence in which neither the reader nor the writer knows whether he or she is philosophizing, is thinking to some end. This is an insight, a philosophical insight, about philosophy: namely, that it is as difficult to stop philosophizing as it is to start. (As difficult, in Wittgenstein's words, as to bring philosophy peace.[9] Most people I know who care about philosophy either do not see this as a philosophical problem or do not believe that it has a solution.)

A convenient way of establishing the sound of Poe's tales is to juxtapose the opening sentences of "The Black Cat" with some early sentences from Descartes's *Meditations*. Here is Descartes:

There is no novelty to me in the reflection that, from my earliest years, I have accepted many false opinions as true, and that what I have concluded from such badly assured premises could not but be highly doubtful and uncertain. . . . I have found a serene retreat in peaceful solitude. I will therefore make a serious and unimpeded effort to destroy generally all my former opinions. . . . Everything which I have thus far accepted as entirely true and assured has been acquired from the senses or by means of the senses. But I have learned by experience that these senses sometimes mislead me, and it is prudent never to trust wholly those things which have once deceived us. . . . But it is possible that, even though the senses occasionally deceive us . . . there are many other things which we cannot reasonably doubt . . . —as, for example, that I am here, seated by the fire, wearing a winter dressing gown, holding this paper in my hands, and other things of this nature. And how could I deny that these hands and this body are mine, unless I am to compare myself with certain lunatics . . . [who] imagine that their head is made of clay, or that they are gourds, or that their body is glass? . . . Nevertheless, I must remember that I am a man, and that consequently I am accustomed to sleep and in my dreams to imagine the same things that lunatics imagine when awake. . . . I realize so clearly that there are no conclusive indications by which waking life can be distinguished from sleep that I am quite astonished, and my bewilderment is such that it is almost able to convince me that I am sleeping.

Now listen to Poe:

For the most wild, yet almost homely narrative which I am about to pen, I neither expect nor solicit belief. Mad indeed would I be to expect it, in a case where my very senses reject their own evidence. Yet, mad am I not—and very surely do I not dream. But tomorrow I die, and today I would unburthen my soul. My immediate purpose is to place before the world, plainly, succinctly, and without comment, a series of mere household events. In their consequences, these events have terrified—have tortured—have destroyed me. Yet I will not attempt to expound them.

The juxtaposition works both ways: to bring out at once Poe's brilliance (and what is more, his argumentative soundness) and Descartes's creepy, perverse calm (given the subjects his light of reason rakes across), his air of a mad diarist.

Moreover, the *Meditations* appear within the content of "The Imp of the Perverse," as indelibly, to my mind, as in "Self-Reliance." Before noting how, let me briefly describe this lesser-known tale. It is divided into two parts, each more or less eight paragraphs in length. The first half is, as Poe says about certain of Hawthorne's tales, not a tale at all but an essay. The essay argues for the existence of perverseness as a radical, primitive, irreducible faculty or sentiment of the soul, the propensity to do wrong for the wrong's sake, promptings to act for the reason that we should not—something it finds overlooked by phrenologists, moralists, and in great measure "all metaphysicianism," through "the pure arrogance of the reason." This phrase "the pure arrogance of the reason," to my ear, signals that Poe is writing a *Critique* of the arrogance of pure reason—as if the task, even after Kant, were essentially incomplete, even unbegun. (This characterization is not incompatible with the appreciation of Poe as a psychologist, but only with a certain idea of what psychology may be.) The second half of "The Imp of the Perverse," which tells the tale proper, begins:

I have said thus much, that in some measure I may answer your question—that I may explain to you why I am here—that I may assign to you something that shall have at least the faint aspect of a cause for my wearing these fetters, and for my tenanting this cell of the condemned. Had I not been thus prolix, you might either have misunderstood me altogether, or, with the rabble, have fancied me mad. As it is, you will easily perceive that I am one of the many uncounted victims of the Imp of the Perverse.

Since we have not been depicted as asking, or having, a question, the narrator's explanation insinuates that we ought to have one about his presence; thus it raises more questions than it formulates.

The tale turns out to be a Poe-ish matter about the deliberately wrought murder of someone for the apparent motive of inheriting his estate, a deed that goes undetected until some years later the writer perversely gives himself away. As for the means of the murder: "I knew my victim's habit of reading in bed. . . . I substituted, in his bedroom candlestand, a [poisoned] wax-light of my own making, for the one which I there found." The self-betrayal comes about when, as he puts it, "I arrested myself in the act." That act is murmuring, half-aloud, "I am safe," and then adding, "yes, if I be not fool enough to make open confession." But "I felt a maddening desire to shriek aloud. . . . Alas! I well, too well understand that, to *think*, in my situation, was to be lost. . . . I bounded like a madman through the crowded thoroughfare. At length, the populace took the alarm, and pursued me."

To the first of my directions for reading "The Imp" I expect nowadays little resistance: both the fiction of the writer's arresting himself and wearing fetters and tenanting the cell of the condemned and the fiction of providing a poisonous wax light for reading are descriptions or fantasies of writing, modeled by the writing before us. There is, or at least we need imagine, no actual imprisoning and no crime but the act of the writing itself. What does it mean to fantasize that words are fetters and cells and that to read them, to be awake to their meaning, or effect, is to be poisoned? Are we being told that writer and reader are one another's victims? Or is the suggestion that to arrive at the truth something in the reader as well as something in the writer must die? Does writing ward off or invite in the angel of death?

I expect more resistance to, or puzzlement at, the further proposal that the fiction of words that are in themselves unremarkable ("I am safe"), but whose saying annihilates the sayer, specifies the claim that "I well, too well understand that, to *think*, in my situation, was to be lost"—which is a kind of negation or perversion of the cogito. Rather than proving and preserving me, as in Descartes, thinking precipitates my destruction. A little earlier Poe's narrator makes this even clearer: "There is no passion in nature so demoniacally impatient, as that of him, who shuddering on the edge of a precipice, thus meditates a plunge. To indulge for a moment, in any attempt at *thought*, is to be inevitably lost; for reflection but urges us to forbear, and *therefore* it is, I say, that we *cannot . . .* we plunge, and are destroyed." If the Whim drawing on Emerson's "Self-Reliance" is to say "I do not think, therefore I do not exist," that of Poe's Imp is to say, "I think, therefore I am destroyed." This connection is reinforced, in this brief passage, by the words *meditates* and *demoniacally.* Poe's undetected, poisoned wax light may even substitute for, or allude to, Descartes's most famous example (of materiality) in the *Meditations,* the piece of melting wax whose identity cannot be determined empirically, but only by an innate conception in the understanding. (That in Poe's tale the act of thinking destroys by alarming the populace and turning them against the thinker and that perverseness is noted as the confessing of a crime, not the committing of it—as if the confessing and the committing were figurations of one another—mark paths of parody and perverseness I cannot trace here. That thinking will out, that it inherently betrays the thinker—[th]inker—is a grounding theme of *Walden.* Its writer declares in the opening chapter, "Economy," that what he prints must in each character "thus unblushingly publish my guilt." He says this upon listing the costs of what he ate for the year. It is as if his guilt consists exactly in keeping himself alive ("getting a living," he says), in his existing, as he exists, and his preserving himself, for example, by writing.)

My third suggestion for reading Poe's tale is that the presiding image collecting the ideas I have cited and setting them in play is given in its title. The title names and illustrates a common fact about language, even invokes what one might think of as an Emersonian theory of language: the possession of language as the subjection of oneself to the intelligible. The fact of language it illustrates is registered in the series of imp words that pop up throughout the sixteen paragraphs of the tale: *impulse* (several times), *impels* (several times), *impatient* (twice), *important, impertinent, imperceptible, impossible, unimpressive, imprisoned,* and, of course, *Imp.* Moreover, *imp.* is an abbreviation in English for *imperative, imperfect, imperial, import, imprimatur, impersonal, implement, improper,* and *improvement.* And *Imp.* is an abbreviation for Emperor and Empress. Now if to speak of the imp of the perverse is to name the imp in English, namely, as the initial sounds of a number of characteristically Poe-ish terms, then to speak of something called the perverse as containing this imp is to speak of language itself, specifically of English, as the perverse. But what is it about the imp of English that is perverse, hence presumably helps to produce, as users of language, us imps?

It may well be the prefix *im-* that is initially felt to be perverse, since, like the prefix *in-*, it has opposite meanings. With adjectives it is a negation or privative, as in *immediate, immaculate, imperfect, imprecise, improper, implacable, impious, impecunious*; with verbs it is an affirmation or intensive, as in *imprison, impinge, imbue, implant, implicate, impersonate*. (It is not impossible that *per-verse*, applied to language, should be followed out as meaning poetic through and through.) In plain air we keep the privative and the intensive well enough apart, but in certain circumstances (say in dreams, in which, according to Freud, logical operations like negation cannot be registered or pictured but must be supplied later by the dreamer's interpretation) we might grow confused about whether, for example, *immuring* means putting something into a wall or letting something out of one, or whether *impotence* means powerlessness or a special power directed to something special, or whether *implanting* is the giving or the removing of life, or whether *impersonate* means putting on another personality or being without personhood.

But the fact or idea of imp words is not a function of just that sequence of three letters. "Word imps" could name any of the recurrent combinations of letters of which the words of a language are composed. They are part of the way words have their familiar looks and sounds, and their familiarity depends upon our mostly not noticing the particles (or cells) and their laws, which constitute words and their imps—on our not noticing their necessary recurrences, which is perhaps only to say that recurrence constitutes familiarity. This necessity, the most familiar property of language there could be—that if there is to be language, words and their cells must recur, as if fettered in their orbits, that language is grammatical (to say the least)—insures the self-referentiality of language. When we do note these cells or molecules, these little moles of language (perhaps in thinking, perhaps in derangement), what we discover are word imps—the initial, or it may be medial or final, movements, the implanted origins or constituents of words, leading lives of their own, staring back at us, calling upon one another, giving us away, alarming—because to note them is to see that they live in front of our eyes, within earshot, at every moment.

But the perverseness of language, working without, even against, our thought and its autonomy, is a function not just of necessarily recurring imps of words but of the necessity for us speakers of language (us authors of it, or imps, or Emperors and Empresses of it) to mean something in and by our words, to desire to say something, certain things rather than others, in certain ways rather than in others, or else to work to avoid meaning them. Call these necessities the impulses and the implications of the saying of our words. There is—as in saying "I am safe," which destroyed safety and defeats what is said—a question whether in speaking one is affirming something or negating it. In particular, in such writing as Poe's, has the impulse to self-destruction, to giving oneself away or betraying oneself, become the only way of preserving the individual? And does it succeed? Is authoring the obliteration or the apotheosis of the writer?

In the passage I cited earlier from "The Black Cat," the writer does not speak of being in fetters and in a cell, but he does name his activity as penning; since the activity at hand is autobiography, he is penning himself. Is this release or incarceration? He enforces the question by going on to say that he will not expound—that is, will not remove something (presumably himself) from a pound, this may mean that he awaits expounding by the reader. Would this be shifting the burden of his existence onto some other? And who might we be to bear such a burden? Mustn't we also seek to shift it? Granted that we need one another's acknowledgment, isn't there in this very necessity a mutual victimization, one that our powers of mutual redemption cannot overcome? Is this undecidable? Or is deciding this question exactly as urgent as deciding to exist?

I will draw to a close by forming three questions invited by the texts I have put together.

First, what does it betoken about the relation of philosophy and literature that a piece of writing can be seen to consist in what is for all the world a philosophical essay preceding, even turning into, a fictional tale— as it happens, a fictional confession from a prison cell? To answer this would require a meditation on the paragraph, cited earlier, in which Poe pivots from the essay to the tale, insinuating that we are failing to ask a question about the origin of the writing and claiming that without the philosophical preface—which means without the hinging of essay and tale, philosophy and fiction—the reader might, "with the rabble, have fancied me mad," not perceiving that he is "one of the many uncounted victims of the Imp of the Perverse." The meditation would thus enter, or center, on the idea of counting, and it is one I have in fact undertaken, under somewhat different circumstances, as part 1 of *The Claim of Reason*.

There I interpret Wittgenstein's *Philosophical Investigations*, or its guiding idea of a criterion, hence of grammar, as providing in its responsiveness to skepticism the means by which the concepts of our language are *of* anything, as showing what it means to have concepts, how it is that we are able to word the world together. The idea of a criterion I emphasize is that of a way of counting something as something, and I put this together with accounting and recounting, hence projecting a connection between telling as numbering or computing and telling as relating or narrating. Poe's (or, if you insist, Poe's narrator's) speaking pivotally of being an uncounted victim accordingly suggests to me that philosophy and literature have come together (for him, but who is he?) at the need for recounting, for counting again, and first at counting the human beings there are, for reconceiving them—a recounting beginning from the circumstances that it is I, some I or other, who counts, who is able to do the thing of counting, of conceiving a world, that it is I who, taking others into account, establish criteria for what is worth saying, hence for the intelligible. But this is only on the condition that I count, that I matter, that it matters that I count in my agreement or attunement with those with whom I maintain my language, from whom this inheritance—language as the condition of counting—comes, so that it matters not only what some I or other says but that it is some particular I who desires in some specific place to say it. If my counting fails to matter, I am mad. It is being uncounted—being left out, as if my story were untellable—that makes what I say (seem) perverse, that makes me odd. The surmise that we have become unable to count one another, to count for one another, is philosophically a surmise that we have lost the capacity to think, that we are stupefied.[10] I call this condition living our skepticism.

Second, what does it betoken about fact and fiction that Poe's writing of the Imp simultaneously tells two tales of imprisonment—in one of which he is absent, in the other present—as if they are fables of one another? Can we know whether one is the more fundamental? Here is the relevance I see in Poe's tale's invoking the situation of Hamlet, the figure of our culture who most famously enacts a question of undecidability, in particular, an undecidability over the question whether to believe a tale of poisoning. (By the way, Hamlet at the end, like his father's ghost at the beginning, claims to have a tale that is untellable—it is what makes both of them ghosts.) In Poe's tale, the invocation of *Hamlet* is heard, for example, in the two appearances of a ghost, who the first time disappears upon the crowing of a cock. And it is fully marked in the second of the three philosophical examples of perversity that Poe's narrator offers in order to convince any reader, in his words, "who trustingly consults and thoroughly questions his own soul" of "the entire radicalness of the propensity in question":

The most important crisis of our life calls, trumpet-tongued, for immediate energy and action. We glow, we are consumed with eagerness to commence the work. . . . It must, it shall be undertaken today, and yet we put it off until to-morrow; and why? There is no answer, except that we feel *perverse*, using the word with no comprehension of the principle. To-morrow arrives, and with it a more impatient anxiety to do our duty, but with this very increase of anxiety arrives, also, a nameless, a positively fearful because unfathomable, craving for delay.

These words invoke Hamlet along lines suspiciously like those in which I have recently been thinking about what I call Hamlet's burden of proof—but no more suspiciously, surely, than my beginning to study Poe while thinking about Hamlet.[11]

    Hamlet studies the impulse to take revenge, usurping thought as a response to being asked to assume the burden of another's existence, as if that were the burden, or price, of assuming one's own, a burden that denies one's own. Hamlet is asked to make a father's life work out successfully, to come out even, by taking his revenge for him. The emphasis in the question "to be or not" seems not on whether to die but on whether to be born, on whether to affirm or deny the fact of natality, as a way of enacting, or not, one's existence. To accept birth is to participate in a world of revenge, of mutual victimization, of shifting and substitution. But to refuse to partake in it is to poison everyone who touches you, as if taking your own revenge. This is why if the choice is unacceptable the cause is not metaphysics but history—say, a posture toward the discovery that there is no getting even for the oddity of being born, hence of being and becoming the one poor creature it is given to you to be. The alternative to affirming this condition is, as Descartes's *Meditations* shows, world-consuming doubt, which is hence a standing threat to, or say condition of, human existence. (I imagine that the appearance of the cogito at its historical moment is a sign that some conditions were becoming ones for which getting even, or anyway overcoming, was coming to seem in order: for example, the belief in God and the rule of kings.) That there is something like a choice or decision about our natality is what I take Freud's idea of the diphasic structure of human sexual development (in "Three Essays") to show—a provision of, so to speak, the condition of the possibility of such a decision. The condition is that of adolescence, considered as the period

in which, in preparation for becoming an adult, one rec
fering rebirth, one's knowledge of satisfactions. This is
me, one speculates about Hamlet's age but thinks of hi
These matters are represented in political thought unde
consent, about which, understandably, there has from t
question of proof.

Finally, what does it betoken about American philos
son and Poe may be seen as taking upon themselves the p
cogito (Emerson by denying or negating it, Poe by perve
ing it) and as sharing the perception that authoring—ph
ing, anyway, writing as thinking—is such that to exist it
acknowledge, the proof of its own existence? I have in e
my mind this betokens their claim to be discovering or rediscovering the
origin of modern philosophy, as sketched in Descartes's *Meditations*, as if
literature in America were forgiving philosophy, not without punishing it,
for having thought that it could live only in the banishing of literature.
What does it mean that such apparent opposites as Emerson and Poe enter such a claim within half a dozen years of one another?

Let us ask what the connection is between Emerson's ecstasies (together with Thoreau's) and Poe's horrors (together with Hawthorne's).
The connection must be some function of the fact that Poe's and
Hawthorne's worlds, or houses and rooms, have other people in them,
typically marriages, and typically show these people's violent shunning,
whereas Emerson's and Thoreau's worlds begin with or after the shunning
of others ("I shun father and mother and wife and brother when my genius calls me") and typically depict the "I" just beside itself. The interest
of the connection is that all undertake to imagine domestication, or inhabitation—as well, being Americans, they might. For Emerson and
Thoreau you must learn to sit at home or to sit still in some attractive spot
in the woods, as if to marry the world, before, if ever, you take on the burden of others; for Poe and Hawthorne even America came too late, or perhaps too close, for that priority.

A more particular interest I have in the connection among these
American writers is a function of taking their concepts or portrayals of domestication and inhabitation (with their air of ecstasy and of horror turned
just out of sight) to be developments called for by the concepts of the ordinary and the everyday as these enter into the ordinary language philosopher's undertaking to turn aside skepticism, in the pains Austin and

Wittgenstein take to lay out what it is that skepticism threatens. In the work of these philosophers, in their stubborn, accurate superficiality, perhaps for the first time in recognizable philosophy, this threat of world-consuming doubt is interpreted in all its uncanny homeliness, not merely in isolated examples but, in Poe's words, as "a series of mere household events."

I end with the following prospect. If some image of marriage, as an interpretation of domestication, in these writers is the fictional equivalent of what these philosophers understand to be the ordinary, or the everyday, then the threat to the ordinary named skepticism should show up in fiction's favorite threat to forms of marriage, namely, in forms of melodrama. Accordingly, melodrama may be seen as an interpretation of Descartes's cogito, and, contrariwise, the cogito can be seen as an interpretation of the advent of melodrama—of the moment (private and public) at which the theatricalization of the self becomes the sole proof of its freedom and its existence. This is said on tiptoe.

6

Finding as Founding: Taking Steps
in Emerson's "Experience"

Claiming, in a companion lecture,[1] the inheritance of a Wittgenstein
who perceives the world to exist in a process of decline as pitiless as that
described by Spengler, hence, say, by Nietzsche, a world beyond recovery
by morality, in which moral relationship itself declines society (though not
perhaps private relationship altogether), I claimed that, into the balance
against this existence, Wittgenstein stations nothing more nor less than a
practice of philosophy—and moreover a practice that is based on the most
unpromising ground, a ground of poverty, of the ordinary, the attainment
of the everyday.

My basis for such stakes, it is more and more clear to me, is the inheritance I ask of Emerson, of his underwriting, say grounding, of this
poverty, this everydayness, nearness, commonness. But since my earlier
inheritance of the later (of Wittgenstein, and before him of Austin) is
equally the basis of my later inheritance of the earlier (of Emerson, and before him of Thoreau), what is basic?

In the present lecture I go on to describe the Emerson in question by
asking in what way, or to what extent, or at what angle, Emerson stands for
philosophy. The location from which I anticipate an answer here is the essay "Experience," published in 1844, a work that good readers of Emerson
generally agree represents some breakthrough in his enterprise.

The question concerning Emerson's standing in or for philosophy is
meant to question what is I believe the most widely fixated, critical gesture
toward Emerson both on the part of his friends and of his enemies, from

the time of James Russell Lowell in *A Fable for Critics* in 1848 to Harold
Bloom in *The New York Review of Books* in 1984, in a review entitled "Mr.
America," namely the gesture of denying to Emerson the title of philosopher. I think of no one else in the history of thought about whom just this
gesture of denial is characteristic, all but universal, as if someone perversely keeps insisting—perhaps it is a voice in the head—that despite all
appearances, a philosopher, after all, is what Emerson is. But, of course,
despite all appearances, it must be Emerson himself whose insistence on
some such question it is so urgent to deny. Yet we know that Emerson was
himself convinced early that his "reasoning faculty" was weak, that he
could never "hope to write Butler's Analogy or an Essay of Hume." And
nothing I find could be more significant of his prose than its despair of
and hope for philosophy. Then maybe he is insisting on something else
just as disturbing, for example, to be pre-philosophical, to call for philosophy, as from his inheritors. But what is the state in which the claim of
philosophy is refused and yet a claim upon philosophy is entered? It
might be quite as remarkable, or rare, as the state of philosophy itself, so
to speak, and no less urgent to deny.

Along with the gesture of denying philosophy to Emerson goes another, almost as common, joined in, with Lowell and Bloom, by so eminent a critic as F. O. Matthiessen and by Emerson's latest biographer, Gay
Wilson Allen, namely, that of describing Emerson's prose as a kind of mist
or fog, as if it is generally quite palpable what it is that Emerson is obscurely reaching for words to say and generally quite patent that the ones
he finds are more or less arbitrary or conventional, as if the greatness of
Emerson's effort simply did not produce a matching achievement of experience and thought, as though he cannot mean anew in every word he says,
as if to bear interpretation were simply beyond him. If you insist on this
view you will seem to find a world of evidence to support it.

In contesting such a view by measuring Emerson's philosophicality, I
should, to be fair, so it may seem, begin with his first famous work, *Nature*,
rather than with the famously personal "Experience." But to begin with
Nature is apt to grant Emerson a relation to philosophy by characterizing
his philosophy as essentially (though doubtless not wholly) neo-Platonic,
whereupon it is just about settled that to master the details of his philosophy will satisfy roughly the same acquired taste as mastering the details of
Plotinus. It is accordingly, I should add, suspiciously convenient for me
that I am at present among those who find *Nature*, granted the wonderful

passages in it, not yet to constitute the Emersonian philosophical voice, but to be the place from which, in the several following years, that voice departs, in "The American Scholar," "The Divinity School Address," and "Self-Reliance." I would characterize the difference by saying that in *Nature* Emerson is taking the issue of skepticism as solvable or controllable whereas thereafter he takes its unsolvability to be the heart of his thinking. At the close of *Nature* we are to "know then that the world exists for you," and the image of "the bark of Columbus near[ing] the shore of America" teaches us that the universe is the property of every individual in it and shines for us. Whereas by the close of "Experience" we learn that "the true romance which the world exists to realize will be the transformation of genius into practical power," which says that the world exists as it were for its own reasons, and a new America is said to be unapproachable.

The identification of Emerson in relation to philosophy begins for me with the perception of him (together with Thoreau) as—so I like to put it—underwriting ordinary language philosophy (I mean especially what J. L. Austin and the later Wittgenstein envision as the role of the ordinary in philosophizing) and somehow at the same time as anticipating the later work of Heidegger, epitomized in his *What Is Called Thinking?* The Heidegger anticipation—specifically through Nietzsche's love of Emerson, and then Heidegger's dominating study of Nietzsche—was broached in my first try at Emerson, "Thinking of Emerson." There Emerson's remark in "Experience," "All I know is reception," is taken to challenge Kant's official view in the *Critique of Pure Reason* that knowledge is active, spontaneous, a matter of synthesizing experience, that is appearances, which alone are receptive, passive; in a motto: there is no intellectual intuition. This places Emerson as a contributor to the Idealist debate that attempts to recuperate Kant's thing in itself by raising again the question of the possibility of such intuition. This is equally a way to place the call, in *What Is Called Thinking?*, for a fateful step back from "representative thinking." As for the underwriting of ordinary language philosophy, that had been in preparation in my work since the first things I published that I still use—the title essay and its companion second essay of *Must We Mean What We Say?*—which identify Wittgenstein's *Investigations* (together with Austin's practice) as inheritors of the task of Kant's transcendental logic, namely to demonstrate, or articulate, the a priori fit of the categories of human understanding with the objects of human understanding, that is, with objects. Within a couple of years, I was attacked so violently for this

Kantian suggestion—on the grounds that it made the study of language unempirical—that a well-placed friend of mine informed me that my philosophical reputation was destroyed in the crib. And now a quarter of a century later, when just about anyone and everyone agrees that the *Investigations* is a Kantian work, I will not even get the solace of being credited with having first pointed it out. (Ah well. If you live by the pen, you perish by the pen.) But the hostility against the suggestion was well placed. Because the Kantian background did not suggest a space for working out my sense of things in citing it in the first place, that Austin's and Wittgenstein's attacks on philosophy, and on skepticism in particular—in appealing to what they call the ordinary or everyday use of words—are counting on some intimacy between language and world that they were never able satisfactorily to give an account of. It was in Emerson and in Thoreau that I seemed to find what I could recognize as this space of investigation, in their working out of the problematic of the day, the everyday, the near, the low, the common, in conjunction with what they call speaking of necessaries, and speaking with necessity.

A critical step for me offered itself in a later try at Emerson, in "Emerson, Coleridge, Kant," principally about Emerson's essay entitled "Fate," in which I find the *Critique of Pure Reason* turned upon itself: notions of limitation and of condition are as determining in the essay "Fate" as they are in Kant, but it is as if these terms are themselves subjected to transcendental deduction, as if not just twelve categories but any and every word in our language stands under the necessity of deduction, or say derivation. The conditions of the concept of condition will thus form part of what the word "condition" itself says, stipulations or terms under which we can say anything at all to one another, the terms or costs of each of our terms, as if philosophy is to unearth the conditions of our diction altogether. Emerson is, I believe, commonly felt to play fast and loose with something like contradiction in his writing; but I am speaking of a sense in which contradiction, the countering of diction, is the genesis of his writing of philosophy. "Aversion" is one of Emerson's Emersonian words for countering; it is roughly his word for what others call "conversion." "Dictation" is Emersonian lingo for *what* he is countering; another of his words for it is "conformity." A summary outburst of the genesis of his writing in "Self-Reliance" is, "Every word they say chagrins us." The vision of *every word* in our—in human—language as requiring attention, as though language as such has fallen from or may aspire to a higher state, a state, say, in which the world is more perfectly expressed, is something that I assume itself has a complex history. The vision in Emerson and Thoreau is essential to their vision that the world as a whole requires attention, say redemption, that it lies fallen, dead; it is thus essential to what we call their romanticism.

Emerson's difference from other nineteenth-century prophets or sages (say Matthew Arnold, Schopenhauer, Kierkegaard), and his affinity with Austin and Wittgenstein (unlike other analytical philosophers, whose distrust of human language goes with the vision not of reinhabiting but of replacing the ordinary) is his recognition of the power of ordinary words— as it were their call—to be redeemed, to redeem themselves, and characteristically to ask redemption from (hence by) philosophy. Emerson will say, or show, that words demand conversion or transfiguration or reattachment, where Wittgenstein will say they are to be led home, as from exile.

But even if it were granted that in some essential and interesting way Emerson provides access both to Wittgenstein and to Heidegger; and even if one granted for the sake of conversation that Wittgenstein and Heidegger establish the passing present of philosophical possibility, so far as I feel I can contribute to it; why especially is it Emerson and Thoreau that I am so insistent on inheriting? Other writers also lie in common behind Wittgenstein and Heidegger—the work of Kant itself, and that of Schopenhauer and of Kierkegaard, not to mention Spengler.

—Yes, but inheriting, by interpreting in some way, the texts of Kant or Schopenhauer or Kierkegaard, not to mention Spengler, will not, so far as I can see, suggest one's credibility as a present philosophical voice, not for an American writer. —Whereas, what? Inheriting by interpreting the texts of Emerson and Thoreau *will*? But you yourself like to say that these writers are repressed by their culture.

—Then, now I am taking precisely that condition to signify their pertinence to the present: I do not, the culture does not, *repress* the thought of Schopenhauer or Kierkegaard or Spengler; they were simply not part of our formation.

I have more than once raised the question, with respect to Thoreau, whether America has expressed itself philosophically. One may feel that this question is pointless, even intellectually retrograde; that America's contribution to, or leadership in, the growing international effort to establish philosophy within or adjacent to the bank of the sciences, natural and cognitive, is philosophy enough for a nation. But that such an ambition leaves out the participation of the writers of my culture that do me most good (Emerson and Thoreau to begin with) means to me that it is not enough.

Again I seem haunted by Wittgenstein's reported reaction in 1931 to the news that Schlick was to teach in an American university: "What can we give the Americans? Our half-decayed culture? The Americans have as yet no culture. But from us they have nothing to learn." Thinking of Wittgenstein against the vision of Spengler, I was, in my companion lecture, "Declining Decline,"[2] impressed by the expression of Wittgenstein's doubts over his own inheritability, whether Europe would continue its discovery of philosophy. The feature of his reaction I am caught by now is the implication that philosophy, as part of culture, can only be inherited by a nation that already possesses that part of culture known as philosophy. But suppose I claim that I am among the inheritors of Wittgenstein. Do I thereby imply the claim that American culture has acquired philosophy within my lifetime, so, since 1926?

The topic of inheritance takes me to Emerson's essay "Experience," which I understand as, among other things, staking Emerson's claim to something like the inheritance of philosophy, not only for himself but for America, a first inheritance. To credit this I will be recurring to something I take Emerson to signify in speaking of his "master-tones" (in "Culture," a companion essay to "Fate" in *The Conduct of Life*, published in 1860)—namely, whatever else, his transfigurations of philosophical terms. I have, for instance, taken his "self-reliance" and his "conditions" to be transfigurations, respectively, of Descartes's thinking of his thinking and of Kant's conditions of the possibilities of experience and of the objects of experience. Other instances will arise, here and elsewhere. It is pertinent now to note that I hear a familiarly quoted statement in "Experience" such as "So grief will make idealists of us,"[3] while of course as a piece of mild worldly wisdom, also as a stern summary or moral of the *Critique of Pure Reason*, thus as meaning that Kant's conception of experience as appearance, hence of a world for us and simultaneously of a world of experience denied or lost to us, will force us to recuperate, such as we can, both worlds by a philosophy of necessary Ideas, of things and matters beyond our knowledge; then philosophy has to do with the perplexed capacity to mourn the passing of the world. (Late in "Experience" this gets fairly explicit: "The life of truth is cold and so far mournful.") I first said roughly this with respect to *Walden*, claiming that the book is built, its edification for us raised on, among some other matters, the identifying of mourning as grieving with morning as dawning, as if grief and grievance are the gates of ecstasy, manifesting philosophical writing as the teaching of the capacity for dawning by itself showing the way of mourning, of the repetitive disinvestment of what has passed. According to Freud, this is the path (back) to the world, a reinvestment of interest in its discovery, something Freud calls its beauty. (The pertinent Freudian text here, even more directly than "Mourning and Melancholia," is "Transience" (1918).) In taking these thoughts to Emerson's "Experience" I am in effect acknowledging Thoreau as Emerson's purest interpreter, no one more accurate, no one else so exclusive.

In an important recent engagement with Emerson's "Experience," Professor Sharon Cameron concentrates on this essay's topic of grief, guided by a necessary question, or a version of one, namely: What happens to Waldo, Emerson's son, referred to in the early pages of the essay and never thereafter? Her answer is in effect that nothing happens and everything happens to him, that he is not forgotten but generates the ensuing topics of the essay, which is thus a testament to his consuming loss, a work of mourning for him, giving to (his?) experience as such the character or structure of grief. She concludes with the suggestion that the "place" of the son in the body of the essay, when he seems forgotten, may be understood in relation to the work of Abraham and Torok on the distinction between the introjection and incorporation of lost objects, work recorded in their book *The Wolf Man's Magic Word*, processes to which Derrida in his Introduction to the English translation gives linguistic registration. While I cannot presently deploy that fascinating material, I will, as I now go on to put together some intuitions I have been developing about "Experience," bear in mind certain of Sharon Cameron's formulations, along with certain of Professor Barbara Packer's from her splendid book *Emerson's Fall*, in which she affirms an earlier insight that Emerson is awfully adept at incorporating and denying (shall we say transcending?) the deaths (of wife, of brother, of son) he has had to absorb.

The works of Cameron and Packer represent so decisive a break with the idea of Emerson's prose as mist or fog that it is the more surprising, even distressing, to find Cameron continuing, in however sophisticated a form, the dissociation of philosophy's pertinence from Emerson's enterprise, even especially from that of "Experience." What she specifies as philosophy, or rather as "philosophical explanations," are ones that attempt to find "contradiction" and "synthesis" in Emerson, terms she says are "not useful to describe Emerson's 'Experience.'" I have said a word about Emerson's precise recapturing of the word *contradiction*. And if "Experience" indeed reopens Kant's case against intellectual intuition, then a piece of its very subject, on the surface although not named, is precisely the necessity of "synthesis," of putting experiences together into a unity in knowing a world of objects.

See how this works itself out in an astounding, obviously key passage from "Experience": "I take this evanescence and lubricity of all objects, which lets them slip through our fingers then when we clutch hardest, to be the most unhandsome part of our condition." Look first at the connection between the hand in "unhandsome" and the impotently clutching fingers. What is unhandsome is, I think, not that objects for us, to which we seek attachment, are, as it were, in themselves evanescent and lubricious; the unhandsome is rather what happens when we seek to deny the stand-offishness of objects by clutching at them, which is to say, when we conceive thinking, say the application of concepts in judgments, as grasping something, say synthesizing. The relation between thinking and the hand is emphasized in Heidegger's *What Is Called Thinking?*, as when he writes, "Thinking is a handicraft," by which I suppose he means both that thinking is practical (no doubt pre-industrial), fruitful work, which must be learned, and also to emphasize that it is work that only the creature with the hand can perform—and most fatefully perform as a mode of necessary, everyday violence. (I assume that Emerson wants the autoerotic force projected in his connection of hand and objects, and I guess that Heidegger does not. I let this pass for now.)

Clutching's opposite, which would be the most handsome part of our condition, is I suppose the specifically human form of attractiveness—*attraction* being another tremendous Emersonian term or master-tone, naming the rightful call we have upon one another, and that I and the world make upon one another (as in "What attracts my attention shall have it," from "Spiritual Laws"). Heidegger's term for the opposite of grasping the world is that of being *drawn* to things. Such affinities between apparently distant thinkers—call them congruences of intellectual landscape—are always surprising, however familiar, since they betoken that a moment of what you might have felt as ineffable innerness turns out to be as shareable as bread, or a particular pond. Now add to the affinity concerning the unhandsome and the attractive the idea of their being part of our condition, our human condition, that is, the condition of our thinking, specifically, our knowing a world of objects, and the affinity of Kant and Emerson with the Wittgenstein of the *Investigations* is outspoken. In claiming the *Investigations* as a Kantian work, I claim for it the work of extending Kant's categories of the understanding into the use of language and its criteria as such, as summarized for the *Investigations* in its paragraph 90:

We feel as if we had to *penetrate* phenomena: our investigation, however, is directed not towards phenomena, but, as one might say, towards the "*possibilities*" of phenomena. We remind ourselves, that is to say, of the *kind of statement* we make about phenomena.

The work of *Philosophical Investigations* is marked by placing the idea of the kind of statement we make in the position Kant establishes for forms of judgment, those functions of unity to which "we can reduce all acts of the understanding":[4] that is, they tell "what kind of object anything is."[5] But in the *Investigations* there is no such system of the understanding, nor a consequent such system of the world, and the demand for unity in our judgments, that is, our deployment of concepts, is not the expression of the conditionedness or limitations on our humanness but of the human effort to escape our humanness—which is also a replacing of a discovery of the *Critique of Pure Reason*. (Say that Wittgenstein has discovered the systematic in the absence of unity.)

The feeling as if we have to penetrate phenomena is evidently produced by a feeling of some barrier to or resistance in phenomena (as if the conditions of a thing's appearance were limitations in approaching it; as if skepticism accurately registered the world's withdrawal from us, say its shrinking), as if language has difficulty in *reaching* phenomena, let alone grasping them. Then all our words are words of grief, and therefore of grievance and violence, counting losses, especially when we ask them to clutch these lost, shrinking objects, forgetting or denying the rightful draw of our attraction, our capacity to receive the world, but instead sealing off the return of the world, as if punishing ourselves for having pain. The feature I am trying to place intuitively within the overlapping of the regions of Kant and Emerson and Wittgenstein lies, I might say, not in their deflections of skepticism but in their respect for it, as for a worthy other; I think of it as their recognition not of the uncertainty or failure of our knowledge but of our disappointment with its success.

Since such intuitions, so far as Emerson can contribute to their articulation—to what he would call their tuition—are tracked in the medium of his essays, let us be more systematic—anyway orderly—in our taking on of the essay "Experience," and start over with it. I mean start at its apparent beginning, its opening question: "Where do we find ourselves?"

Who, in what straits, asks such a question? Of whom? And the question has itself to be asked in the perplexed, say disoriented, state the essay goes on to describe. Before the essay's beginning, its prefacing poem is about something called "the lords of life"—something like a priori categories of human life, those of Use, Surprise, Surface, Dream, Succession, Wrong, Temperament—and explicitly about a male child with a puzzled look, walking "among the legs of his guardians tall" (presumably these lords), whom Nature takes by the hand and to whom Nature whispers "Darling, never mind. . . . The founder thou; these are thy race!" (Is this a child? He is called "little man." Is he also the one described, along with the lords of life, as "the inventor of the game/Omnipresent without name"? That compound condition or predicate—omnipresent without name— might be Waldo's in the essay.) Before the opening question about finding ourselves, then, we are alerted that the mind of the writer is on founding. So while the essay is about grief and mourning or incorporation as illustratable, so to speak, through the death of a young son, from the beginning this circumstance, if perplexed, is to be considered in the light of the essay as a work, or claim, of founding. Founding what?

For one thing, if the opening question asking about finding ourselves is an invitation to ask where we are at the beginning of a piece of writing, hence to ask what the perplexed (foundered) state of reading is (an invitation furthered by the next, apparently answering, sentence, "In a series of which we do not know the extremes"—remembering perhaps that the volume in which this piece of writing appeared was entitled *Essays: Second Series*); and if my guiding thought is sound that Emerson's writing is to be read as a call for philosophy; then something being found, or say established, is a relation to philosophy. And if so we already know one cause of the perplexity is the consequent necessity to establish, or reconceive, what founding is, what philosophical foundation is (or grounding, since mustn't the treads we are on end or begin somewhere?), and specifically to conceive what it means to intuit founding in a child (is it conceivably a foundling?) and in an idea of finding ourselves.

Is the child of the poem Waldo? Of what is a child, or a Waldo, the founder? (By the way, the name *Waldo* entered the Emerson family early and was maintained in each generation to commemorate the founder of the Waldensian sect of dissenters, a fact important to our writer.[6] Of what significance this may be to Thoreau's moving two years after this series of essays was published to find Walden, I do not guess.) Why is Waldo never named in the essay but simply described as "my son"? This question forces others: Why is the son invoked at all? How do the topics of the essay generate him? Why are there so many children generated in the essay? What are its topics? What are the topics of an Emerson essay? I let the questions pour a little to indicate that their answers are not to be learned before learning the work of the essay, but rather that their answers, along with those to questions yet unforeseeable, are the very work, the trials, of the essay itself. My guiding question accordingly is why an essay constituted by its quest for its topics, as if in search for a right to them, becomes a medium for philosophy, or for something as close as possible to it.

Taking it for example that the question "Where do we find ourselves?" is a question of one lost, or at a loss, and asked while perplexed, as between states, or levels, yet collected enough to pose a question or perplexity, let us pick two startling sentences of the essay as explicit answers the writer gives as to his whereabouts, as to where he may be discovered, and as to what he has found: "It is very unhappy, but too late to be helped, the discovery we have made that we exist. That discovery is called the Fall of Man." And two paragraphs earlier: "I am ready to die out of nature and be born again into this new yet unapproachable America I have found in the West." Since both Milton and Columbus appear among the many sequences of names recited in the essay, I would like to take it as uncontroversial that the expulsion from Eden is something being invoked as a place lost, and hence that existing in the world is discovered as being thrown for a loss; and uncontroversial that finding a new America in the West while being, or because, lost is remembering or repeating something Columbus did, repeating it otherwise than in *Nature*. (Is it conceivable that we are all foundlings?) Then controversy should appear. (I note parenthetically Emerson's characteristic use of the word *call*, taken over by Thoreau. It might here be Emerson's way of saying that it is our unnecessary unhappiness or suffering that we call the Fall of Man. We might call the event of knowing that we exist something else. (As Thoreau does, or so I claim for him in *The Senses of Walden*: "[T]he besideness of which ecstasy speaks is my experience of my existence, my knowledge 'of myself as a human entity.'"[7]) If you take to heart Kant's fascinating document "Conjectural Beginning of Human History," you might find yourself speaking of the event—the discovery of humankind as not at home in nature—as the Rise of Man. Then it becomes an open question why we are chronically or constitutionally unhappy, excessive sufferers.)

Why is this new America said to be yet unapproachable? There are many possibilities, three obvious ones. First, it is unapproachable if he (or whoever belongs there) is already there (always already), but unable to experience it, hence to know or tell it, or unable to tell it, hence to experience it. Second, finding a nation is not managed by a landfall; a country must be peopled, and "nation" speaks of birth. There is no nation if it has only one inhabitant. Emerson's sentence speaks of being born again, out of nature and into his discovery; and "born again" implies that there is (or was) another, one from which to be born. Are two enough? Third, this new America is unapproachable by a process of continuity, if to find it is indeed (to be ready) to be born again, that is to say, suffer conversion; conversion is to be turned around, reversed, and that seems to be a matter of *discontinuity*. "Aversion" is the name Emerson gives to his writing in "Self-Reliance"—or the name he gives to self-reliance in relation to conformity.

And it is, I take it, the condition under which anything new can be said, or cause experience. When "Self-Reliance" says in effect "Self-reliance is the aversion of conformity,"[8] it means that this writing finds America, as it stands, or presents itself, to be repellent, or say unattractive; and it means that America so finds this writing. Emerson by no means, however, just shrinks from America, because this "aversion" turns not just away, but at the same time, and always, toward America. The aversive is an Emersonian calculation of the unapproachable, a reckoning of it as the forbidding. What about America is forbidding, prohibitive, negative—the place or the topic of the place? Is the problem about it that it is uninhabitable or that it is undiscussable—and the one because of the other? And is this a way of saying that America "is uncultivated"? Then is the writer of "Experience" cultivating America? And so is he declaring that he too is uncultivated? (The writer of "Circles" had prophesied: "A new degree of culture would instantly revolutionize the entire system of human pursuits."[9]) It would be as if to declare that he has—hence that we have—no language (of our own). Can that be *said* (by us)? Can it be shown? The classical British Empiricists had interpreted what we call experience as made up of impressions and the ideas derived from impressions. What Emerson wishes to show, in these terms, is that, for all our empiricism, nothing (now) makes an impression on us, that we accordingly have no experience (of our own), that we are inexperienced. Hence Emerson's writing is meant as the provision of experience for these shores, of our trials, perils, essays.

Then Emerson's writing is (an image or promise of, the constitution for) this new yet unapproachable America: his aversion is a rebirth of himself into it (there will be other rebirths); its presence to us is unapproachable, both because there is nowhere *else* to go to find it, we have to turn toward it, reverse ourselves; and because we do not know if our presence to it is peopling it. "Repeopling the woods" is a way Thoreau names his task as a writer. A characteristic naming Emerson gives to his task as a writer is implied in the following passage from "The American Scholar": "Those . . . who dwell and act with [the American scholar and artist] will feel the force of his constitution in the doings and passages of the day better than it can be measured by any public and designed display." The identification this writer proposes between his individual constitution and the constitution of his nation is a subject on its own. The endlessly repeated idea that Emerson was only interested in finding the individual should give way to or make way for the idea that this quest was his way of founding a nation, writing its constitution, constituting its citizens. But why then would the writer say "I found" (a new America) as if in answer to the opening question "Where do we find?" (ourselves). If we consider that what we now know, know now, of this writer is this writing, that says we and that says I, then wherever he is we are—otherwise how can we hear him? Do we? Does his character make an impression on us? Has he achieved a new degree of culture? To have us consider this is a sensible reason for his saying "I," as it were abandoning us. Where do we find ourselves?

How are these findings of losses and lost ways, this falling and befalling, images of, or imaged by, the loss of a child? Is the idea of the child as founder continued from the poem into the body of the essay or does the essay contradict the poem, showing that its writer has found nothing?

Let us bear in mind the writer's caution about himself that runs "One would not willingly pronounce these words in their hearing" (the same "their" or "they" whose every word chagrins us), and what and how to pronounce and when to renounce are matters never away from this prose from the time of "The Divinity School Address." In the present context the writer has just mentioned the words "love" and "religion," and his reluctance to pronounce is a treatment of the theme of old and new that laces the text of "Experience"—old and new testaments, old and new philosophy, old and new births, old and new individuals, old and new Englands, old and new worlds. Put this further with the Kantian function: if the world is to be new, then what creates what we call the world—our experience and our categories ("notions" Emerson says sometimes; let us say our every word)—must be new, that is to say, repronounced, renounced. In "The American Scholar" this is something called "thinking"; in the *Philosophical Investigations* this thinking takes the form of bethinking ourselves of our criteria for applying words to a world, and this is something Wittgenstein explicitly characterizes as requiring a turning around (I, of course, conceive it as Emersonian aversion). And now compute the Columbus and the Adam and Eve functions: How do you know what names are used in a new world? Who are the native speakers of our tongue?

Is the idea of a new world intelligible to mere philosophy? Philosophy can accept the existence of other worlds, of various similarities to our own, I mean to this one. But new? That at once seems to speak of something like a *break* with this one, or a transformation or conversion of it. And that sounds as if something is to be *done* to this world. Can mere philosophy *do* anything? Marx's idea—voiced the same year Emerson was composing "Experience," in the Introduction to *The Critique of Hegel's Theory of Right*—that the working class is the inheritor of German philosophy means, let us say, that a certain group of human beings are now, given the conditions of the present developed over the stages of world history, in a position at last to put the ideals of philosophy into practice, and human history will at last begin. For Emerson, in the American nineteenth century, which represents, or should, a break in human history, the conditions of a philosophical practice are set before *us*, the group of human beings who find themselves here. (Here—under *this* constitution. Which? Is Emerson writing a new one, or ratifying the old?) "We see young men who owe us a new world, so readily and lavishly they promise." Philosophy has from Plato to Kant known of two worlds; these are plenty to know. Here and now there is no reason the other is not put into practice, brought to earth. America has deprived us of reasons. The very promise of it drives you mad, as with the death of a child.

Our philosophical experience now, finding ourselves here, necessitates taking up philosophically the question of practice. This experience necessitates the ending of the essay "Experience," which accepts the question, "Why not realize your world?" The answer of the final sentence—"The true romance which the world exists to realize will be the transformation of genius into practical power"—does not exactly shift the burden from the genius onto the world, but reaches from Plato's vision of a Philosopher-King to Kant's question of how the pure will can be practical, keeping the question open. For Emerson, as for Kant, putting the philosophical intellect into practice remains a question for philosophy. For a thinker such as John Dewey it becomes, as I might put it, merely a problem. That is, Dewey assumes that science shows what intelligence is and that what intelligent practice is pretty much follows from that; the mission of philosophy is to get the Enlightenment to happen. For Emerson the mission is rather, or as much, to awaken us to why it is happening as it is, negatively not affirmatively. "For skepticisms are not gratuitous or lawless, but are limitations of the affirmative statement, and the new philosophy must take them in and make affirmations outside of them, just as it must include the oldest beliefs." In a new world everything is to be lost and everything is to be found. The commonest criticism of Emerson is that he is denying the tragic. His commonest criticism of us is that we are denying—we deny our affirmations (say their individuality) and we deny our negations (say our skepticisms).

The first and last answers in "Experience" to the question of realizing philosophy's worlds are recommendations to ignorance—not as an excuse but as the space, the better possibility, of our action. In the second paragraph: "We do not know today whether we are busy or idle." And in the last paragraph this is summarized as: "Far be from me the despair which prejudges the law by a paltry empiricism;—since there never was a right endeavor but it succeeded." Then the issue is whether an endeavor is right, for example, whether this writing will be left by the writer in such a way that it succeeds. In doing what? In achieving philosophy? In approaching America? In getting Waldo's death nearer?

A measure of the paltriness of our empiricism is that among Kant's categories of the experience of a world there is nothing exactly like the "lords of life"—Use and Surprise, Surface and Dream, Temperament, Succession, Reality, and so on. These are categories in which not the objects of a world but the world as a whole is, as it were, experienced; an earlier Emerson word for these categories is moods. Perhaps we can say attitudes. In the *Tractatus Logico-Philosophicus*, Wittgenstein toward the end says that "if good or bad acts of will do alter the world, . . . their effect must be that it becomes an altogether different world. It must, so to speak, wax and wane as a whole. The world of the happy is different from that of the unhappy."[10] Emerson may be understood to be saying that: the world of the temperament open to surprise is different from that of the one closed; the mood of the one prepared to be useful to the world is different from that of the one prepared to adapt to it; the world of the dreaming from that of the dreamless; the world of the one willing for succession from that of the one wedded to fixation; and so on. The existence of one of these worlds of life depends on our finding ourselves there. They have no foundation otherwise. No grown-up philosophy can secure the permanence of any, but grown-ups can destroy or deny any. Their chagrin is the aversion of our joy. Emerson gives directions for the translation from old to new in the sentences that precede the one that names his new unapproachable America.

When I converse with a profound mind . . . or have good thoughts, I do not at once arrive at satisfactions, as when, being thirsty I drink water . . . ; no! but I am first apprised of my vicinity to a new and excellent region of life. By persisting to read or to think, this region gives further sign of itself, as it were in flashes of light, in sudden discoveries of its profound beauty and repose. . . . But every insight from this realm of thought is felt as initial, and promises a sequel. I do not make it [the promise? the realm of thought?]; I arrive there, and behold what was there already [always already?]. I make! O no! I clap my hands in infantine joy and amazement before the first opening to me of this august magnificence, old with the love and homage of innumerable ages, young with the life of life, the sunbright Mecca of the desert.

Taking a "region of life" to be a world ruled by a lord of life, I will follow the writer's instruction in reading and thinking (that is, the instruction to *persist* to read and to think), prompted by a sign or omen that the region of the essay "Experience" gives of itself initially and suddenly, namely, that the writer is unwilling or unable to pronounce the name of his dead son. (Unwilling or unable in "their" hearing? In ours, of course.) If we may know that the son's name was Waldo, we may know further (as reported in G. W. Allen's *Waldo Emerson*) that Waldo was the father's preferred name for himself. So that what may be unnamed by the father is some relation between father and son, something, as it were, before nameable griefs. What comes "before" the nameable Emerson calls sometimes sentiment and sometimes presentment, as if sentiments appear in a structure of omens. That the father withholds the pronouncing of a relation to a son accordingly discloses two paths for reading and thought: that of the incidence and insistence on children and birth throughout the essay; and that of the idea of the nameless.

I can hardly pause to verify the presence of births buried in the essay: I list the birth of Osiris as something that happened during days we might have found profitless; the birth of Mohammed coded in the mention of "the sunbright Mecca of the desert"; and the writer's birth into his unapproachable America. And then of the sound of Wordsworth's "Intimations Ode" and its idea that "our birth is but a sleep and a forgetting" (from which we might wake and find ourselves on a stair), I note merely its prefacing poem, with the words "The child is father to the man," in connection with the prefacing poem of "Experience" and its child as founder, so in this connection as founder of the father; and to mark that I find no limit to the knowledge writers will have of one another (if this causes anxiety it is an anxiety toward one's own unconscious), I confess that the difficult remark "For contact with [reality] we would even pay the costly price of sons and lovers" strikes me as an allusion to, or interpretation of, *The Winter's Tale*, in which the death of a son and a loving wife are the cost of a refusal to recognize contact with the reality of a birth.

Since the connection between "Experience" and *The Winter's Tale* is that in Shakespeare the significance of a dead five- or six-year-old son is also buried throughout the work, and since I take the Shakespeare to represent the problematic of skepticism in terms of a father's doubt whether the child is his, I am bound to consider whether in "Experience" its problematic of skepticism is comparably represented in the identity of the dead son and the father's certainties. This brings me to the function of the nameless, where one line of reasoning would go this way. The little man of the poem, say it is Waldo, is either Omnipresent without name or else the founder of this omnipresence. Then just after founding America and having "described life as a flux of moods," the writer "must now add that there is that in us which changes not," a "cause, which refuses to be named," whose unbounded substance is not covered by "quaint names" such as "Fortune, Minerva, Muse, Holy Ghost." "Every fine genius has essayed to represent [this unchanging cause] by some emphatic symbol, as, Thales by water, . . . Zoroaster by fire, Jesus and the moderns by love." Is the genius-essayist of "Experience" representing the cause that refuses to be named, by the emphatic love of a dead son whose passing he cannot get nearer to him? Emerson calls such a representation a generalization and goes on to say:

In our more correct writing we give to this generalization the name of Being, and thereby confess that we have arrived as far as we can go. Suffice it for the joy of the universe that we have not arrived at a wall, but at interminable [unnameable?] oceans.

Generalization is an Emersonian tone or function most fully computed in "Circles," where the generation of new circles is associated with what we ordinarily call generalizations and genesis and generations; and also with the idea of "general" as meaning the multitude and as meaning a ranking officer and a ranking term; and equally with the idea of generosity. And if the figure of a circle is the self-image of an Emerson essay, then one generation in question refers to the genre of the Emerson essay. The writer says in the lines just quoted that the correct, furthest generalization has not arrived at a wall. Has it conceivably arrived at a Waldo? I mean, is the correct identification of Waldo to be as an emphatic symbol of Being? Then what is symbolized in the inability to mourn him? He was perhaps the father's most generous generation, his farthest generalization. Then is the fate of skepticism sealed by the death of Waldo, or is this fate open to the mourning of Waldo? In what sense is the writer unable to mourn? If "Experience," like *Walden*, is a testament, it is the promise of a gift in view of the testator's death. Then the gift is the young Waldo's promise, as kept or founded in the old Waldo. Founded how?

I will sketch my intuition that what is nameless in the essay is the anticipation of a particular birth. Begin with the essay's remarkable statement of pregnancy, near its middle, after a paragraph in which the writer has said, "All writing comes by the grace of God, and all doing and having":

In the growth of the embryo, Sir Everard Home I think noticed that the evolution was not from one central point, but coactive from three or more points. . . . Life has no memory. That which proceeds in succession might be remembered, but that which is coexistent, or ejaculated from a deeper cause, knows not its own tendency. So it is with us. . . . Bear with these distractions, with this coetaneous growth of the parts; they will one day be *members*, and obey one will.

(I call attention to the deliberately odd, physicalized, etymonic use of "distractions." Emerson is forcing a picturing of the parts, say pre-members, as *torn away*, as if originating in dismemberment. We must surely remember this.) Someone who resists the thought that this passage is a description of an Emerson essay, and of what it takes to read one—for example that the "us" in "So it is with us" names us as writer and readers—is not apt to be impressed by the various hints of this identification, say by the naming in the preceding paragraph of the origin of writing in God's arranging for our surprises, or in the paragraph following by the phrase concerning every genius who essays to represent, or by the joining of the two ideas of growth or evolution he names succession and coexistence, each of which and especially both together describe the fact and the action of words and sentences on or by one another.

There are for me decisive further hints in the clauses "the evolution [of the embryo] was not from one central point" and in the phrase "obey one will." The former abbreviates the image from "Circles" that, as said, I figure to be one of an Emersonian essay's self-images, a something "whose center is everywhere and whose circumference is nowhere." Emerson of course cites this as Augustine's definition of God; its precise application to Emerson's textuality is that every sentence of an essay from him may be taken to be its topic, and that there is no end to reading it. Put otherwise (rather as suggested in "The Divinity School Address"), an Emersonian essay is a finite object that yields an infinite response. The phrase "obey one will" harks back, to my ear, to what I call the theory of reading in "Self-Reliance," the part of it that is epitomized in Emerson's formula "Who has more obedience than I masters me," a statement of mastery as listening that pictures mastery as of a text. From which it follows that what the essay is remembering, or membering, the one will it creates itself to obey, and creates in order to obey, is that which puts it in motion, the will of a listening, persisting reader. That would be, would, so to speak, give birth to, experience.

(Suppose that the derivation of the word *experience*—its own experience, as it were—goes through ideas of peril, trial, birth, way or journey, approach, and so forth [ideas that are all, according to the American Heritage Dictionary's Appendix on Indo-European Roots, developments of the root *per*]. Then what I have been, and will be, saying suggests that the [historical, but not past] synthesis named by and named in the word *experience* is reproduced, or recounted, or resynthesized in Emerson's essay of that name. This recounting would be an alternative to Kant's of his idea that "the conditions of the *possibility of experience* in general are at the same time the *possibility of the objects of* experience."[11] Kant's demonstration requires what he calls a "schematism" to show how objects are subsumed under or represented in a concept. Emerson's schematism, let me call it, requires a form or genre that synthesizes or transcendentalizes the genres of the conversion narrative, of the slave narrative, and of the narrative of voyage and discovery. For Emerson the forms that subsume—undertake—subjects under a concept [the world under a genre] become the conditions of experience, for his time. My association of Emerson with Kant on the necessity of a schematism [or temporalization] of forms [for Kant, the forms of judgment, which mark concepts; for Emerson the genres of texts, which mark narratives] is a proposal for work to be done, I hope by others. Kant says in the section of the first *Critique* called "The Schematism of the Pure Concepts of Understanding" that "the schemata are thus nothing but *a priori* determinations of time in accordance with rules" [determinations of permanence or succession or coexistence or determinateness in time], which relates the order of categories to the order of "all possible objects."[12] Emerson's notation of the determination of time that is necessary to contemporary experience—to the world's now making an impression upon us—is the stepping from Old to New, matters of successions that require conversion, and the aspiration of freedom, and discovery [arrivals, hence departures, abandonings]. In "The American Scholar," conversion and its companion idea transfiguration are Emerson's predicates of thinking. An Emersonian conceptual unfolding of thinking as a conversion or transfiguration [of making an impression, mattering]—as from an Intuition of what counts to a Tuition of how to recount it—is one within which the Kantian "lines" between the intelligible and the sensible [say, with Kant, the active and the passive], and between objects for us and things in themselves, are no longer placeable. I would like to say that Emerson's "Experience" announces and provides the conditions under which an Emerson essay can be experienced—the conditions of its own possibility. Thus to announce and provide conditions for itself is what makes an essay Emersonian.)

I seem to myself obedient to "Experience" in taking the essay's idea of itself as pregnant to be declared in the passages that relate the son now dead to the writer-father's body: "When I receive a new gift, I do not macerate my body to make the account square, for if I should die I could not make the account square"; and "Something which I fancied was a part of me, which could not be torn away without tearing me, nor enlarged without enriching me, falls off from me and leaves no scar." These passages are a man's effort to imagine—to fancy—giving birth.

This effort is continued in the periodic imagery of getting bigger, from a fairly literal or allegorical moment like "The subject exists, the subject enlarges; all things sooner or later fall into place" to the more famous, Emersonian cracks such as "The great and crescive self, rooted in absolute nature, supplants all relative existence and ruins the kingdom of mortal friendship and love." That it is pregnancy and birth he is imagining here as supplanting mortal with immortal roots is prepared in the preceding sentence, "But the longest love or aversion has a speedy *term*" (my emphasis), and, in the paragraph containing the clause "use what language we will, we can never say anything but what we are," he goes on to describe a traveler who increases our knowledge of our location as a "new-comer" and says "every other part of our knowledge is to be pushed to the same extravagance, ere the soul attains her *due sphericity*" (my emphasis again).

The most beautiful of these quite phantasmic experiences of pregnancy is in the endlessly remarkable paragraph declaring his readiness to "be born again into this new yet unapproachable America" he had found. The sentence preceding that declaration and succeeding the one on the sunbright Mecca, is: "I feel a new heart beating with the love of the new beauty." The heart of which Waldo is new? Is skepticism at an end? A new beauty is announced. Is ugliness at an end? Here anyway is the new and excellent region of life our new thinking and conversation may apprize us of.

What I might call the most metaphysical passage to be seen in this sunbright light, the light of losing and having a son, contains the explicit reversal of Kant on knowing: "All I know is reception." It continues: "I am and I have: but I do not get, and when I have fancied that I had gotten anything, I found I did not." Without pursuing this invitation to think about the structural relationships of epistemology with economy, of knowing with owning and possessing as the basis of our relation with things, I note just the plain difference of direction, as it were, in having a child and getting (that is, begetting) a child, and the implication that for something to belong to me I must, whatever men think, found it, belong to it, as others then may. ("Whatever men think": for example, about mixing their labor with things.) In this light, the remark two paragraphs earlier "It is a main lesson of wisdom to know your own from another's" appears as a father's doubt, outside the anxiety of a mother's.

Is there a reason that my fantasizing in response to Emerson's fantastic sentences takes up Emerson's imagining his giving birth somehow as a man rather than as somehow a woman? After all, mothers appear in "Experience" as often as fathers; and as "Dearest Nature . . . whispered Darling" in the prefacing poem, so later the essayist says to his "dearest scholar," "Thou, God's darling," and it seems to me right to think of this as whispered. I find a precedent for thinking of male birth here, for which I do not argue, in the Book of Jeremiah:

> Then the word of the Lord came unto me, saying,
> Before I formed thee in the belly I knew thee; and
> before thou camest forth out of the womb I sanctified
> thee, *and* I ordained thee a prophet unto the nations.
> Then said I, Ah, Lord God! Behold, I cannot speak: for

I *am* a child.
But the Lord said unto me, Say not, I am a child: for
thou shalt go to all that I shall send thee, and whatsoever
I command thee thou shalt speak. . . .
Then the Lord put forth his hand, and touched my
mouth. And the Lord said unto me, Behold, I have put
my words in thy mouth.[13]

My idea is that the belly in which God formed Jeremiah is his own, and
that the effect of spiritual takeover in putting his words in the prophet's
mouth is not (here, at any rate) that of feminizing him, but of infantilizing
him. To feel small for the moment, wordless, abashed, say crushed, before
certain writing seems to me a sign of reading its claim correctly. Emerson
produces such (prophetic) writing. It is evidently a form of the sublime.
What are founding fathers? What, in particular, did they do to "bring
forth" "on this continent" a new nation "conceived in liberty"?

Perhaps we are far enough along in the region of the thought of this
writing to look for land by taking up, and turning somewhat, three of the
most abashing, let us say, dumbfounding statements the essayist makes in
response to the son's death—turn them toward the call for philosophy and
for America, and then formulate provisionally further answers to the question of where we find ourselves.

Take first: "I grieve that grief can teach me nothing, nor carry me one
step into real nature." This is typically taken to be the confession of a private fault, an inability on Emerson's part to mourn: some will then adduce
his apparently innate coolness of spirit; others will add that here he is
numb with grief. But whatever his description of his state in his letters and
journals in the days after Waldo's death (when he famously wrote, "I grieve
that I cannot grieve"[14]), the writer here, two years later, states that he is
grieving, and twice, with the first a kind of grievance against grief, for its
own dumbness; as if he is still recovering from illusions that grief has
something to teach, for example that there exists some known and established public source of understanding and consolation, call this religion, or
that there is some measured distance to the world known and established
by the few, call this philosophy. These illusions are to be transcended: "The
elements already exist in many minds around you of a doctrine of life
which shall transcend any written record we have."

Take next: "Nothing is left us now but death." Does this mean that
life is not left us, is over, now that Waldo is dead? But now, before all, he,

the father, is writing; we find ourselves, it happens, here, in this series of essays, of words, of steps or platforms of rising and falling moods and powers. A testament is writing in view of one's death; but if he is writing it he is not dead, and that remains his mystery. As if he is thinking: If Waldo had been who I took him for, and if grief had been what I imagined, I would have joined him in death. Then by my life I am forced to make sense of his death, of this separation, hence of his life, hence of mine, say how to face going on with it, with the *fact* that I do, now, go on; how to orient it in the West, how to continue the series by taking a step, up or down, out of or into nature. But isn't to learn what death is, what mortality is, an old task of philosophy? And if the loss of the world—of say being—is philosophy's cause, which it tries to overcome even as it causes; and if I am to overcome philosophy; then to make sense of Waldo's life I have to declare myself a philosopher. But then if I have found a new America, then I have to declare myself the first philosopher of this new region, the founder of the nation's thought. Hence my son is my founder and his death is to be made sense of as the death of a founder and of a founder's son, for example, as we might imagine the relation of Isaac's promised death to Abraham's mission. Must I take Waldo's death as a sacrifice (a "martyrdom" he says, thinking of Osiris?) to my transformation? But the fruit of what happened "seven years ago," the time of Waldo's birth, is to "have an effect deep and secular as the cause." It must be immanent. A secular sacrifice would be for a transcendence not to a higher realm, but to another inhabitation of this realm—an acknowledgment, let us say, of what is equal to me, an acceptance of separateness, of something "which I fancied was a part of me, which could not be torn away without tearing me."

If you permit my fantasizing for Emerson here, you will not deny me one further step within it, to think that giving birth to Waldo will enact this life of separation, if it enacts the giving over of him, the promise of him, to others, putting the life of separation into practice. ("Was it Boscovich who found out that bodies never come in contact? Well, souls never touch their objects.") He can enact this practice if writing can, if his writing is his body in which he can bury Waldo, and the likes of you and me are accordingly, under certain conditions, given to discover him as if he were a new America, as if we are apprized of a new and excellent region, of a new being. Whatever this discovery takes is what reading Emerson takes. It may yield philosophy.—Does one expect less of a writer whom we have never settled, who retains so much secrecy, who asks of us transcendence, transformation, aversion, the response to an infinite object, the drawing of a new circle, the rememberment of fragments torn from his work, from us? He cannot name his successor.

Let's come back to earth and listen briefly to the third response to the son's death: "I cannot get it nearer to me." Of course this may again be taken as adding one more image to Emerson's isolation from the event or his exclusion from its experience. But suppose he is speaking not—or not just—privately but philosophically, saying, as he puts it, what is necessary, charting that, as philosophy will. Then his saying is at least double. As in the case of his unapproachable America, and as I say in the case of the world withdrawn before skepticism, there is no nearer for him to get since he is already there; somehow that itself is what is disappointing, that this is what there is. And he is saying something about the term *near*, a charged tone for him.

He has from the beginning, in "The American Scholar," sought the near as one of the inflections of the problematic of the common, the low, the familiar, which is to say, among other things, of the here, in our poverty, rather than the there, in their pomp of emperors. In specifying his inability to get it nearer he is leaving a direction open. I cannot get "it" nearer (as in general I do not get, but I am and I have); if it is to become nearer *it* must come nearer, draw closer.

But what can this mean? With respect to approaching America it means: I cannot approach it alone; the eventual human community is between us, or nowhere. With respect to the present world of the senses, in which we are fallen, expelled, it means whatever "All I know is reception" means. Then it means whatever overcoming thinking as clutching means, and if this is what Heidegger and Wittgenstein are driving at, it specifies the place at which philosophy is to be overcome. In favor of what? Not in favor, evidently, of science or poetry or religion, from each of which this writing distinguishes itself. In favor, then, of philosophy itself, in the face of the completed edifice of philosophy as system and as necessary, unified foundation. Every European philosopher since Hegel has felt he must inherit this edifice and/or destroy it; no American philosopher has such a relation to the history of philosophy. If the generation after Hegel has announced the completion of philosophy, American writers must be free to discover whether the edifice of Western philosophy is as such European or whether it has an American inflection. (Here is where Emerson's and Thoreau's attraction to Eastern philosophy is crucial, as an experiment can be crucial, a crossroads past which there is no return. America's search for philosophy continues, by indirection, Columbus's great voyage of indirection, refinding the West by persisting to the East.)

What happens to philosophy if its claim to provide foundations is removed from it—say the founding of morality in reason or in passion, of society in a contract, of science in transcendental logic, of ideas in impressions, of language in universals or in a formalism of rules? Finding ourselves on a certain step we may feel the loss of foundation to be traumatic, to mean the ground of the world falling away, the bottom of things dropping out, ourselves foundered, sunk on a stair. But on another step we may feel this idea of (lack of) foundation to be impertinent, an old thought for an old world. (The idea of foundation as getting to the bottom once and for all of all things is a picture Thoreau jokes about in describing, in "The Pond in Winter" and "Conclusion" in *Walden*, the time he took measurements of the bottom of Walden, and times such measurements become controversial.) The step I am taking here is to receive the work of "Experience" as transforming or replacing founding with finding and to ask what our lives would look like if the work is realized.

Let us finish these moments by starting an answer, one that experiments with a pair of ideas the essay deploys in working out this transformation or replacement, the ideas of indirection and of succession.

Indirection names the direction I said is left open in the writer's confession, "I cannot get it nearer"; it is precisely the direction of reception, of being approached, the attractive, handsome part of our condition. Specifications of this theme of indirection, or of the angular, pervade the essay. (Think of indirection as the negation of direction; rhetorically it will express itself in various reversals, especially of assertion.) They appear impressively in the rest of the paragraph that speaks of objects slipping through our fingers as the unhandsome part of our condition:

Nature does not like to be observed [here is another motto, in an Emersonian master tone, for the *Critique of Pure Reason*, where perceptions, or say observations, without concepts are blind], and likes that we should be her fools and playmates [which thus will make for fooling and playing with language, so make for intellectual comedy]. We may have the sphere for our cricketball, but not a berry for our philosophy [turned around, this means you cannot know even a berry by observation (one of Berkeley's examples was a cherry) and that if you turn observation around you may, I'm glad he says here, "have the sphere," achieve a reception of the globe; you may even learn to say a new conception]. Direct strokes she [that is nature] never gave us power to make; all our blows glance [since they are observations], all our hits are accidents [meaning for one thing that no hit is of anything we should any longer call the essence]. Our relations to each other are oblique and casual [put otherwise, they are by inclination and fateful accident, you could say, by intellectual melodrama].

The idea of indirection is not to invite us to strike glancingly, as if to take a sideswipe; it is instead to invite us, where called for, to be struck, impressed. (The Greek word naming the river of forgetfulness, which may be translated to mean hidden, may also be translated to mean indirect. No Polonius, Emerson by indirections finds out indirection. Nor is the idea of indirectness here captured by particular forms of figurative language, though in a sense it may mean indirect discourse, as if in our philosophizing we are reporting what the sphere says.

 The idea of succession forms a pair with the idea of indirection, because both concern the idea that "[n]ature does not like to be observed." (In the New Testament it is the attainment of heaven that will not be observed—as if what replaces that journey for Emerson, as for Nietzsche and for Marx, is the attainment of earth. This happens no more by doing than by undoing something, trickier steps.) Emerson names "Succession" as lord of life, a term or condition of our relation to the world as a whole. The term incorporates or spans, together with America's ideas of success, Kant's problematic of succession (of inner and outer senses, of temporality, remembering, in "Experience," "We must be very suspicious of the deceptions of the element of time"), and provides a critique of both America and Kant that would show how to recover from the condition they leave us in, say how to recount the condition. The stories are each well known, if not perhaps well joined together—that Kant's idea of succession and America's idea of success are each depriving us of a world more important than the important and undoubted world they each provide. For Emerson this is not a cue for nostalgia, say for ceding intelligence to sentiment; it is instead the cause of the presentiment, or omen, of philosophy. One place his philosophical response shows up, as usual without notice, is at the close of "Experience," where Emerson directs at himself the imagined inquiry, "Why not realize your world?" and directly refuses it, or refuses it directly (he says there, "polemically"). After going on to enter the claim, or tautology, "There never was a right endeavor but it succeeded," he places the injunction, "Patience, patience, we shall win at the last." This hardly seems much of a polemic, but let us try it out.

Take more of the final paragraph:

> I know that the world I converse with in the city and in the farms, is not the world I *think*. I observe that difference, and shall observe it. One day I shall know the value and law of this discrepance. But I have not found that much was gained by manipular attempts to realize the world of thought. Many eager persons successively make an experiment in this way, and make themselves ridiculous. They acquire democratic manners, they foam at the mouth, they hate and deny. Worse, I observe that in the history of mankind there is never a solitary example of success,—taking their own tests of success. I say this polemically, or in reply to . . . despair which prejudges the law by a paltry empiricism;—since there never was an endeavor but it succeeded. Patience and patience, we shall win at the last.

This is a reasonably treacherous Emersonian texture of summary, in which the task of his prose turns to casting together scenes that allow certain inversions and diminutions of his current essay's series of master tones—the repeated words or tones in the few sentences just cited are *know, observe, realize, world, law, make, think* and *thought, success* and *succeeded* and *successively, experiment* and *empiricism, manipular* and *manners*—as if to show us our breathlessness and obscurity he must allow himself to be taken as taken by breathlessness and obscurity. I call attention here to two passages.

In saying (praying), "Far be from me the despair which prejudges the law [of the discrepance between the world of thought and the world of observation—Kant's two worlds whose simultaneous inhabitation differentiates the human] by a paltry empiricism," Emerson is turning on his essay's prayer for despair, for getting grief near. As if he is praying: There is despair and despair, experience and experience; near be to me the despair which judges the law of two worlds by a great and significant empiricism. And in repeating the tone of finding—"I have not found that much was gained by manipular attempts to realize the world"—Emerson is replying to the inquiry "Why not realize your world?" in terms of the essay's opening inquiry about finding ourselves, together with one of his earliest foundings concerning the unhandsomeness of our condition. As if he is saying: I have been responding to *this* inquiry about realization from the opening words of the essay. *This*, before you, is the work (in fact, and in promise) of realizing my world.

Since Emerson is here imagining his reader (a matter to be specified) at the end still to wish to inquire after a realization that is (or specifically fails to be) offered in every sentence, Emerson must imagine his offers as rejected. Then he must reject the inquiry philosophically, that is, he must reply polemically—not in revenge, but as controversy, turning the question back in unphilosophical haste. To imagine the offers in his words destroyed (in this way unrealized)—by imagining them to inspire not gratitude but disappointment, as if in naming precisely what his readers wish for, he is depriving them of a world, not showing them theirs; the irony is perfect— is to imagine that nothing will fill the void of America. Then I find myself abashed before Emerson's forbearance: "Patience, patience." Even if said mostly to himself, the words are to be announced, say as part of the struggle against a perfect irony, recognizing that cynicism and disillusion are in a democracy politically devastating passions.

He is at an end of the words at our disposal; his spade is turned.[15] And the thing that cannot be said cannot be shown; nothing here is secret. What is now before us, unapproachable, is now to be acknowledged or to be avoided, now to happen or not to. Poetry, it is said, is making, say work. That ought not to be taken as an answer to the question of what poetry is, but as an incitement to consider the question: first the question what poetic making or work is. An essential of the work before us is the teaching or exemplification of what work is (Emerson's work; let us say philosophical work)—of what it is about our work, and our ideas of work, that keeps the things we most want to happen from happening. If Waldo's death has not happened to this writer, has his birth? Has America happened? Doubtless the question is romantic. Then the question is posed: Is there a way alternative to the romantic to ask the question? If you do not produce such an alternative; and if nevertheless you desire to keep hold of the question; then you will have not only to conclude that we are not beyond the demands of romanticism, but you will have to hope that the demands of romanticism are not beyond us.

Emerson's emphatic call to patience should threaten a familiar idea of Emersonian power, for Emerson makes power look awfully like (from a certain platform, look exactly like) passiveness. I would like to say that it is the philosophical power of passiveness that Emerson characteristically treats in considering what he calls "attraction," as important to him as gravity is to Newton. Since in the figure of Waldo the power of passiveness, say passion, is shown as mourning, Waldo means: Philosophy begins in loss, in finding yourself at a loss, as Wittgenstein more or less says. Philosophy that does not so begin is so much talk ("this talking America" is how

"Experience" puts it). Loss is *as such* not to be overcome, it is interminable, for every new finding may incur a new loss. (Foundation reaches no farther than each issue of finding.) Then philosophy ends in a recovery from a terminable loss. Philosophy that does not end so, but seeks to find itself before or beyond that, is to that extent so much talk. The recovery from loss is, in Emerson, as in Freud and in Wittgenstein, a finding of the world, a returning of it, to it. The price is necessarily to give something up, to let go of something, to suffer one's poverty. Emerson is describing this procedure in saying: "Life itself is a mixture of power and form. . . . To finish the moment, [to live in wisdom, is] to find the journey's end in every step of the road." A finding in every step is the description of a series, perhaps in the form of a proof, or a paragraph.

And here we reach our momentary end, since we are beginning again at our beginning. "The *last*," at which we shall win, if we are patient, is an instruction about philosophical patience or suffering or reception or passion or power. It speaks of lasting as enduring, and specifically of enduring as on a track, of following on, as a succession of steps (which bears on why a shoemaker's form is a last). Hence it speaks of a succession as a leaving of something, a walking away, as the new world is a leaving of an old, as following your genius is leaving or shunning something. Is this pragmatic? (Is this walking, knowing how to *go* on, philosophizing without leaps? But suppose the leaps are uses of the feet to dance (not, say, to march)—as when one uses the hands to clap (not to clutch). But Nietzsche's leaping and dancing, like Emerson's dancing and standing and sitting, and like Thoreau's sitting long enough in some attractive spot, pose further questions of the posture of thinking, following, succeeding, in particular, questions of *starting* to think.)

Now listen again to the answer to the opening question, "Where do we find ourselves?" in its succeeding two sentences: "In a series of which we do not know the extremes," and "We wake and find ourselves on a stair," that is, a step. Only it takes the lasting of the paragraphs of an essay to realize that this is an answer. The most renowned phrase for what I was calling the power of passiveness—a power to demand the change of the world as a whole, Emerson sometimes calls it revolution, sometimes conversion—is what Thoreau will call civil disobedience. This phrase notes the register of lasting as it appears in a public crisis, call it a tyranny of the majority. Emerson may seem to confine himself on the whole to lasting's appearance not at the public end of crisis but at the private end, call this the tyranny of thinking. Yet he says that he would write on the lintels of the door-post (in "Self-Reliance"). Perhaps he is now writing so. Is that a public place?

It may well be thought that I would not have landed so hard on Emerson's idea of "lasting" apart from Heidegger's ideas of getting on the way, and of staying or dwelling, and of leaping and of stepping back; and I have welcomed the association of Emerson's ideas of loss and turning (and, I would add, of series) with their roles in Wittgenstein's *Investigations*. What seems to me evident is that Emerson's finding of founding as finding, say the transfiguration of philosophical grounding as lasting, could not have presented itself as a stable philosophical proposal before the configuration of philosophy established by the work of the later Heidegger and the later Wittgenstein, call this the establishing of thinking as knowing how to go on, being on the way, onward and onward. At each step, or level, explanation comes to an end; there is no level to which all explanations come, at which all end. An American might see this as taking the open road. The philosopher as the hobo of thought.

But if we say that the work represented in Heidegger's *What Is Called Thinking?* and in Wittgenstein's *Investigations* gives ways the philosophy Emerson calls for will look, then there is—is there not?—a prior, simpler question we should have faced head on: How can philosophy—in the form of the call for philosophy—look like *Emerson's* writing? This still may remain incredible. But suppose the question is by now expressible as: Why must philosophy, or its call, at a certain moment in history, in a certain place, look Emerson's way? (If *this* calls philosophy, what writing is off limits?)

Answering this question will require locating the tasks for thought and for writing the meeting of which (or the unearthing or bearing of which) will be imagined to cause the look of Emerson's prose: tasks such as the transfiguring of founding as finding, or grounding as lasting; the conversion of American success and Kantian succession into a passive practice, the power of mourning; the composing of a testament, so a bequeathing, specifically of a promise; the stepwise overcoming of skepticism, say of the immeasurable distance from the world, by the process of nearing as indirection, so an instruction in mortality, finitude; an establishing of founding without a founder, a ground on which the power of mastery is common, is mastery of the common, the everyday. (Emerson might have called each such task an argument, as in his saying—in "The Poet," another essay on foundation and necessity and condition—a poem is made not by meters but by meter-making argument, so: philosophical prose is made not by arguments but by a philosophy-making argument.)

Then I hear a final question that may well be posed to me now: Don't you really believe that the process of indirection is writing itself, any writing whose seriousness engages such tasks as you have begun listing, tasks whose authority already depends on writing, say even literature, as if you would give philosophy and literature into one another's keeping? And isn't this really just the line you took in *The Senses of Walden* where Thoreau's claim to philosophy is said to be a function of his claims of writing, as to awaken the voice? And isn't your conviction in all this encouraged by recent foreign developments, for all your exasperation over them, because you too, after all, thinking everything is language, and by no means formal language?

—It is true that when I hear Emerson saying (in "Self-Reliance"), "We lie in the lap of immense intelligence, which makes us receivers of its truth and organs of its activity," I know that while others will take this "intelligence" to be an allusion to God or to the Over-Soul and a little condescend to it, I take it as an allusion to, or fantasy of, our shared language, and I aspire to descend to it. (I do not deny that the directions are linked).

—So doesn't this just affirm that nothing other than language, on your view, counts?

—In a way that is utterly false and in a way utterly true. What I think can be said is that while of course there are things in the world other than language, for those creatures for whom language is our form of life, those who are what "Experience" entitles "victims of expression"—mortals—language is everywhere we find ourselves, which means everywhere in philosophy (like sexuality in psychoanalysis).

—Found for philosophy, I clap my hands in infantine joy, thus risking infantilization, leaping free of enforced speech, so succeeding it. Thus is philosophy successful.

Aversive Thinking: Emersonian Representations in Heidegger and Nietzsche

In taking the perspective of the Carus Lectures as an opportunity to recommend Emerson, despite all, to the closer attention of the American philosophical community, I hope I may be trusted to recognize how generally impertinent his teachings, in style and in material, can sound to philosophical ears—including still, from time to time, despite all, my own. But what else should one expect? My recommendation is bound to be based—unless it is to multiply impertinence—on something as yet unfamiliar in Emerson, as if I am claiming him to remain a stranger. In that case, to soften his strangeness would be pointless—which is no excuse, I do realize, for hardening it. About my own sound it may help to say that, while I may often leave ideas in what seems a more literary state, sometimes in a more psychoanalytic state, than a philosopher might wish—that is, that a philosopher might prefer a further philosophical derivation of the ideas—I mean to leave everything I will say, or have, I guess, ever said, as in a sense provisional, the sense that it is to be gone on from. If to a further derivation in philosophical form, so much the better; but I would not lose the intuitions in the meantime—among them the intuition that philosophy should sometimes distrust its defenses of philosophical form.

It is common knowledge that Emerson's "The American Scholar" is a call for Man Thinking, something Emerson contrasts with thinking in "the *divided* or social state," thinking, let us say, as a specialty. I do not know of any commentary on this text that finds Emerson to be *thinking* about the idea of thinking. Uniformly, rather, it seems to be taken that he and his readers understand well enough what it is he is calling for, that it is something like thinking with the whole man; and I suppose this can be taken so for granted because there has been, since Emerson's time, or the time he speaks for, a widespread dissatisfaction with thinking as represented in Western philosophy since the Enlightenment, a dissatisfaction vaguely and often impatiently associated, I believe, with an idea of romanticism. And of course there has been, in turn, a reactive impatience with this dissatisfaction. Emerson is, in his way, locating himself within this struggle when he calls upon American thinkers to rely on and to cheer themselves: "For this self-trust, the reason is deeper than can be fathomed,—darker than can be enlightened." As if he anticipates that a reader might suppose him accordingly to be opposed to the Enlightenment, he will famously also say, "I ask not for the great, the remote, the romantic; . . . I embrace the common, I sit at the feet of the familiar, the low," a claim I have taken as underwriting ordinary language philosophy's devotion to the ordinary, surely one inheritance of the Enlightenment.

Existentialism—in the years in which it seemed that every mode of thinking antagonistic to analytical philosophy was called Existentialism—was famous for some such dissatisfaction with philosophical reason, expressed, for example, by Karl Jaspers in his book on Nietzsche, originally published in 1935:

That the source of philosophical knowledge is not to be found in thinking about mere objects or in investigating mere facts but rather in *the unity of thought and life*, so that thinking grows out of the provocation and agitation of the whole man—all this constitutes for Nietzsche's self-consciousness the real character of his truth: "I have always composed my writings with my whole body and life"; "All truths are bloody truths to me."[1]

("Cut these sentences and they bleed."[2]) Philosophy, as institutionalized in the English-speaking world, has not much felt attacked by nor vulnerable to such criticism, partly because the style and animus of the criticism is so foreign as to suggest simply other subjects, but partly, and sufficiently, because surely since Frege and the early Russell, analytical philosophy can see what thinking is, or should be: namely, reasoning, expressed in a certain style of argumentation.

In taking on Emerson's view of thinking I will not be interested in advocating his view over, or characterizing it against, views more familiar to us (say a view of reason as rationality), but rather in asking attention to an attitude toward or investment in words that Emerson's view seems to depend upon, an attitude allegorical of an investment in our lives that I believe those trained in professional philosophy are trained to disapprove of. The disapproval of the attitude interests me as much as the attitude itself. If, as professional philosophers, we were asked whether philosophizing demands of us anything we would think of as a style of writing, our answer, I guess, would waver, perhaps because our philosophical motivation in writing is less to defend a style than to repress style or allow it only in ornamental doses. In speaking of disapproval, accordingly, I am not raising a question of taste, of something merely not for us, but a question of intellectual seriousness and illicitness. However glad we may be to think of ourselves as intellectually fastidious, I do not suppose we relish the idea of ourselves as intellectual police.

I should perhaps confess that an ulterior stake of mine in speaking of Emerson's attitude to words is that—to begin specifying a suggestion already made—I find J. L. Austin and the later Wittgenstein to participate in a region of that attitude, the region that places so heavy an investment in the words of a natural language as to seem quite antithetical to sensible philosophizing. It was half a lifetime ago that I began writing philosophy by preparing a paper ("Must We Mean What We Say?") for this division of our philosophy association defending J. L. Austin's practice with ordinary language against criticisms of it articulated by Benson Mates, criticisms notably of Austin's apparently insufficient empirical basis for his claims to know what we say and mean when. I did not really answer Mates's criticisms because I could not account for that investment in the ordinary. I still cannot. This failure pairs with my inability to answer Barry Stroud's question to me twenty years later, at another association meeting, about whether my *Claim of Reason* didn't amount to a claim to find a general solution to skepticism. I wanted to answer by saying that by the end of the first two parts of that book I had convinced myself not only that there is no such solution, that to think otherwise is skepticism's own self-interpretation, but that it seemed to me, on the contrary, work for an ambitious philosophy to attempt to keep philosophy open to the threat or temptation to skepticism. This left me what I named as Nowhere, and it led me, in Part Four of my book, to particular territories customarily associated with literature—especially to aspects of Shakespearean and of certain romantic texts—in which I seemed to find comic and tragic and lyric obsessions with the ordinary that were the equivalent of something (not everything)

philosophy knows as skepticism. Emerson became more and more prominent an inhabitant of these regions. His investment in the ordinary is so
constant and so explicit that, perhaps because of the very strangeness and
extravagance of his manner, it may indicate afresh why a philosopher interested in the manner might spend portions of a reasonable lifetime looking for an account of it.

The first half of this lecture takes its bearing from pertinences Emerson's "American Scholar" address bears to Heidegger's sequence of lectures
translated as *What Is Called Thinking?* (all citations of Heidegger are from
this text); the second half continues the discussion broached in my Introduction of that moral perfectionism for which Emerson's writing is definitive, particularly in connection with its dominating influence on, among
others, Nietzsche.

Emerson's sense of thinking is, generally, of a double process, or a
single process with two names: transfiguration and conversion. For instance (still in "The American Scholar"), "A strange process, . . . this by
which experience is converted into thought, as a mulberry leaf is converted
into satin. The manufacture goes forward at all hours." And again:

The actions and events of our childhood and youth are now matters of calmest observation. . . . Not so with our recent actions,—with the business which we now
have in hand. . . . Our affections as yet circulate through it. . . . The new deed . . .
remains for a time immersed in our unconscious life. In some contemplative hour
it detaches itself . . . to become a thought of the mind. Instantly it is raised, transfigured; the corruptible has put on incorruption.

Transfiguration is to be taken as a rhetorical operation, Emerson's figure for
a figure of speech—not necessarily for what rhetoricians name a known figure of speech, but for whatever it is that he will name the conversion of
words. In "Self-Reliance" he calls the process that of passing from Intuition
to Tuition,[3] so it is fitting that those who find Emerson incapable of
thought style him a philosopher of Intuition, occluding the teacher of Tuition. Tuition is what Emerson's writing presents itself to be throughout;
hence, of course, to be articulating Intuition. It is when Emerson thinks of
thinking, or conversion, as oppositional, or critical, that he calls it aversion.[4] This bears relation not alone to Emerson's continuous critique of religion but to Kant's speaking of reason, in his always astonishing "Conjectural Beginning of Human History," as requiring and enabling "violence"
(to the voice of nature) and "refusal" (to desire), refusal being a "feat which

brought about the passage from merely sensual to spiritual attractions," uncovering "the first hint at the development of man as a moral being."[5] And Emerson's aversion bears relation to Heidegger's discussion of why thinking in his investigation of it "is from the start tuned in a negative key."[6]

Accordingly, a guiding thought in directing myself to Emerson's way of thinking is his outcry in the sixth paragraph of "Self-Reliance": "The virtue in most request is conformity. Self-reliance is its aversion." I gather him there to be characterizing his writing, hence to mean that he writes in aversion to society's demand for conformity, specifically that his writing expresses his self-consciousness, his thinking as the imperative to an incessant conversion or refiguration of society's incessant demands for his consent—his conforming himself—to its doings, and at the same time to mean that his writing must accordingly be the object of aversion to society's consciousness, to what it might read in him. His imperative is registered in the outcry a few paragraphs later, "Every word they say chagrins us." Emerson is not, then, as the context might imply, expressing merely his general disappointment at some failure in the capacity of language to represent the world but also expressing, at the same time, his response to a general attitude toward words that is causing his all but complete sense of intellectual isolation. It is his perfectionism's cue.

The isolation is enacted in "The American Scholar," whose occasion is enviably if not frighteningly distinctive. Whoever Emerson invokes as belonging to the class of scholars that commencement day at Harvard in the summer of 1837—himself, his audience (whether as poets, preachers, or philosophers)—the principal fact about the class is that it is empty; the American Scholar does not exist. Then who is Emerson? Suppose we say that what motivates Emerson's thinking, or what causes this call for the American Scholar, is Emerson's vision of our not yet thinking. Is this plain fact of American history—that we are, we still find ourselves, looking for the commencement of our own culture—worth setting beside the intricate formulation whose recurrences generate Heidegger's *What Is Called Thinking?*: "Most thought-provoking in our thought-provoking time is that we are still not thinking" (*Das Bedenklichste in unserer bedenklichen Zeit ist, dass wir noch nicht denken*).[7] It probably does not matter that the translation cannot capture the direct force in the relation of *bedenklich* to *denken* and the senses of *bedenklich* as doubtful, serious, risky, scrupulous—it would mean capturing the idea of the thing most critically provoking in our riskily provocative time to be that we are still not really provoked, that nothing serious matters to us, or nothing seriously, that our thoughts are unscrupulous, private. (Emerson's remark in his "Divinity School Address" echoes for me: "Truly speaking, it is not instruction, but provocation, that I can receive from another soul."[8] What translation will capture the idea of provocation here as calling forth, challenging?) Nor, hence, capture the surrealistic inversion of the Cartesian thought that if I am thinking then I cannot be thinking that perhaps I do not think. In Heidegger, if I am thinking then precisely I must be thinking that I am (still) not thinking. I say the translation may not matter because one who is not inclined, as I am, at least intermittently, to take Heidegger's text to be a masterpiece of philosophy will not be encouraged—on the contrary—to place confidence in a mode of argumentation which invests itself in what is apt to seem at best the child's play of language and at worst the wild variation in and excesses of linguistic form that have always interfered with rationality. For someone who has not experienced this play in Heidegger, or in Emerson, the extent of it can from time to time appear to be a kind of philosophical folly.

I summarize two instances from the essay "Experience" to suggest the kind of practice that has convinced me that Emerson's thought is, on a certain way of turning it, a direct anticipation of Heidegger's. Emerson writes: "I take this evanescence and lubricity of all objects, which lets them slip through our fingers then when we clutch hardest, to be the most unhandsome part of our condition." You may dismiss, or savor, the relation between the clutching fingers and the hand in *handsome* as a developed taste for linguistic oddity, or you might further relate it to Emerson's recurring interest in the hand (as in speaking of what is at hand, by which, whatever else he means, he means the writing taking shape under his hand and now in ours) and thence to Heidegger's sudden remark "Thinking is a handicraft," by which he means both that thinking requires training and makes something happen, but equally that it makes something happen in a particular way since the hand is a uniquely human possession: "The hand is infinitely different from all grasping organs—paws, claws, fangs."[9] (It matters to me in various ways to recall a seminar of C. I. Lewis, "The Nature of the Right," given at Harvard in the academic year 1951–52—the year Heidegger delivered the lectures constituting *What Is Called Thinking?*—in which Lewis emphasized the hand as a trait of the human, the tool-using trait, hence one establishing a human relation to the world, a realm of practice that expands the reaches of the self. The idea seemed to me in my greenness not to get very far, but it evidently left me with various impressions, among others one of intellectual isolation. Lewis's material was published posthumously under the title, "The Individual and the Social Order."[10]) Emerson's image of clutching and Heidegger's of grasping emblematize their interpretation of Western conceptualizing as a kind of sublimized violence. (Heidegger's word is *greifen*; it is readily translatable as "clutching.") Heidegger is famous here for his thematization of this violence as expressed in the world dominion of technology, but Emerson is no less explicit about it as a mode of thinking. The overcoming of this conceptualizing will require the achievement of a form of knowledge both Emerson and Heidegger call reception, alluding to the Kantian idea that knowledge is active, and sensuous intuition alone passive or receptive. (Overcoming Kant's idea of thinking as conceptualizing—say analyzing and synthesizing concepts—is coded into Emerson's idea that our most unhandsome part belongs to our condition. I have argued elsewhere (in "Emerson, Coleridge, Kant"[11]) that Emerson is transfiguring Kant's key term "condition" so that it speaks not alone of deducing twelve categories of the understanding but of deriving—say schematizing—every word in which we speak together (speaking together is what the word *condition* says), so that the conditions or terms of every term in our language stand to be derived philosophically, deduced).

Now reception, or something received, if it is welcome, implies thanks, and Heidegger, in passages as if designed to divide readers into those thrilled and those offended, harps on the derivation of the word *thinking* from a root for *thanking* and interprets this particularly as giving thanks for the gift of thinking, which is what should become of philosophy. Does it take this thematization to direct attention to one of Emerson's throwaway sentences that, as can be said of essentially every Emersonian sentence, can be taken as the topic of the essay in which it finds itself, in this case "Experience"? "I am thankful for small mercies." To see that this describes the thinking that goes on in an Emersonian sentence you would have to see the joking tautology in linking his thankfulness with a mercy, that is to say a *merci*, and to recognize "small mercy" as designating the small son whose death is announced at the beginning of "Experience," an announcement every critic of the essay comments on, a child never named in the essay but whose death and birth constitute the lines of the father's investigation of experience—and it is the philosopher's term *experience* Emerson is (also) exploring, as in Kant and in Hume—an effort to counteract the role of experience as removing us from, instead of securing us to, the world. The idea, again argued elsewhere (in "Finding as Founding"[12]), is that Emerson's essay "Experience" enacts the father's giving birth to Waldo—the son that bears Emerson's name for himself, hence declares this birth (as of himself) as his work of writing generally, or generously. The clearer the intricacies become of the identification of the child Waldo with the world as such, the deeper one's wonder that Emerson could bring himself to voice it socially, to subject himself either to not being understood or to being understood—yet another wonder about intellectual isolation. I am myself convinced that Emerson knew that such devices as the pun on "thankful" and "mercy" were offensive to philosophical reason. So the question is why he felt himself bound to give offense. (An opening and recurrent target of Dewey's *Experience and Nature* is thinkers who take experience to "veil and screen" us from nature. Its dissonance with Emerson is interesting in view of Dewey's being the major American philosopher who, without reservation, declared Emerson to be a philosopher—without evidently finding any use for him. For Dewey the philosophical interpretation of experience was cause for taking up scientific measures against old dualisms, refusing separation. For Emerson the philosophical interpretation of experience makes it a cause for mourning, assigning to philosophy the work of accepting the separation of the world, as of a child.)

It is in Nietzsche, wherever else, that some explanation must be sought for the inner connection between a writer (such as Heidegger) who calls for thinking knowing the completed presence of European philosophy or, say, facing its aftermath, as if needing to disinherit it, and a writer (such as Emerson) who calls for thinking not knowing whether the absence of the philosophical edifice for America means that it is too late for a certain form of thinking here or whether his errand just is to inherit remains of the edifice. Nietzsche is the pivot because of his early and late devotion to Emerson's writing, together with his decisive presence in Heidegger's *What Is Called Thinking?* But no matter how often this connection of Nietzsche to Emerson is stated, no matter how obvious to anyone who cares to verify it, it stays incredible, it is always in a forgotten state. This interests me almost as much as the connection itself does, since the incredibility must be grounded in a fixed conviction that Emerson is not a philosopher, that he cannot be up to the pitch of reason in European philosophy. The conviction is variously useful to American as well as to European philosophers, as well as to literary theorists. When one mind finds itself or loses itself in another, time and place seem to fall away—not as if history is transcended but as if it has not begun.

The reverse of the unhandsome in our condition, of Emerson's clutching and Heidegger's grasping—call the reverse the handsome part— is what Emerson calls being drawn and what Heidegger calls getting in the draw, or the draft, of thinking. Emerson speaks of this in saying that thinking is partial, Heidegger in speaking of thinking as something toward which the human is inclined. Heidegger's opening paragraphs work inclination into a set of inflections on *mögen, vermögen,* and *Möglichkeit*: inclination, capability, and possibility. Emerson's "partiality" of thinking is, or accounts for, the inflections of partial as "not whole," together with partial as "favoring or biassed toward" something or someone. Here is Emerson weaving some of this together:

Character is higher than intellect. Thinking is the function. Living is the functionary. . . . A great soul will be strong to live, as well as strong to think. Does he lack organ or medium to impart his truths? He can still fall back on this elemental force of living them. This is a total act. Thinking is a partial act. Let the grandeur of justice shine in his affairs. Let the beauty of affection cheer his lowly roof. Those "far from fame," who dwell and act with him, will feel the force of his constitution.

("Affairs," "lowly roof," and "constitution" are each names Emerson is giving to functions of his writings.) A number of clichés, or moments of myth, are synthesized here, opening with a kind of denial that virtue is knowledge, continuing with the existentialist tag that living is not thinking, picking up a romantic sound ("lowly roof") to note that strong thoughts are imparted otherwise than in educated or expert forms, and hitting on the term "partial" to epitomize what he calls at the beginning of his address "the old fable" "that the gods, in the beginning, divided Man into men, as the hand was divided into fingers, the better to answer its end" (thus implying that Man has an end, but that to say so requires a myth).

When Emerson goes on to claim to have "shown the ground of his hope in adverting to the doctrine that man is one," the apparent slightness of this, even piousness, in turning toward a doctrine, as if his hopes are well known, and well worn, may help disguise the enormity of the essay's immediate claim for its practice, that is, for its manner of writing. The passage (citing thinking as partial) proposes nothing *more*—say something total—for thinking to be; it declares that *living* is total, and if the living is strong it shows its ground, which is not to say that it is *more* than thinking, as if thinking might leave it out. Thinking *is*—at its most complete, as it were—a partial act; if it lacks something, leaves something out, it is its own partiality, what Kant calls (and Freud more or less calls) its incentive and interest (*Triebfeder*).

Since the lives of this people, Emerson's people, do not yet contain thinking, he cannot, or will not, sharing this life, quite claim to be thinking. But he makes a prior claim, the enormous one I just alluded to, namely, to be providing this incentive of thinking, laying the conditions for thinking, becoming its "source," calling for it, attracting it to its partiality, by what he calls living his thoughts, which is pertinent to us so far as his writing is this life; which means, so far as "the grandeur of justice shine(s)" in the writing and "affection cheer(s)" it. Then this lowly roof, in which the anonymous will dwell with him, will provide them with the force of his constitution—there is no further fact, or no other way, of adopting it. (To follow out the idea of Emerson as [re]writing the constitution of the nation, or amending it, in the system of his prose, is a tale I do not get to here.) This provisionality of his writing—envisioning its adoption, awaiting its appropriation in certain ways (it cannot *make* this happen, work as it may)—is the importance of his having said, or implied, that since in the business we now have in hand, through which our affections as yet circulate, we do not know it, it is not yet transfigured, but remains in "our unconscious life," the corruptible has not yet put on incorruption.[13] But what is this corruptible life, this pretransfigurative existence of his prose, unconscious of itself, unconscious to us? It is, on the line I am taking, one in which Tuition is to find its Intuition, or in which Emerson's thinking finds its "material" (as psychoanalysis puts it). In the opening two paragraphs of "The American Scholar" it accepts its topics in hope, and understands hope as a sign, in particular of "an indestructible instinct," yet an instinct that thinking must realize as "something else." I suppose this to mean that thinking is replacing, by transfiguring, instinct (as Nietzsche and as Freud again will say).

The opening reluctance and indefiniteness of Emerson's definition of his topic in "The American Scholar," his notation of this anniversary event as the "sign of the survival of the love of letters amongst a people too busy to give to letters any more" (than love and hope and instinct), suggest to me that Emerson means that his topics are our everyday letters and words, as signs of our instincts; they are to become thought. Then thinking is a kind of reading. But thought about what? Reading for what?

Sign suggests representation. How can "The American Scholar" represent the incentive of thinking—constitute a sign of its event—without at the same time presenting thinking, showing it? If thinking were solving problems, the incentive would be the problems or could be attached to the solutions. But Emerson's crack about our being "too busy to give to letters any more" exactly suggests that we are precisely busy solving things. When he opens by defining the anniversary on which he is speaking as one of hope and perhaps not enough of labor, he means of course that our labors (including those of what we call thinking) are largely devoted elsewhere than to letters—which is what everyone who cared was saying in explanation of the failure of America to found its own letters, its own writing, and its own art. But Emerson also means that founding letters demands its own labor and that we do not know what this (other) labor (the one that produces letters) is, that it is also a mode of thinking. Labor—as a characterization of thinking—suggests brooding. An interplay between laboring as reproductive and as productive (say as the feminine and the masculine in human thought) suggests Emerson's relentlessness concerning the interplay of the active and the receptive, or passive, in our relating to the world. (Thinking as melancholy reproduction characterizes Hamlet.) The other labor of thinking—devoted to letters—is, accordingly, one that requires a break with what we know as thinking. (Wittgenstein says our investigation has to be turned around; Heidegger says we have to take a step back from our thinking.) The incentive to this other mode will presumably consist in recognizing that we are not engaged in it, not doing something we nevertheless recognize a love for, an instinct for. Then Emerson's task is to show to that desire its satisfaction, which is to say: This writing must illustrate thinking. This means at the least that it must contain thought about what illustration is, what an example is.

In "The American Scholar" Emerson's transfiguration of illustration is his use of the word "illustrious." For example: "[The scholar] is one who raises himself from private considerations ["innermost" he sometimes says] and breathes and lives on public ["outermost"] and illustrious thoughts." In Emerson's way of talking, this is a kind of tautology. It is a favorite idea of Emerson's that the passage from private to public ideas is something open to each individual, as if there is in the intellectual life the equivalent of the Moral Law in the moral life, an imperative to objectivity. In "Self-Reliance" he imagines a man who is able to reachieve a certain perspective that society talks us (almost all of us) out of, as one whose opinions would be "seen to be not private but necessary," and in "The American Scholar" he phrases what he will call the ground of his hope that man is one by saying "the deeper [the scholar] dives into his privatest, secretest presentiment, to his wonder he finds this is the most acceptable, most public, and universally true." The contrast to the superficially private, which the most private can reach, Emerson characterizes sometimes as necessary, sometimes as universal, thus exactly according to the characteristics Kant assigns to the a priori. I suppose Emerson knows this. But why would Emerson speak of illustrating the a priori conditions of thinking as illustrious? Surely for no reason separate from the fact that the illustration of thinking as attaining to the necessary and universal illustrates the conditions shared by humanity as such; such thoughts are illustrious exactly because they are completely unexceptional, in this way representative.

This thought produces some of Emerson's most urgent rhetoric, some of the most famous. In the opening paragraph of "Self-Reliance": "To believe your own thought, to believe that what is true for you in your private heart is true for all men,—that is genius." "In every work of genius we recognize our own rejected thoughts; they come back to us with a certain alienated majesty." Self-evidently no one is in a position to know more about this than any other, hence in no position to *tell* anyone of it, to offer information concerning it. (This is the Ancient Mariner's mistake, and his curse.) So pretty clearly Emerson is not talking about science and mathematics. Then what is he talking about? Whatever it is, he properly—conveniently, you might think—describes himself as *showing* his ground. But if his ground, or anyone's, will prove to be unexceptional (except for the endlessly specifiable fact that it is one's own life on that ground), why the tone of moral urgency in showing it, declaring it? Is thinking—something to be called thinking—something whose partiality or incentive is essentially moral and perhaps political?

Let us confirm Emerson's transfiguration of the illustrative in its other occurrence in "The American Scholar": "The private life of one man shall be a more illustrious monarchy, more formidable to its enemy, more sweet and serene in its influence to its friend, than any kingdom in history." The idea is that the illustrious is not, or shall not be, merely a particular result of monarchy but monarchy's universal cause, and the paradox alerts us to consider that while of course monarchy is derived as the rule of one (for whoever is still interested in that possibility), it may also come to be seen to speak of the *beginning* or *origin* of one, of what Emerson calls "one man," the thing two sentences earlier he had called "the upbuilding of a man," that is, of his famous "individual." (Hence the paradox of a private life as an illustrious monarchy is to be paired with the argument, as between Jefferson and Adams, of the natural aristocrat. Both knew that *that* was a paradoxical idea—as if democracy has its own paradox to match that of the philosopher king. The Adams-Jefferson exchange is invoked in a complementary context in my *Pursuits of Happiness.*[14]) When this process of upbuilding, or origination, is achieved, then, as the final sentence of "The American Scholar" puts it, "A nation of men will for the first time exist"—or as Marx put the thought half a dozen years after Emerson's address, human history will begin. For Emerson you could say that this requires both a constitution of the public and an institution of the private, a new obligation to think for ourselves, to make ourselves intelligible, in every word. What goes on inside us now is merely obedience to the law and the voices of others—the business Emerson calls conformity, a rewriting of what Kant calls heteronomy. That no thought is our own is what Emerson signals by interpreting the opening fable of his essay, concerning the gods' original division of Man into men, to mean that "Man is thus metamorphosed into a thing." That we are already (always already) metamorphosed sets, I suppose, the possibility and necessity of our transfiguration. Then what were we before we were metamorphosed? (Emerson not only speaks of our conversion, which is to say, rebirth; he also says that we are unborn. This is worth brooding over.)

If we are things, we do not belong to Kant's realm of ends; we do not regard ourselves as human, with human others. For Kant the realm of ends might be seen as the realization of the eventual human city. As for Kant, for Emerson this vision is an inception of the moral life. What is the entrance to the city?

Here we cross to the second part of this lecture, to follow out a little the questionable tone of moral urgency in Emerson's descriptions of thinking. My thought is that a certain relation to words (as an allegory of my relation to my life) is inseparable from a certain moral-like relation to thinking, and that the morality and the thinking that are inseparable are of specific strains—the morality is neither teleological (basing itself on a conception of the good to be maximized in society) nor deontological (basing itself on an independent conception of the right), and the thinking is some as yet unknown distance from what we think of as reasoning. An obvious moral interpretation of the image of figuring from the innermost to the outermost is that of moral perfectionism (on a current understanding) at its most objectionable, the desire to impose the maximization of one's most private conception of good on all others, regardless of their talents or tastes or visions of the good.

I remarked that moral perfectionism has not found a secure home in modern philosophy. There are various reasons for this homelessness, and, as I have said, the title perfectionism covers more than a single view. Taking Emerson and Nietzsche as my focal examples here, and thinking of them, I surmise that the causes for the disapproval of perfectionism will orbit around two features or themes of their outlook. (1) A hatred of moralism—of what Emerson calls "conformity"—so passionate and ceaseless as to seem sometimes to amount to a hatred of morality altogether. (Nietzsche calls himself the first antimoralist; Emerson knows that he will seem antinomian, a refuser of any law, including the moral law.) (2) An expression of disgust with or a disdain for the present state of things so complete as to require not merely reform, but a call for a transformation of things, and before all a transformation of the self—a call that seems so self-absorbed and obscure as to make morality impossible: What is the moral life apart from acting beyond the self and making oneself intelligible to those beyond it?

A thought to hold onto is that what Emerson means by "conformity" is to be heard against Kant's idea that moral worth is a function of acting not merely in conformity with the moral law but for the sake of the law. Kant famously, scandalously, says that a mother who cares for her child out of affection rather than for the sake of the moral law exhibits no moral worth. Kant does not say that this woman exhibits no excellence of any kind, just not of the highest kind, the kind that makes the public life of mutual freedom possible, that attests to the realm of ends. Emerson's perception can be said to be that we exhibit neither the value of affection nor the worth of morality (neither, as it were, feminine nor masculine virtues), but that our conformity exhibits merely the fear of others' opinions, which Emerson puts as a fear of others' eyes, which claps us in a jail of shame.[15]

This in turn is to be heard against John Rawls's impressive interpretation of Kant's moral philosophy, in which he presents Kant's "main aim as deepening and justifying Rousseau's idea that liberty is acting in accordance with a law that we give to ourselves" and emphasizes that "Kant speaks of the failure to act on the moral law as giving rise to shame and not to feelings of guilt."[16] A text such as Emerson's "Self-Reliance" is virtually a study of shame and perceives what we now call human society as one in which the moral law is nowhere (or almost nowhere) in existence. His perception presents itself to him as a vision of us as "bugs, spawn," as a "mob";

Nietzsche will say (something Emerson also says) "herd." It is a violent perception of a circumstance of violence. How do we, as Emerson puts it, "come out" of that?[17] How do we become self-reliant? The worst thing we could do is rely on ourselves as we stand—this is simply to be the slaves of our slavishness: it is what makes us spawn. We must become averse to this conformity, which means convert from it, which means transform our conformity, as if we are to be born (again). How does our self-consciousness— which now expresses itself as shame, or let us say embarrassment—make us something other than human? I have elsewhere (in "Being Odd, Getting Even"[18]) tried to show that Emerson is taking on philosophy's interpretation of self-consciousness in its versions in both Descartes and Kant.

In Descartes, self-consciousness, in the form of thinking that I think, must prove my existence, human existence. When in "Self-Reliance" Emerson says that we dare not (as if we are ashamed to) say "I think," "I am," as if barred from the saying of the *cogito ergo sum*, his implication is that we do not exist (as human), we as if haunt the world. And I find this pattern in Emerson (of discovering our failing of philosophy as a failure of our humanity) also to be interpreting Kant's idea of freedom as imposing the moral law upon oneself. It is for Emerson not so much that we are ashamed because we do not give ourselves the moral law— which is true enough—but that we do not give ourselves the moral law because we are already ashamed, a state surely in need of definition, as if we lack the right to be right. Again, it is not that we are ashamed of our immorality: we are exactly incapable of being ashamed of *that*; in that sense we are shameless. Our moralized shame is debarring us from the conditions of the moral life, from the possibility of responsibility over our lives, from responding to our lives rather than bearing them dumbly or justifying them automatonically. That debarment or embarrassment is for Emerson, as for Kant, a state other than the human, since it lacks the humanly defining fact of freedom. That we are perceived as "bugs" says this and more. Bugs are not human, but they are not monsters either; bugs in human guise are inhuman, monstrous.

How does Emerson understand a way out, out of wronging ourselves? That is, how does Emerson find the "almost lost . . . light that can lead [us] back to [our] prerogatives"—which for Emerson would mean something like answering for ourselves? Here is where Emerson's writing, with its enactment of transfigurations, comes in. Its mechanism may be seen in (even as) Emersonian perfectionism.

Perfectionism makes its appearance in Rawls's *A Theory of Justice* as a teleological theory and as having two versions, moderate and extreme.[19] In the moderate version its principle is one among others and "[directs] society to arrange institutions and to define the duties and obligations of individuals so as to maximize the achievement of human excellence, in art, in science, and culture."[20] Then how shall we understand Emerson's and Nietzsche's disdain for the cultural institutions, or institutionalized culture, of the day (including universities and religions and whatever would be supported by what Rawls describes as "public funds for the arts and sciences"[21]), a disdain sometimes passionate to the point of disgust? The distribution of nothing of high culture as it is now institutionalized is to be maximized in Emersonian perfectionism, which is in that sense not a teleological theory at all. What Nietzsche calls "the pomp of culture" and "misemployed and appropriated culture" is, on the contrary, to be scorned. It makes no obvious sense to ask for some given thing to be maximized in what this perfectionism craves as the realm of culture, the realm to which, as Nietzsche puts it, we are to consecrate ourselves, the path on which, as Emerson puts it, we are to find "the conversion of the world." There is, before finding this, nothing to be maximized. One can also say that the good of the culture to be found is already universally distributed or else it is nothing—which is to say, it is part of a conception of what it is to be a moral person. Emerson calls it genius; we might call this the capacity for self-criticism, the capacity to consecrate the attained to the unattained self, on the basis of the axiom that each is a moral person.

The irrelevance of maximization (as a particular teleological principle) should be clearer still in what Rawls calls the extreme version of perfectionism, in which the maximization of excellence is the sole principle of institutions and obligations. As I noted earlier, *A Theory of Justice* epitomizes this extreme version by a selection of sentences from Nietzsche. They are from the third untimely meditation, "Schopenhauer as Educator":

Mankind must work continually to produce individual great human beings—this and nothing else is the task. . . . For the question is this: how can your life, the individual life, retain the highest value, the deepest significance? . . . Only by your living for the good of the rarest and most valuable specimens.[22]

This sounds bad. Rawls takes it straightforwardly to imply that there is a separate class of great men (to be) for whose good, and conception of good, the rest of society is to live. Rawls is surely right to reject this as a principle of justice pertinent to the life of democracy. But, as I also noted, if Nietzsche is to be dismissed as a thinker pertinent to the founding of the democratic life, then so, it should seem, is Emerson, since Nietzsche's meditation on Schopenhauer is, to an as yet undisclosed extent, a transcription and elaboration of Emersonian passages. Emerson's dismissal here would pain me more than I can say, and if that is indeed the implication of *A Theory of Justice*, I want the book, because of my admiration for it, to be wrong in drawing this implication from itself.

In Nietzsche's meditation, the sentence "Only by your living for the good of the rarest and most valuable specimens" continues with the words "and not for the good of the majority." However, the majority is then characterized still further in that sentence; it is not part of constitutional democracy that one is to live for the good of the majority—something Rawls's book is the demonstration of for those committed to democracy. If not for the good of the majority, then is one to live for the good of each (for each societal "position")? I suppose this is not captured in the idea of making rational choices that have justifiably unequal benefits for all (measured by the Difference Principle, Rawls's second principle of justice), but it may yet be a life taken within the commitment to democracy. There will doubtless be perfectionisms that place themselves above democracy or that are taken in the absence of the conditions of democracy. The former might describe a timarchy, an oligarchy, or a dictatorship. These are not my business, which is, rather, to see whether perfectionism is necessarily undemocratic. I might put my thought this way: the particular disdain for official culture taken in Emerson and in Nietzsche (and surely in half the writers and artists in the one hundred and fifty years since "The American Scholar," or say since romanticism) is itself an expression of democracy and commitment to it. Timocrats do not produce, oligarchs do not commission, dictators do not enforce, art and culture that disgust them. Only within the possibility of democracy is one committed to living with, or against, such culture. This may well produce personal tastes and private choices that are, let us say, exclusive, even esoteric. Then my question is whether this exclusiveness might be not just tolerated but treasured by the friends of democracy.

There are two further problems with the final sentence among those Rawls quotes from Nietzsche concerning living for rare specimens and not for the majority. First, Nietzsche's word translated as "specimens" is *Exemplare* (faithfully translated as "exemplars" later in *Untimely Meditations*, by the same translator from whom Rawls takes his Nietzsche sentences. The biological association of "specimens" suggests that the grounds for identifying them (hence for assessing their value) are specifiable independently of the instance in view, of its effect on you; its value depends upon this independence; specimens are samples, as of a class, genus, or whole; one either is or is not a specimen. Whereas the acceptance of an exemplar, as access to another realm (call it the realm of culture; Nietzsche says, echoing a favorite image of Emerson's, that it generates "a new circle of duties"), is grounded not in the relation between the instance and a class of instances it stands for but in the relation between the instance and the individual other—for example, myself—for whom it does the standing, for whom it is a sign upon whom I delegate something. ("Archetype," translatable as "exemplar," is the word Kant associates with the Son of God in *Religion within the Bounds of Reason Alone*[23]) Second, when Nietzsche goes on, in the sentences following the one about exemplars, to begin characterizing the life of culture, it must in a sense be understood as a life lived for the good of the one living it. It accordingly demands a certain exclusiveness; its good is inherently not maximizable (transportable to other lives). But it is not inherently unjust, requiring favored shares in the distribution of good. Its characteristic vice would not be envy (a vice methodologically significant for *A Theory of Justice*) but perhaps shirking participation in democracy. Then the question becomes: If it is not shirking, then *what* is its participation? Nietzsche continues, after the sentences Rawls quotes, as follows:

The young person should be taught to regard himself as a failed work of nature but at the same time as a witness to the grandiose and marvellous intention of this artist. . . . By coming to this resolve he places himself within the circle of *culture*; for culture is the child of each individual's self-knowledge and dissatisfaction with himself. Anyone who believes in culture is thereby saying: "I see above me something higher and more human than I am; let everyone help me to attain it, as I will help everyone who knows and suffers as I do."[24]

In the next sentence the "something higher," the desire for which is created in self-dissatisfaction, is marked as "a higher self as yet still concealed from it." It is my own, unsettlingly unattained.

Maximization is roughly the last thing on the mind of the suffering individual in this state of self-dissatisfaction, the state of perceiving oneself as failing to follow oneself in one's higher and happier aspirations, failing perhaps to have found the right to one's own aspirations—not to the deliverances of rare revelations but to the significance of one's everyday impressions, to the right to make them one's ideas. It is a crucial moment of the attained self, a crossroads; it may be creative or crushing. To look then for the maximization of a given state of culture is to give up looking for the reality of one's own. To be overly impatient philosophically with this crisis is to be overly impatient with the explorations of what we call adolescence. Emerson and Nietzsche notably and recurrently direct their words to "youth" as words against despair, showing that they themselves have survived the incessant calls to give over their youthful aspirations. For youth to be overly impatient with these calls is to be overly impatient with the adults who voice them; it is a deflection of the interest of the contest with adulthood, of the crisis in giving consent to adulthood, say with the arrogation of one's voice in the moral life, the law.[25] Since democracy is the middle or civil world of political possibilities—not ceding its demands for itself either to possibilities defined courteously or violently (neither to diplomacy nor to rebellion), it may be taken to be the public manifestation of the individual situation of adolescence, the time of possibilities under pressure to consent to actualities. The promise of Emerson and of Nietzsche is that youth is not alone a phase of individual development but—like childhood for the earlier romantics—a dimension of human existence as such.

When Nietzsche says, in the words of his passage last quoted, describing the young person as a failed work of nature and as a witness, "for culture is the child of each individual's self-knowledge and dissatisfaction with himself," and imagines one who seeks this child to pray that everyone will help him or her to attain it, could it be clearer that the "something higher and more human" in question is not—not necessarily and in a sense not ever—that of someone *else*, but a further or eventual position of the self now dissatisfied with itself? (The quantification is old-fashioned. Not, "there is a genius such that every self is to live for it," but, "for each self there is a genius." I am thinking particularly of the passage in "Self-Reliance" where Emerson reports that his genius calls him;[26] it calls him, it turns out, to his own work, which, it happens, is writing. I do not imagine this to be some other person calling him.) Nietzsche goes on: "Thus only he who has attached his heart to some great man is by that act *consecrated to culture*; the sign of that consecration is that one is ashamed of oneself without any accompanying feeling of distress, that one comes to hate one's own narrowness and shrivelled nature."[27] The perfectionist idea of culture is projected in contrast to this idea of "one's own nature." The sense is that the move from the state of nature to the contract of society does not, after all, sufficiently sustain human life. If the idea of unshriveling our nature is that of transforming our needs, not satisfying them as they stand, the moral danger that is run may seem to be that of idealistic moralism, forgetting the needs of others as they stand. Since the task for each is his or her own self-transformation, the representativeness implied in that life may seem not to establish a recognition of others in different positions, so to be disqualified as a moral position altogether. "Representativeness" invokes one of Emerson's "master-tones," both as characterized in his writing and as exemplified by his writing. And I think we can say: Emerson's writing works out the conditions for my recognizing my difference from others as a function of my recognizing my difference from myself.

Nietzsche's idea of "attaching one's heart," here to some great man, is, let us say, acting toward him in love, as illustrated by Nietzsche's writing of his text on Schopenhauer. But the author of that text is not consecrating himself to Schopenhauer—Schopenhauer, as everyone notes, is scarcely present in the text. If what you consecrate yourself to is what you live for, then Nietzsche is not living for Schopenhauer. It is not Schopenhauer's self that is still concealed from the writer of this text. The love of the great is, or is the cause of, the hate of one's meanness, the hate that constitutes the sign of consecration. "The fundamental idea of culture, insofar as it sets for each one of us but one task [is]: to promote the production of the philosopher, the artist and the saint *within us* and without us and thereby to work at the perfecting of nature."[28] This is said to set one in the midst of "a mighty community." Obviously it is not a present but an eventual human community, so everything depends on how it is to be reached.

Many, with Rawls, have taken Nietzsche otherwise than as calling for the further or higher self of each, each consecrating himself /herself to self-transformation, accepting one's own genius, which is precisely not, it is the negation of, accepting one's present state and its present consecrations to someone fixed, as such, "beyond" one. Perhaps it was necessary for Nietzsche to have left himself unguarded on this desperate point.

Emerson provides an explanation and name for this necessary ambiguity in the passage of "The American Scholar" of which Nietzsche's passage on the relation to greatness is a reasonably overt transcription (with sensible differences):

The main enterprise of the world for splendor, for extent, is the upbuilding of a man . . . [i]n a century, in a millennium, one or two men; that is to say, one or two approximations to the right state of every man. All the rest behold in the hero or the poet their own green and crude being,—ripened; yes, and are content to be less, so *that* may attain to its full stature.

But Emerson does not say that this contentment is the best or necessary state of things. For him, rather, it shows "[w]hat a testimony, full of grandeur [in view of what we might become], full of pity [in view of what we are], is borne to the demands of his own nature [by the poor and the low. The poor and the low are] to be brushed like flies from the path of a great person, so that justice shall be done by him to that common nature which it is the dearest desire of all to see enlarged. . . . He lives for us, and we live in him." (Emerson is unguarded; we are unguarded.) As we stand we are apt to overrate or misconstrue this identification. Emerson continues:

Men, such as they are, very naturally seek money or power. . . . And why not? for they aspire to the highest, and this, in their sleepwalking, they dream is highest. Wake them and they shall quit the false good and leap to the true, and leave governments to clerks and desks. This revolution is to be wrought by the gradual domestication of the idea of Culture. . . . Each philosopher, each bard, each actor has only done for me, as by a delegate, what one day I can do for myself.

Here there simply seems no room for doubt that the intuition of a higher or further self is one to be arrived at in person, in the person of the one who gives his heart to it, this one who just said that the great have been his delegates and who declares that "I" can one day, so to speak, be that delegate. I forerun myself, a sign, an exemplar.

In the so-called Divinity School address, delivered the year after "The American Scholar," Emerson will in effect provide the originating case of our repressing our delegation and attributing our potentialities to the actualities of others, the case of "Historical Christianity['s] dwell[ing], with noxious exaggeration about the *person* of Jesus," whereas "the soul knows no persons." Evidently Emerson is treating this form of worship or consecration, even if in the name of the highest spirituality, as idolatry. (Here is a site for investigating the sense that perfectionism is an attempt to take over, or mask, or say secularize, a religious responsibility, something Matthew Arnold is explicit in claiming for his perfectionism in *Culture and Anarchy,* something Henry Sidgwick criticizes Arnold for in "The Prophet of Culture.")

In Emerson's way of speaking, "one day" ("Each philosopher . . . has only done, as by a delegate, what one day I can do for myself") always also means today; the life he urgently speaks for is one he forever says is not to be postponed. It is today that you are to take the self on; today that you are to awaken and to consecrate yourself to culture, specifically, to domesticate it gradually, which means bring it home, as part, now, of your everyday life. This is perfectionism's moral urgency; why, we might say, the results of its moral thinking are not the results of moral reasoning, neither of a calculation of consequences issuing in a judgment of value or preference, nor of a testing of a given intention, call it, against a universalizing law issuing in a judgment of right. The urgency is expressed in Emerson's sense of fighting chagrin in every word, with every breath. If calculation and judgment are to answer the question Which way?, perfectionist thinking is a response to the way's being lost. So thinking may present itself as stopping, and as finding a way *back,* as if thinking is remembering something. (This is a kind of summary of the way I have read Emerson's "Experience" in my "Finding as Founding."[29])

The urgency about today is the cause of Emerson's characteristic allusions to the gospels. In "The American Scholar" it is rather more than an allusion: "For the ease and pleasure of treading the old road . . . [the scholar instead] takes the cross of making his own"—a road Emerson characterizes in that passage as one of poverty, solitude, stammering, self-accusation, and "the state of virtual hostility in which he seems to stand to society, and especially to educated society." In "Self-Reliance" the parody is as plain as the allusion: "I shun father and mother and wife and brother when my genius calls me. I would write on the lintels of the door-post, *Whim.*" The shunning reference is to the call to enter the kingdom of heaven at once, today, to follow me, to let the dead bury the dead.[30] Emerson's parody mocks his own preachiness, and while it acknowledges that the domestication of culture is not going to be entered on today, yet it insists that there is no reason it is postponed: that is, no one has the reason for this revolution if each of us has not. It is why he perceives us as "[bearing] testimony, full of grandeur, full of pity, . . . to the demands of [our] own nature," a remark transcribed in Nietzsche as "[regarding oneself] as a failed work of nature but at the same time as a witness to the grandiose and marvellous intention of this artist."[31] Bearing testimony and witnessing are functions of martyrdom. In moral perfectionism, as represented in Emerson and in Nietzsche, we are invited to a position that is structurally one of martyrdom—not, however, in view of an idea of the divine but in aspiration to an idea of the human.

What can this mean? (Whatever it means it suggests why I cannot accede to the recent proposal, interesting as it is in its own terms, of taking perfectionism to be exemplified by the well-rounded life. See the essay by Thomas Hurka.[32]) And how does thinking as transfiguration bear on it? Which is to ask, how does Emerson's way of writing, his relation to his reader, bear on it? Which in turn means, how does his writing represent, by presenting, the aspiration to the human?

Before going on to sketch an answer to this pack of questions, it may be well to pause to say another word about my sense that the view Emerson and Nietzsche share, or my interest in it, is not simply to show that it is tolerable to the life of justice in a constitutional democracy but to show how it is essential to that life. What is the pertinence, for example, of perfectionism's emphasis, common from Plato and Aristotle to Emerson and Thoreau and Nietzsche, on education and character and friendship for a democratic existence? That emphasis of perfectionism, as I have said, may be taken to serve an effort to escape the mediocrity or leveling, say vulgarity, of equal existence, for oneself and perhaps for a select circle of like-minded others. There are undeniably aristocratic or aesthetic perfectionisms. But in Emerson it should, I would like to say, be taken as part of the training for democracy. Not the part that must internalize the principles of justice and practice the role of the democratic citizen—that is clearly required, so obviously that the Emersonian may take offense at the idea that this aspect of things is even difficult, evince a disdain for ordinary temptations to cut corners over the law.

I understand the training and character and friendship Emerson requires for democracy as preparation to withstand not its rigors but its failures, character to keep the democratic hope alive in the face of disappointment with it. (Emerson is forever turning aside to say, especially to the young, not to despair of the world, and he says this as if he is speaking not to a subject but to a monarch.) That we will be disappointed in democracy, in its failure by the light of its own principles of justice, is implied in Rawls's concept of the original position in which those principles are accepted, a perspective from which we know that justice, in actual societies, will be departed from, and that the distance of any actual society from justice is a matter for each of us to assess for ourselves. I will speak of this as our being compromised by the democratic demand for consent, so that the human individual meant to be created and preserved in democracy is apt to be undone by it.

Now I go on to my sketch in answer to how Emerson's writing (re)presents the aspiration to the human, beginning from a famous early sentence of "Self-Reliance" I have already had occasion to cite: "In every work of genius we recognize our own rejected thoughts; they come back to us with a certain alienated majesty." The idea of a majesty alienated from us is a transcription of the idea of the sublime as Kant characterizes it. Then the sublime, as has been discussed in recent literary theory, bears the structure of Freudian transference.[33] The direction of transference—of mine to the text, or the text's to me in a prior countertransference (or defense against being read)—seems to me an open question. In either case reading, as such, is taken by Emerson as of the sublime.

This comes out in Emerson's (and Thoreau's) delirious denunciation of books, in the spectacle of writing their own books that dare us to read them and dare us not to, that ask us to conceive that they do not want us to read them, to see that they are teaching us how—how not to read, that they are creating the taste not to be read, the capacity to leave them. Think of it this way: If the thoughts of a text such as Emerson's (say the brief text on rejected thoughts) are yours, then you do not need them. If its thoughts are not yours, they will not do you good. The problem is that the text's thoughts are neither exactly mine nor not mine. In their sublimity as my rejected—say repressed—thoughts, they represent my further, next, unattained but attainable self. To think otherwise, to attribute the origin of my thoughts simply to the other, thoughts which are then, as it were, implanted in me—some would say caused—by let us say some Emerson, is idolatry. (What in "Politics of Interpretation" I call the theology of reading is pertinent here.[34])

In becoming conscious of what in the text is (in Emerson's word) unconscious, the familiar is invaded by another familiar—the structure Freud calls the uncanny, and the reason he calls the psychoanalytic process itself uncanny. Emerson's process of transfiguring is such a structure, a necessity of his placing his work in the position of our rejected and further self, our "beyond." One of his ways of saying this is to say "I will stand here for humanity," as if he is waiting for us to catch up or catch on. When this is unpacked it turns out to be the transfiguration of a Kantian task. To say how, I track for a moment Emerson's play, pivotally and repeatedly in "Self-Reliance," on inflections of standing up and understanding in relation to standing for and in relation to standards.

"Standing for humanity," radiating in various directions as *representing* humanity and as *bearing* it (as bearing the pain of it) links across the essay with its recurrent notation of postures and of gaits (leaning and skulking among them—postures of shame) of which *standing*, or uprightness, is the correction or conversion that Emerson seeks, his representative prose. This opens into Emerson's description of our being drawn by the true man, as being "constrained to his standard."[35] (Emerson says he will make "this" true—I assume he is speaking of his prose—and describes the true man as "measuring" us.) Now *constraint*, especially in conjunction with *conformity*, is a Kantian term, specifically noting the operation of the moral law upon us—of the fact that it applies only to (is the mark of) the human, that is, only to a being subject to temptation, a being not unmixed in nature, as beasts and angels are unmixed. If you entertain this thought, then the idea of "standard" links further with the Kantian idea that man lives in two worlds, that is, is capable of viewing himself from two "standpoints" (in Kant's term). It is this possibility that gives us access to the intelligible world—the realm of ends, the realm of reason, of the human— "beyond" the world of sense. If Emerson assigns his pages as standards (flags and measures) and if this is an allusion to, an acceptance of, the Kantian task of disclosing the realm of ends, the realm of the human, then what is its point?

The point of contesting the Kantian task is presumably to be taken in the face of its present failure, or parody, its reduction to conformity. In picking up its standard—and transfiguring it—Emerson finds the intelligible world, the realm of ends, closed to us as a standpoint from which to view ourselves individually (our relation to the law no longer has *this* power for us). But at the same time he shows the intelligible world to be entered into whenever another represents for us our rejected self, our beyond, causes that aversion to ourselves in our conformity that will constitute our becoming, as it were, ashamed of our shame. Some solution. Well, some problem.

Kant describes the "constraint" of the law as an imperative expressed by an ought.[36] For Emerson, we either *are* drawn beyond ourselves, as we stand, or we are *not*; we stand for something, we are attracted to a standard we recognize as ours, or we do not; we recognize our reversals or we do not;

there is no ought about it. It remains true that being drawn by the standard of another, like being impelled by the imperative of a law, is the prerogative of the mixed or split being we call the human. But for Emerson we are divided not alone between intellect and sense, for we can say that each of these halves is itself split. We are halved not only horizontally but vertically—as that other myth of the original dividing of the human pictures it—as in Plato's *Symposium*, the form of it picked up in Freud, each of us seeking that of which we were originally half, with which we were partial.

Here, in this constraint by recognition and negation, is the place of the high role assigned in moral perfectionism to friendship. Aristotle speaks of a friend as "another myself." To see Emerson's philosophical authorship as taking up the ancient position of the friend, we have to include the inflection (more brazen in Nietzsche but no less explicit in Emerson) of my friend as my enemy (contesting my present attainments). If the position of that loved one were not also feared and hated, why would the thoughts from that place remain rejected? If one does not recognize Emerson in his version of such a position, his writing will seem, to its admirers, misty or foggy; to its detractors, ridiculous. (*Almost* everyone gets around to condescending to Emerson.)

How can philosophy have, in such a fashion, worked itself into the position of having to be accepted on intimate terms before it has proven itself? It seems the negation of philosophy.

If Emerson is wrong in his treatment of the state of conformity and of despair in what has become of the democratic aspiration, he seems harmless enough—he asks for no relief he cannot provide for himself—whatever other claims other perfectionisms might exert. But if Emerson is right, his aversion provides for the democratic aspiration the only internal measure of its truth to itself—a voice only this aspiration could have inspired, and, if it is lucky, must inspire. Since his aversion is a *continual turning away* from society, it is thereby a continual turning *toward* it. Toward and away; it is a motion of seduction—such as philosophy will contain. It is in response to this seduction from our seductions (conformities, heteronomies) that the friend (discovered or constructed) represents the standpoint of perfection.

The idea of the self as always to be furthered is not expressed by familiar fantasies of a noumenal self, nor of the self as entelechy, either final or initial. May one imagine Emerson to have known that the word *scholar* is related in derivation to *entelechy* (through the idea of holding near or holding back, as if stopping to think)—so that by the American Scholar he means the American self? Then, since by Cartesian and by Kantian measures the self in America does not exist, America does not exist—or, to speak in proper predicates, is still not discovered as a new, another, world.

And the question might well arise: Why does Emerson take on the Cartesian and Kantian measures? Why does he put his English on the terms of philosophy? Instead of transfiguring these terms, why not take the opportunity of America as one of sidestepping philosophy, as one more European edifice well lost? Why does Emerson care, why ought we to care, whether he is a philosopher? Why care when we come to his page, his standard, whether the encounter with our further self, the encounter of reading, the access to an intelligible world, is a philosophical one? Evidently because the gradual domestication of culture he calls for—what he names his revolution—is a philosophical one. How?

How is this domestication—call it finding a home for humanity; Emerson and Thoreau picture it as building a house, another edification—how is this a task for philosophy? We may take for granted Plato's description of his task in the *Republic* as creating a "city of words," hence accept it that philosophy in the Western world unfolds its prose in a depicted conversation concerning the just city. Emerson's house of words is essentially less than a city, and while its word is not that of hope, its majesty is not to despair, but to let the "grandeur of justice shine" in it, and "affection cheer" it. Kant had asked, What can I hope for? Emerson in effect answers, for nothing. You do not know what there is hope for. "Patience—patience [suffering, reception]"; "abide on your instincts"[37]—presumably because that is the way of thinking. For him who abides this way, "the huge world will come round to him"—presumably in the form in which it comes to Emerson, one person at a time, a world whose turning constitutes the world's coming around—the form in which you come to your (further) self.

In coming to Emerson's text from a certain alienated majesty, we (each of us as Emerson's reader) form an illustrious monarchy with a population of two. It illustrates the possibility of recognizing my finitude, or separateness, as the question of realizing my partiality. Is the displacement of the idea of the whole man by an idea of the partial man worth philosophy?

I see it this way. Emerson's perception of the dispossession of our humanity, the loss of ground, the loss of nature as our security, or property, is thought in modern philosophy as the problem of skepticism. The overcoming or overtaking of skepticism must constitute a revolution that is a domestication for philosophy (or redomestication) because, let us say, neither science nor religion nor morality has overcome it. On the contrary, they as much as anything cause skepticism, the withdrawal of the world. *Is* philosophy left to us, even transformed? Well, that is my question. I think it is philosophy's question, which accordingly now comes into its own—as if purified of religion and of science.

I can formulate my interest in Emerson's situation in the following way. Domestication in Emerson is the issue, or urgency, of the *day*, today, one among others, an achievement of the everyday, the ordinary, now, here, again, never again. In Wittgenstein's *Philosophical Investigations* the issue of the everyday is the issue of the siting of skepticism, not as something to be overcome, as if to be refuted, as if it is a conclusion about human knowledge (which is skepticism's self-interpretation), but to be placed as a mark of what Emerson calls "human condition," a further interpretation of finitude, a mode, as said, of inhabiting our investment in words, in the world. This argument of the ordinary—as what skepticism attacks, hence creates, and as what counters, or recounts, skepticism—is engaged oppositely in a work such as Heidegger's *What Is Called Thinking?*; hence the argument of the ordinary is engaged between these visions of Wittgenstein and of Heidegger. (It may present itself as an argument between skepticism and sublimity, between transfiguration down and transfiguration up.) It is why I am pleased to find Emerson and his transfigurations of the ordinary to stand back of both Wittgenstein and Heidegger. They are the two major philosophers of this century for whom the issue of the ordinary, hence of skepticism, remains alive for philosophy, whose burden is philosophy's burden; it is, to my mind, utterly significant that in them—as in Emerson—what strikes their readers as a tone of continual moral urgency or religious or artistic pathos is not expressed as a *separate* study to be called moral philosophy, or religious philosophy, or aesthetics. The moral of which—or the aesthetics of which—I draw as follows: what they write is nothing *else* than these topics or places of philosophy, but is always nothing but philosophy itself. Nothing less, nothing separate, can lead us from, or break us of, our shameful condition. Philosophy presents itself as a (an untaken) way of life. This is what perfectionists will find ways to say.

Then, needless to say, in calling for philosophy Emerson is not comprehensible as asking for guardianship by a particular profession within what we call universities. I assume what will become "philosophy itself" may not be distinguishable from literature—that is to say, from what literature will become. Then that assumption, or presumption, is, I guess, my romanticism.

I come back to earth, concluding by locating what I have been saying in relation to a passage from John Stuart Mill's *On Liberty* that should be common ground among professional philosophers. I adduce it with the thought that what I have been saying suggests to me that perfectionism, as I perceive the thing that interests me, is not a competing moral theory but a dimension of any moral thinking. Kant found an essential place for perfection in his view of it at the end, as it were, of his theory, as an unreachable ideal relation to the moral law to be striven for; in Emerson this place of the ideal occurs at the beginning of moral thinking, as a condition, let us say, of moral imagination, as preparation or sign of the moral life. And if the precondition of morality is to be established in personal encounter, we exist otherwise in a premoral state, morally voiceless. Mill's passage, while no doubt not as eager to court the derangement of intellect as Emerson's prose has to be, is no less urgent and eloquent in the face of human dispossession and voicelessness:

In our times, from the highest class of society down to the lowest, every one lives as under the eye of a hostile and dreaded censorship. Not only in what concerns others, but in what concerns themselves, the individual, or the family, do not ask themselves—what do I prefer? . . . or, what would allow the best and highest in me to have fair play, and enable it to grow and thrive? They ask themselves, . . . what is usually done? I do not mean that they choose what is customary in preference to what suits their own inclination. It does not occur to them to have any inclination except for what is customary. Thus the mind itself is bowed to the yoke: even in what people do for pleasure, conformity is the first thing thought of; they like in crowds; they exercise choice only among things commonly done; peculiarity of taste, eccentricity of conduct, are shunned equally with crimes: until by dint of not following their own nature, they have no nature to follow: their human capacities are withered and starved; they become incapable of any strong wishes or native pleasures, and are generally without either opinions or feelings of home growth, or properly their own. Now is this, or is it not, the desirable condition of human nature?[38]

I call attention to the toll of that Millian word "desirable." In a passage in *Utilitarianism*, Mill famously conceives the claim that anything is desirable—on analogy with the claim that anything is visible or audible—to rest finally on the fact that people do, or presumably under specifiable circumstances will, actually desire it. Philosophers in the years I was in graduate school never used to tire of making fun of that passage from *Utilitarianism.* Yet the drift of it still strikes me as sound. According to it, the question at the conclusion of the quotation from *On Liberty* becomes: Do you, or would you, his reader, under any circumstances, desire this censored condition of mankind? It is perfectionism's question, its reading of the cry of freedom, for a life of one's own, of one's choice, that one consents to with one's own voice. The eloquence of Mill's passage is to awaken its friend to the question, to show that it is a question. The implication seems to be that until we each give our answers to the question, one by one, one on one, we will not know what it is to which—long before we begin our calculations of pleasure and of pain—we are giving our consent.

Hope against Hope

This is a most happy occasion for me and I do not wish to mar it by speaking of unhappy things.[1] But I will not belittle it by using it to speak of anything less than what matters most to me as a teacher and a writer and a citizen. One of these matters I share in common with every thinking person on earth, the imagination, or the refusal of imagination, of nuclear war, the most famous issue now before the world. Another matter is, in comparison, one of the most obscure issues of the world, and I share it, at most, with a few other obscure persons: the inability of our American culture to listen to the words, to possess them in common, of one of the founding thinkers of our culture, Ralph Waldo Emerson, an inability which presents itself to me as our refusal to listen to ourselves, to our own best thoughts. The particular odd matter I am moved to speak about by this occasion—on which a faculty is gathered to honor students, before their proud families, joined gratefully by me together with my family—is how this famous matter of destructiveness and this obscure matter of the repression of thinking have conjoined in my mind.

The precipitating cause of this conjunction was my coming into two sets of documents over the past summer. The first set consisted in two essays on Emerson published last year, one by one of our most influential literary critics, Harold Bloom of Yale, the other by one of our most prolific and celebrated novelists, John Updike.[2] The second set of documents consisted in material concerning a form of Christian fundamentalism that believes nuclear war will be the fulfillment of the biblical image of Armageddon as given in the book of Revelation, that accordingly a final war is scheduled between us and our enemies in which the stakes are the victory of cosmic good over cosmic evil. (If you disagree with, or disapprove of, what I will be saying, I hope you can at least regard it as of a certain interest in showing the kind of heaping and hooping together of contrary appeals and protests and accusations and denunciations that compete for our attention every day, each asking for the loan of our voices because each is demanding the right to speak for us. It seems that the more total our access to information becomes, the more complete becomes our ignorance of why it is given us, what it means, whom to believe, and what fruitful action we could take on its basis.) Since President Reagan is reported on a number of occasions to have endorsed this fundamentalist view—sometimes called "end-time theology," the view that in our time we will see the end of time—it is understandably a question for many of us whether his administration has the will and the taste to muster and be constant to whatever practical wisdom is within human command on the subject of nuclear war. The material on endtime theology was sent to me at my request by a friend and student of religious education who has enlisted in the labors of nuclear education. I should say at the outset that I agree with the sense of many of those similarly enlisted, to whom I feel indebted, that the idea of a final nuclear war as God's own instrument and plan for humankind is an expression of despair. This will hardly imply that we have nothing to fear; on the contrary, it implies that despair, always a mortal temptation, is now itself a mortal danger, since it is precisely a climate of despair that will ease the fulfillment of our worst fears.

This is where the repression of Emerson's thinking comes to mind, for it was precisely despair that was the climate in which Emerson felt he wrote and which his writing was meant to withstand and disperse. He calls this mood "secret melancholy." His disciple Thoreau, sharing the vision, called it "quiet desperation" and said famously that this is the life led by the mass of men. I imagine that some of you will wish to reply in something like the following way: "But now things are different. In Emerson's and Thoreau's day there were many things to be feared but there was no external cause such as we now living have for hopelessness. For them it still made sense to say that the external threats of life do not cause despair, that on the contrary despair is itself the ultimate spiritual threat. Emerson could say: The office of the scholar is to cheer and raise us; the post of the poet is the delight in common influences, so that their metamorphosis through him excites in us an emotion of joy. But for us, an Emersonian cheerfulness and hopefulness would simply express a childish ignorance of our real situation." The trouble with this reply is that it was always the reply to Emerson; he is forever taken by his detractors, and not by them alone, to ignore the tragic facts of life. Whereas Emerson seems to take despair not as a recognition of life, not even a tragic recognition of it, but as a fear of life, an avoidance of it. I persist in thinking this is correct, then and now.

Call this my (American) faith. It is not optimism. I see that I hang on to it as for dear life in one of the first essays I wrote that I still use, just over twenty years ago, concerning the interplay of what may be called literature with what may be called philosophy, a reading of Samuel Beckett's play *Endgame*, first performed in the mid-1950s, a play that pretty obviously takes place at some end of the world, among the survivors of some holocaust. I quote a few lines from myself of twenty-one years ago: "*Endgame* [suggests] . . . that we think it is right that the world end. Not perhaps morally right, but inevitable; tragically right. In a world of unrelieved helplessness, where Fate is not a notable [trio of] Goddess[es] but an inconspicuous chain of command, it would be a relief to stop worrying and start loving the Bomb."[3] This does not deny that our times are different from Emerson's times but it suggests that their differences lie not in our occasions for despair but in our means for expressing and enacting it. To quote one more sentence from my essay on Beckett's *Endgame*: "[The Bomb] has finally provided our dreams of vengeance, our despair of happiness, our hatreds of self and world, with an instrument adequate to convey their destructiveness, and satisfaction."[4] The idea is that world-destroying revenge is a kind of despair caused by an illusory hope, or an illusory way of hoping—a radical process of disappointment with existence as a whole, a last glad chance for getting even with life. It frightened me then to find myself having such thoughts, and now the organized cultivation of the wish for the end of time works to harden the fright.

Is Emerson really up to finding the measure of hope even here? To answer this I have to specify how I find what I called "our best thoughts" are to be discovered in Emerson. It will depend on seeing his words as those of something like a philosopher. Since that form of accuracy is generally not granted him, I will need to say why I insist upon it.

When I spoke, interpreting Beckett, of the Bomb as satisfying our dreams of vengeance, I was taking it that, for example, Nietzsche had spotted our vengefulness, our gloomy self-destructiveness, about as near the end of the nineteenth century as we are near the end of the twentieth, in his prediction, or warning, of nihilism, the will to nothingness. And near the end of the century before Nietzsche's, in 1794, Immanuel Kant, in an essay I had quite forgotten until the thoughts I am reporting on here led me back to it, very fully expressed his offense both as a philosopher (which I share) and as a Christian (which I am not in a position to share, but to admire and rejoice in) at the efforts he saw around him to link the end of the world to human means. Kant's essay is entitled "The End of All Things," and it undertakes to show, as the author of the monumental *Critique of Pure Reason* might be expected to do, that the idea of an apocalyptic end of the world is absolutely unknowable by us (exactly as unknowable as the ultimate nature of the world or of ourselves). It is unknowable exactly *because* the end of all things implies the end of time, and the human capacity for *knowledge* takes place only *within* time as one of its necessary conditions. The end of time is, however, according to Kant, *conceivable*; it is not a meaningless idea; and, moreover, the idea in its generality—only in its generality—is necessitated by human aspiration itself. Our moral and religious natures *must* aspire to the perfection for which they have been created, and they *must* understand themselves as capable of changing in the direction of perfection, and this perfection has in view the goal and end of moral struggle. Moral struggle, however, cannot end within time, in which change is called for; so the human being is bound to conceive in some way or other of an end to change and an end to struggle, and hence in some way of an end to time. But for Kant this moral struggle is an inner one of each soul with itself, in its fallenness, so that any apocalyptic end must be taken to be an allegory or figure of that struggle, not a moralized (literalized) outer substitute for it. To know the conflict between the allegorical or figurative and the literal may be taken to be the first lesson of reading. So to learn reading has now become a matter of literal life and death. Preachers of nuclear "end-time" theology pretty clearly believe that there will be change *after* the war they speak of, so it is not the end of time, not the final war, they are imagining, but just the end of one more war; and they are not imagining the end of a nuclear so-called war because they speak of a group of exceedingly contented survivors of their war.

But to suppose that the human being can know or seriously predict what the end of days will be, as we can know or predict the end of a given day, is for Kant, as said, not only philosophically offensive but Christianly offensive. This is because it leads men to imagine that they can fashion the human means of bringing about God's purposes for humankind. "The end of all things which pass through men's hands even if their purposes are good is folly, i.e., the use of means which are opposed to the purposes they are supposed to serve. [This] practical wisdom . . . abides alone with God." Moreover, the result of taking the means into human hands, Kant says, will destroy the hope of Christianity. "If Christianity promises rewards . . . as if it were an offer to bribe, as it were, to exhibit good conduct; . . . Christianity would not be worthy of love. Only a desire for such actions as arise from disinterested motives can inspire human respect toward the one who does this desiring; and without respect there is no true love." The result will be that "Christianity, though indeed intended to be the universal world religion, would not be favored by the workings of fate to become so, and the (perverse) end of all things (in a moral point of view) [i.e., an end of all things for which we are responsible, not God] will come to pass." So how can we translate God's wisdom, as to his purposes for us, into human, practical wisdom? Kant's advice is to recognize that the hope of securing ourselves against the folly of supposing ourselves to have laid hold of God's plan lies only "through trials and frequent change of plans" and "as fellow citizens [not through the exercise of authority, to] draw up plans and agree on them for the most part, [to] demonstrate in a trustworthy way that truth is of concern to [us]."

From Kant to Emerson is an immeasurable step. Emerson himself took the step in one direction, saying that the title *Transcendentalism*, which names what he calls his and his friends' "American Idealism," comes directly from Kant's use of the term *transcendental*.[5] In saying that the step is immeasurable, I mean that we are in no position to measure it. In the first of what is becoming a set of essays in which Emerson figures prominently, I say that he "challenges the basis of the argument of the *Critique of Pure Reason*," indeed, that he is therewith challenging philosophy as such. I also say that to challenge philosophy is something the major modern philosophers since Descartes and Locke have typically done, but I recognize that almost no one would now grant Emerson the intellectual stamina to challenge Kant philosophically. If he indeed were entering a challenge to Kant, it could only be on some literary or spiritual ground or other. I also say that if—as uncontroversially, in our century, Heidegger and Wittgenstein do—you challenge philosophy philosophically, then the answer to the question whether what you are composing is or is not philosophy is necessarily unstable. (If you challenge philosophy as such, how can what you are doing remain philosophy? But if what you are doing does not remain philosophy, how can it challenge anything philosophically?) Anyone who considers Emerson will want to know what kind of writing it is that Emerson has produced. My answer, in effect, is that since the answer to this question, to be correct, must be unstable, and since this instability is a function of Emerson's challenge of philosophy, this instability constitutes Emerson's capture of philosophy for America. (My effort is accordingly not to ask us to restrict our intellectual attention to our native writers but to recognize Emerson, in founding thinking for America—discovering America in thinking—as finding our own access to European thought.)

So I was likely not to be satisfied with the recent essays I have cited by Bloom and Updike, both of which turn the title of "philosopher" from Emerson, both of which question Emerson's essays as pieces of writing without allowing that writing itself to recognize the question and to participate in it, and both of which—most astoundingly to me—pretty much on the whole take what Emerson says at face value, without supposing the demand of interpretation. Their similarities on these and other points are the more notable since Bloom loves Emerson and he has put us in his debt for having done as much as anyone has done in the past two decades to bring Emerson back to his culture's attention, whereas Updike is one more in the line of artful detractors of Emerson, who from time to time are moved to get him in perspective by condescending to him. Bloom's praise of Emerson is not exactly praise for the wrong reason, but let me say for a stinted reason, and this, I cannot but feel, helps to keep condescension toward him in respectable orbit. It helps to keep our culture, unlike any other in the West, from possessing any founding thinker as a common basis for its considerations. If one were to say, truly enough, that Emerson is himself responsible for his disreputable, or overly reputable, appearances, then I say that Emerson should be the first for us to enlist in understanding that about him. He may, for example, exactly wish to write in order to deprive us of a philosophical founder, of all foundation of a certain sort. This may not, well understood, exactly be a bad thing. But it is an uncannily philosophical thing.

As evidence for Emerson's demand of interpretation, take the famously quoted passage from "Self-Reliance" which both Bloom and Updike requote (Bloom a little more extensively):

Then again, do not tell me, as a good man did to-day, of my obligation to put all poor men in good situations. Are they *my* poor? I tell thee, thou foolish philanthropist, that I grudge the dollar, the dime, the cent, I give to such men as do not belong to me and to whom I do not belong. There is a class of persons to whom by all spiritual affinity I am bought and sold; for them I will go to prison, if need be; but your miscellaneous popular charities; the education at college of fools; the building of meeting-houses to the vain end to which many now stand; alms to sots; and the thousand-fold Relief Societies;—though I confess with shame I sometimes succumb and give the dollar, it is a wicked dollar, which by and by I shall have the manhood to withhold.

Updike at once replies, "A doctrine of righteous selfishness is here pro-pounded." Bloom takes a little longer to say so, stopping first to remark that "Emerson meant by his 'class of persons' such as his friend Henry Thoreau, the mad poet Jones Very, and his precursor, the Reverend William Ellery Channing, which is not exactly . . . Ronald Reagan, and the Reverend Jerry Falwell." But Bloom continues: "Self-Reliance translated out of the inner life and into the marketplace is difficult to distinguish from our current religion of selfishness, as set forth so sublimely in the re-cent grand epiphany at Dallas" (i.e., I imagine, the last Republican na-tional convention).

    Was *selfishness* so much more clearly in evidence at the Republican than at the Democratic national convention? And is Emerson really so dif-ficult to distinguish from those who may be taken to be parodies of him? Not so difficult, it seems to me, apart from a suspicion that his parodists may just be right about him: Bloom says that "Emerson is more than pre-pared to give up on the great masses that constitute mankind"; but then where does Emerson expect his readers to come from, and why does he write as he does, which so often offends what you might call the elite, the educated classes? One may well feel that Emerson leaves himself too open to the purposes of his parodists; then that should specifically be under-stood and assessed. Let's look at the passage I just again requoted. Emerson does not say he does not give to the poor; on the contrary, he says he does (sometimes he succumbs, he says; no one, I suppose, gives to *every* cause that presents itself). Nor does the difficult question "Are they *my* poor?" imply that he recognizes no poor as his for charity; on the contrary, the question implies that some poor are his. Thoreau and Very are no doubt among those whom Emerson would say he belongs to and who belong to him. They are his, his equals, let us say; which suggests that a charitable dollar is wicked because it is given to unequals, because it supports what it is that keeps them down; which further suggests that when Emerson adds

of the wicked dollar, "which by and by I shall have the manhood to withhold," he does not exactly mean that he will further harden his heart but
that by and by he will live in a society that has achieved manhood, that one
day humankind will not require the dole from one another. So to style such
as Thoreau, Very, and Reverend Channing as his poor seems arch.

To see who Emerson's poor are, we can adduce the sentences preceding the ones I quoted, perhaps no less familiar:

I shun father and mother and wife and brother when my genius calls me. I would
write on the lintels of the door-post, *Whim.* I hope it is somewhat better than
whim at last, but we cannot spend the day in explanation. . . . Then again, do not
tell me . . . of my obligation to . . . all poor men.

Shunning father and mother is what Jesus required of who would belong
to him, and in that context the cry of the poor is of those that you have
always with you ("but me ye have not always"[6]). The spirit in which that
is said has always demanded interpretation and is itself appropriatable for
selfish ends. It no less requires interpretation in Emerson's case, unless
one supposes him not merely righteously selfish but a moral lunatic, raising the issue of the poor only in order to glory in his riches. Emerson addresses his remark about the poor to "thou foolish philanthropist"; Jesus'
remark about always having the poor with you was addressed to Judas Is-
cariot, who had just criticized Mary, the sister of Martha and Lazarus, for
anointing Jesus' feet with costly ointment. Judas was there undertaking
to instruct Jesus in the claims of charity. Emerson is accordingly placing
the most extreme pressure on his discernment of when and where to encounter the poor.

Emerson's poor are those to whom he has preached poverty and who
have listened to him. These are ones he calls (American) scholars, to whom
he had given warning in his earlier, most famous address to them:

The office of the scholar is to cheer, to raise, and to guide men by showing them
facts amidst appearances. . . . Long he must stammer in his speech; often forego
the living for the dead. Worse yet, he must accept—how often!—poverty and solitude. For the ease and pleasure of treading the old road, accepting the fashions, the
education, the religion of society, he takes the cross of making his own, and, of
course, the self-accusation, the faint heart, the frequent uncertainty and loss of
time, which are the nettles and tangling vines in the way of the self-relying and
self-directed; and the state of virtual hostility in which he seems to stand to society, and especially to educated society.

Are these the accents of self-congratulation to be heard in the kind of Dallas event Bloom cites, from which he says it is difficult to distinguish Emerson's view? Bloom speaks of Self-Reliance as "the American religion [Emerson] founded." Emerson's casting his genius figuratively in the role of Jesus, whose severe call he obeys, supports the idea; but Emerson's figuration here, while drawn in deadly earnest, at the same time shows him laughing at himself, at the position history has prepared for him. As he is laughing, and in deadly earnest, when he imagines writing "Whim" on the lintels of the door-posts. Performers at political conventions of the sort Bloom imagines, and those who prophesy world doom for their enemies and escape for themselves, are not laughing at themselves. To put writing on the lintels and the door-posts is the Old Testament command specifically at the time of Passover, as a sign to the angel of death to pass the house and spare its first born; and generally to put writing on the doorpost is a sign of faithfulness to God's command to "lay up these my words in your heart and in your soul and . . . write them upon the door posts of thine house."[7] Emerson's laughing use of Whim is a stumbling block to the perception of him, and he surely meant it to be. Here is Updike:

Totalitarian rule . . . offers a warped mirror in which we can recognize, distorted, Emerson's favorite concepts of genius and inspiration and whim; the totalitarian leader is a study in self-reliance gone amok, lawlessness enthroned in the place where law and debate and checks and balances should be. . . . The extermination camps are one of the things that come between us and Emerson's optimism.

Quite apart from this whimsical picture of totalitarian leadership, how is Emerson recommending so much as the private breaking of law in his passage about writing "Whim"? (When he does recommend disobedience to law there is no doubt about it, as in his outraged denunciation of the Fugitive Slave Act, whose support by Daniel Webster Emerson took as a betrayal of principle.[8])

Take three facts about the picture Emerson sketches for us: that when his genius calls him he shuns family ties; that what it calls him to do he cannot explain beyond writing "Whim" in a place of his own that is both public and dedicated to the sacred; and that what he does under that sign is done in hope ("I hope it is better than whim at last"). What I understand him specifically called by his genius to do, on the occasion on which he writes "Whim," is exactly to *write*: it is what he does; it constitutes his part in all our encountering of him; the passages before us are accordingly precisely what has become of his hope that his writing will be better than whim at last; and self-evidently *before* he produces his words in hope and notes their effect (their effect as creating their own readers, which may or may not in include his relations) he cannot post them as the justification for producing them, and what more can he *say* beforehand, before finding his words, than to stammer "Whim" and "hope"? If he *knew* he could produce inspired writing whenever he closed his door to his mother and father and wife and brother and miscellaneous relief societies and listened alone to his genius and wrote—if he knew this he would not require hope. But then why raise the issue of the poor at all?

I have mostly given my answer, that Emerson asserts that what he is withdrawing in order to do is done for the poor. This announces his act as moral, as announcing moral principles whose application will rebuke those who rebuke him for failing his moral obligations. There are two complementary moral principles implied in Emerson's scene. One is: to claim that an action is so important that you must shun your domestic obligations to perform it, you must be able to communicate the hope in which it is undertaken and you must be ready to declare publicly that you are without further explanation, or authority. A public declaration of your uncertainty will limit what it is you can ask people to do, and subject them to. You will have, if you are in political power, to take those over whose lives you have the power of life and death into your confidence. Speaking in confidence is the precise opposite of speaking in slogans and out of untold secrets; in confidence is the way to speak to fellow citizens. The further principle is: to claim your action as called out by your genius you must be comprehensible as serving the poor; the action must weigh itself at every moment against the visible suffering of the world. These seem to me principles upon which I would be happy to see those in political power over us act.

Do I press Emerson's meaning further than his words warrant? Updike says that Emerson's discourse is disconnected and that his affrontive assertions mark "the creation of a new religion"; Bloom's calling Self-Reliance Emerson's American religion says of him that "by no means the greatest American writer, perhaps more an interior orator than a writer, he is the inescapable theorist of virtually all subsequent American writing." But Bloom, for all the magnificence he allows Emerson's achievement, leaves the achievement incomprehensible by the implicit denial that Emerson is capable of comprehending his own writing, I mean accounting for it philosophically. My insistence that Emerson's achievement is essentially a philosophical one concentrates a number of claims. (1) His language has that accuracy, that commitment to subject every word of itself to criticism, endlessly, with nothing held safe, that is the blessing or the curse of philosophy—it is not a commitment religion may make, sometimes to its credit, sometimes not. (2) "Self-Reliance" in particular constitutes a theory of writing and reading whose evidence its own writing fully provides, before its role in subsequent American writing, and without which its role is incredible, as for many people it must always be; it before all describes its own prose, asserts itself as the foundation of its own existence, as Descartes had asserted *his* argument for self-reliance, his *cogito ergo sum*, as his foundation for his existence, hence as the basis of his philosophy. Emerson broadly alludes to Descartes's *cogito* argument, virtually repeats it—"I think," "I am," Emerson says in "Self-Reliance," or rather rebukes us for failing to say—another fact unnoticed, I believe, because of the endlessly repeated rumor that Emerson was not much of a thinker. (How *eager* his culture has been, top to bottom, to nourish this rumor! What's in it?) (3) The relation of Emerson's writing (the expression of his self-reliance) to his society (the realm of what he calls conformity) is one, as "Self-Reliance" puts it, of mutual aversion: "The virtue in most request is conformity. Self-reliance is its aversion." Naturally Emerson's critics take this to mean roughly that he is disgusted with society and wants no more to do with it. But the idea of self-reliance as the aversion of conformity figures each side in terms of the other, declares the issue between them as always joined, never settled. But then this is to say that Emerson's writing and his society are in an unending argument with one another—that is to say, he writes in such a way as to *place* his writing in his unending argument (such is his loyal opposition)—an unending turning away from one another, but for that exact reason a constant keeping in mind of one another, hence endlessly a turning *toward* one another. So that Emerson's aversion is like, and unlike, religious conversion. (4) His prose not only takes sides in this aversive conversation, but it also enacts the conversation, continuously creating readings of individual assertion that mutually turn from and toward one another (for example, the poor as rejected, his poor as embraced; the writing of "Whim" as the decision between life and death; the preaching of aversion as what Kant called a trustworthy demonstration of our concern for community and truth). This is perhaps what most immediately gives to Emerson's prose its sometimes maddening quality of seeming never to come to a point. It is one of Updike's chief complaints about the prose;

Bloom forgives Emerson for it. But for me Emerson's prose enacts in this way the state of democracy—not because it praises the democratic condition we have so far achieved, but because its aversive stance toward our condition only makes sense on the assumption of democracy as our life and our aspiration. Only within such a life and aspiration is a continuity of dialogue with one another, and with those in power over us, a possibility and duty. What could it mean to find in Emerson our founding thinker and not find in him *this* founding aspiration?

When Emerson teaches that actions we take to define our lives, on which we stake the life and death of our families and our societies, should be taken in hope and on such claim to authority as only we alone, in our uncertainty, can bring to it, he is teaching what Kant called "practical wisdom." It gives me hope—if small in our dangerous world, still concrete, clear, persistent, as large as my difficult sensibility can absorb. He tells me that those who have power over us who do not communicate to us their persistent hope of peace are despairing of peace, and are placing what they call their hope in a favorable roll of scientific or magic dice. This is no more genuine hope than praying for such a favorable outcome is genuine prayer. They are caught by their power, by their images of themselves, by what they believe to be their public's expectations of them, our expectations. We must help to teach them otherwise, teach them hope, and first one another.

What Is the Emersonian Event?
A Comment on Kateb's Emerson

(The following was my contribution to a panel at the American Political Science Association on August 20, 1993, celebrating the announcement of a new book by George Kateb on Emerson's politics.[1] The three brief citations I have taken from Kateb are from the portion of his manuscript that he chose to send me as a proposed text for my response, a text of seventy-three pages entitled "Emerson's Philosophy of Self-Reliant Activity." Since this was a typescript, it may vary from the published text, and the citations I discuss even vanish. The version I studied, in any case, contains elements of a view of Emerson that I find widely shared, but develops it more systematically, more carefully, and, if I may say so, more affectionately than I know of anywhere else. It accordingly seemed important to me, since I strongly disagree with certain aspects of the view, but in ways I have found it difficult to articulate, to take the occasion to let it prompt me, if I could, to get my thoughts clearer about so significant a locus of issues.)

Set in my ways, and doubtful that I would have something to say of interest to this gathering, I nevertheless found Bonnie Honig's invitation to participate on this panel irresistible, as she noted that it would allow me to help celebrate the appearance of the work of one old friend, George Kateb, on Emerson and to invoke the memory of a still older friend, Judith Shklar, whose words to me about many things, but in recent years often about Emerson, ring in my ears: "My dear Stanley,"—I'm sure many of you can invoke the stern yet playful tone for yourself—"let us say that everything you have said about Emerson is true. You will still not have told the story unless you can tell the politics of this writing." I felt she was right; I made various excuses, and some beginnings; but I have never been as explicit as I will try to be now.

George Kateb and I agree on two, perhaps the two most fundamental, issues in reading Emerson—to begin with, that Emerson is a figure of democratic inspiration and aspiration. Kateb puts this, for example, by saying: "Emerson's guiding sense is that society exists for individuals, not the other way round. Only democracy, among societies, is devoted to this precept." A way I have found I wanted to make this out is to argue that Emersonian perfectionism—place it as the thought that "the main enterprise of the world for splendor, for extent, is the upbuilding of a man"—is not an elitist call to subject oneself to great individuals (to the "one or two men" "in a century, in a millennium") but to the greatness, the thing Emerson calls by the ancient name of the genius, in each of us; it is the quest he calls "becoming what one is"[2] and, I think, "standing for humanity." And Kateb and I agree, further, that this fact of democratic inspiration is of essential importance to Emerson's work. But I believe we may differ in how this importance is to be articulated.

His manuscript begins by noting that it continues from a text I have not seen in which it is argued that Emerson's idea of self-reliance occurs in two states, ones Kateb calls the mental and the active. In the text before me, Kateb goes on to distinguish various forms within the state of active (not merely intellectual or spiritual) self-reliance, among which he argues that there is a ranking to be understood, beginning with primitive self-help, moving through the pursuit of wealth and other worldly ambitions, to culminate in the discovery of work of one's own, one's vocation. This ranking is, if I understand, meant to be in service of asking and answering Kateb's question: "What provision has Emerson made for a self-reliant individual to work with others, to cooperate and collaborate? There is no doubt that the very idea of association disturbs self-reliance when association moves out of a small circle of friends and includes numbers of people, many of them strangers or only acquaintances." I shall not contest Kateb's proposed ranking of the states of active self-reliance, nor do I challenge its pertinence to the question whether "you can be politically active and still be self-reliant." But my sense is that however important these questions may be to political theory and practice, they are not, so formulated and elaborated, ones to which Emerson's writing makes a very distinctive or distinguished contribution. Some of his readers who share this sense may be expected to conclude: so much the worse for Emerson's claims upon our attention as a political sensibility.

Here I merely report that I find I do not exactly recognize in Kateb's account the Emerson I have come to know in the work I have devoted to Emerson's writing. I assume that Kateb would report something similar from his side of things. So what? Aren't we always being told that everyone who cares for such things has his or her own Emerson? But in the present case I would hate to leave it at that. Not simply because Kateb's account is so civilized and attractive, nor just because we are in agreement in a fundamental commitment to a democratic Emerson, but essentially because, given these affinities, I am perplexed by the disproportionateness of my sense of distance from his account. I feel there must be some systematic explanation for this, I mean some explanation of a sense of systematic difference in play, and, moreover, one that is internal to an understanding of what Emerson's writing is designed to do, as if Emerson courts such disagreements, and among friends.

Let us see what certain apparent disagreements between us look and sound like, and try to guess, in these few minutes, how much they are apt to matter.

Kateb writes early: "Emerson's work lowers hope for self-reliant activity, while also lowering the dignity of activity in comparison to self-reliant thinking. Yet he does not desert self-reliant activity. To the contrary, he urges it onward." But recall this from "The American Scholar": "Men, such as they are, very naturally seek money or power. . . . And why not? for they aspire to the highest, and this, in their sleepwalking, they dream is highest. Wake them and they shall quit the false good and leap to the true. . . . This revolution is to be wrought by the gradual domestication of the idea of Culture." Waking men to enable them to quit does not sound like urging them on.

But we know—do we not?—that one can generally find for every characteristic citation in Emerson another that contradicts it. It is said—and said that Emerson says—that he contradicts himself, that he is inconsistent. I do not know that anyone has ever granted to Emerson there the power of the Cretan paradoxically to be denying his own denial. In any case, Kateb evidently does not believe that Emerson's language is untrustworthy, and neither do I. (I have, however, elsewhere worried over Emerson's idea of contradiction—in relation to his idea of condition—and I am sure that we who care about the Emersonian text will sometime have to make explicit how we choose citations from it—from which texts, and at what length.[3])

In speaking of Emerson urging action on, Kateb, I suppose, is remembering such familiar passages or gestures of cheering Emerson such as this from "Experience": "Sanity and revelations" seem to say "never mind the defeat; up again, old heart! . . . there is victory yet for all justice." Or as this, from "Self-Reliance": "If our young men miscarry in their first enterprises, they lose all heart, . . . men say [they are] *ruined.* . . . Let a Stoic . . . tell [a man] . . . that the moment he acts from himself, tossing the laws, the books, idolatries and customs out the window, we pity him no more but thank and revere him." In such cases Emerson urges on self-reliant activity not in its successes, so-called, but in its so-called defeats. And what is more, in a case of waking us from the fruits of a successful aspiration that Emerson grants it is natural for us to have, he is in effect combating nature in us (he does not recommend that we *become* the rose that rebukes us); and in the cases of defeated expectations what he urges upon us seems to be in the one case perfect *inaction*—"Patience, patience"—which is to say, passion and suffering (politically suspicious advice, to say the least), and in the other he expects acting from the self to achieve the predicates of the most perfect thinking (thankfulness and reverence).

Is Emerson therefore opposed both to defeat *and* to success? And is this part of his supposed contradiction or inconsistency? I take the question to be a sign of Emerson's sense—even vision—that we do not know what human activity is, specifically not its difference from human passivity. We do not know that every human action is a reaction, hence has passivity or suffering within it; and that every reaction is an action, since it has the power of communication in it. The thought is epitomized in such a formulation as this from "Self-Reliance": "the fact which is the upshot of all history, that there is a great and responsible Thinker and Actor moving wherever moves a man,"[4] where "moves a man" is studiedly at once active and passive—as if to say that human action is a dimension of a being that thinks, as human sexuality is a dimension of an animal self-divided.

Again, on that early page, Kateb writes: "Self-reliant thinking is an embrace of contrast and contradiction, while action . . . must choose and exclude." Then how shall we understand Emerson's outburst in "Spiritual Laws": "I say, do not choose"? Emerson goes on to gloss this by saying:

This is a figure of speech by which I would distinguish what is commonly called *choice* among men, and which is a partial act, the choice of the hands, of the eyes, of the appetites, and not a whole act of the man. But that which I call right or goodness, is the choice of my constitution; and that which I call heaven, and inwardly aspire after, is the state or circumstance desirable to my constitution; and the action which I in all my years tend to do, is the work for my faculties.

Let us take it that what Kateb calls vocation in Emerson makes its appearance here as "the work for my faculties" and, being "the choice of my constitution," is not accomplished by "what is commonly called choice among men." Will Kateb wish to say that this does not contradict his saying that, in contrast to thinking, "action must choose," because he can make an exception to choice in the case of vocation, the highest form of self-reliant activity? But the exception would show that there is not the essential difference between thinking and acting that Kateb has projected; moreover, it is an Emersonian thought that the only choice that has genuine necessity in it (about which there is a genuine "must") is precisely that of vocation.

In "Self-Reliance" Emerson had found: "Our housekeeping [the business Thoreau establishes as our "economy"] is mendicant, our arts, our occupations, our marriages, our religion we have not chosen, but society has chosen for us." So does Emerson know whether he is asking us to choose or is asking us not to? How may we think about this?—undoubtedly bearing in mind that "To think is to act" ("Spiritual Laws"), and doubtfully having in mind, if you're like me, Heidegger's formulation: "Thinking is a handicraft." Is anything to be done about the circumstance in which we both must choose and yet have no choice? Evidently there is nothing we can choose to do about this circumstance—nothing, that is to say, against our habitual picture of what it is to choose and to do something.

Is Emerson to be understood as leaving us with nothing more than the choice to suffer? And politically wouldn't that be—forgive this—insufferable? I believe this is where many feel left in reading Emerson. Within such a feeling, his urging us to self-reliance, no matter how refined, will appear cruel, and his incessant efforts to lift our spirits seem grating. If there is more to him here it must lie in his perception of suffering, hence, without doubt, of joy.

With this open for now, I go back to my sense that George Kateb and I are differing—however far we agree in the fact of Emerson's importance for political thinking—in the way we define the Emersonian event. I have indicated how I see Kateb's way in his present text—through the ranking of states and modes of self-reliance to assess the possibility of political participation. I conclude with some remarks about how I see my way.

I begin with what is at once the most obvious and the most obscure fact about Emerson, that he writes, and in the attractive and repellant way he writes; that this is his vocation, what he does and what he suffers. I go on to claim that writing is Emerson's constant model for what Wittgenstein more or less calls the human life form, that each essay of Emerson investigates an aspect of what an essay—or passage of human life—is. "The American Scholar" proposes that writing is thinking, and that both are, at their best, aversive and partial; "The Divinity School Address" proposes that writing is the inheritor and perhaps destroyer of communion; "Compensation," ridiculing a preacher's sermon on the Last Judgment for its "[assumption] that judgment is not executed in this world," proposes by implication that serious writing—Emerson's for the moment—is the *present* judgment of the world, thus identifying his readers as the dead, hence giving them an understandable cause to take offense at his words, or find them grating; "Self-Reliance," as I have gone over perhaps too many times, in accusing us of being too timid to say "'I think,' 'I am'" (which is to say, too timid to perform Descartes's "Cogito ergo sum," and therewith to prove our existence), in effect accuses us, so to speak, of not existing (Emerson sometimes calls this inanition[5]), and goes on to show how the proof works, which turns out to be by letting yourself know the existence of others, modeled in his claim to have written a text in which others are known, that is, know themselves, or as he puts it, find their thoughts returning to them; in "Fate," as I have argued, there is the most intricate demonstration, by thunderously deliberate silence, that our inability to recognize the existence of the slave has brought us to a state Emerson pictures as suffocation (linking it with my claim that *Walden* predicts the Civil War); and, for a last instance, "Circles," in effect proposing that an essay is a circle, suggests that each Emerson essay draws a circle around each other.

Is there politics somewhere here? There is, I think, a useful picture of the political, or prepolitical, to be found. Go back to Kateb's picture (of Emerson's idea) of political activity in his saying that "the very idea of association disturbs [an individual's] self-reliance when association moves out of a small circle of friends and includes numbers of people, many of them strangers or only acquaintances." The picture is of self-reliance as essentially unsociable, a condition in which the individual puts distance between himself or herself and society at large. But this is not the unique topology of Emerson's writing.

Each of the countless identifications he makes of his relation to his readers takes them one by one, as a book does. In a sense he makes a circle with each reader; and in a sense he and the reader make two circles, each around the other, depending on whose turn it is; but in a sense there is no circle yet since there are only two points, a writer and a reader, which determines just a line. If we say, letting the writer pass, that there must be a connection among the readers, we can imagine, if not a circle, then some other closed figure in two-dimensional space. In that case I note three features of this figure to counter Kateb's "small circle of friends." First, there is, as I imagine it, no intuitive size of the figure enclosing us, since each of us keeps on encountering, here and there, and always with surprise, other Emersonian ears. Hence there is some minimum number of occupants of the figure that each of us members can vouch for, but there is no assignable maximum number; there may be millions. (People keep telling me that there cannot be millions of people who actually understand Emerson. How do they know?) Second, even if the membership is thought of as small, it does not consist of known friends of Emerson. No reader of Emerson is a priori closer to him than any other, and no one is closer to him than a true reader (for them, for what he calls "[his] poor," this writer declares that he shuns mother and father, sister and brother). Third, if we conceive that sharing the Emersonian text creates a kind of community, I picture it as essentially invisible, or perhaps I should say, as a set of strangers to one another, since no one knows whether he or she will be able to convey her or his membership. Emerson's words may at any time go dead for me, or I to them. If I say it takes a kind of faith to wait for their or our awakening, I must add that faith in *this* unseen is different from its predecessors since, in moments, I know, if I know anything about myself, that I am one of those unseen. (Perhaps "essentially invisible" means "essentially audible." Both imply some kind of distance, or present displacement.)

So my question becomes: Is there some conceivable political importance for an invisible group whose size is unknowable and whose composition is undeclarable? One way for me to answer, or to keep the question alive, is to say that it is important if Socrates's idea of a "city of words" is important. Which is to claim that if, as I suppose, this imagined city of perfect justice, in whose public affairs alone Plato's Socrates imagines the philosopher can participate, is realized by the text called Plato's *Republic*, then a democratic successor of it, as it were, is the Emersonian essay. A drastic difference is that imagining the perfected democratic city does not exempt us from acting in the present scene of imperfection (one that is, for example, as Rawls expresses the matter, at best in partial compliance with the principles of justice). On the contrary, this imagining is what enables us to act, that is, to exist in freedom from a despair of democracy; there is no one other than the likes of us either to act within the present city or to imagine its difference from itself. It is a freedom that depends upon our not letting others tell us—not the closest friend—whether our actions, of mind and body, are successful or not, whether they are worth the candle or not. The necessity of our (a citizen's, one whose consent is invested) participation in a democracy is not expressed by saying, as Kateb insists, that we "must" act. You may or may not take an explicit side in some particular conflict, but unless you find some way to show that this society is not yours, it is; your being compromised by its actions expresses the necessity of your being implicated in them. That you nevertheless avoid express participation or express disavowal is what creates that ghost-state of conformity Emerson articulates endlessly, as our being inane, timid, ashamed, skulkers, leaners, apologetic, noncommittal, a gag, a masquerade, pinched in a corner, cowed, cowards fleeing before a revolution. These are among the contraries at once to thinking *and* to acting aversively; which is to say, by Emerson's definition of self-reliance (namely as the aversion of conformity), contraries of self-reliance, in word or in deed. Writing from self-reliance is thus simultaneously an emblem or instance of the self-reliant in word and in deed, in words that are deeds. I would like to say, in philosophy. So we are to remember that an aversive address may be taken toward oneself as much as toward any institution. Not thus to address the self is to harbor conformity, and I think Emerson invites us to see this as a political choice.

It is as a contribution to the city of words that I am concerned to preserve the order of words of the Emersonian text. Put otherwise, it is Emerson as a philosopher whose pertinence to democracy I am concerned to assess, the thinker—one among others—of the democratic city of words: "I know that the world I converse with in the city and in the farms, is not the world I *think*." These worlds are not in communication, but eclipse one another. Their location with respect to one another seems sometimes so far as to assure despair, sometimes so near as to threaten madness, that it is not nearer. Since the human being inhabits both worlds—this duality, for Emerson as for Kant, defines the human; for Wittgenstein, as well, if differently—the hope of the one lies in not denying the other, which each would love to do. It is the measure of Emerson's strength, and the value of his writing, that it bears the suffering of this perception of our separation from ourselves, that he records it—as I have argued elsewhere—in the power of his self-aversive sentences, as each converts and transfigures our common language.

This doubleness, of worlds, of words, offers a reading of a saying Emerson invokes in "The American Scholar": "But the old oracle said, 'All things have two handles: beware of the wrong one.'"[6] The oracle's saying itself has two handles, for beyond the warning to stop and think of another side, there is the warning that each side in isolation is wrong. Emerson continues: "In life, too often, the scholar errs with mankind and so forfeits his privilege." I read this—apart from interesting ambiguities—to say that the scholar errs who is unable or unwilling to maintain the aspirations of humankind because unable or unwilling to bear the spectacle of their oblivion.

Emerson's Constitutional Amending:
Reading "Fate"

What follows is the latest installment of a project, or experiment, of about a dozen years' standing, to reappropriate Emerson (I sometimes call this overcoming his repression) as a philosophical writer. I am aware of a number of reasons for my interest in such a project. Since Emerson is characteristically, almost obsessively, said—by his admirers as well as by his detractors—not to be a philosopher, my thought was that if I could understand this denial I would learn something not only about Emerson, and not only about American culture, but something about philosophy, about what makes it painful.

If the thought of Emerson's work as constituting philosophy—or, as I sometimes put it, as calling for philosophy—is considered, then something further could be considered. It is more or less obvious, and is given more or less significance by various philosophers, that Western philosophy has, roughly since the death of Kant, been split between two traditions, call them the German and the English traditions; and each of these has its internal splits. I take Wittgenstein to be the culmination of one line of English-speaking philosophy arising from the work of Frege and Russell; and I take Heidegger to be the culmination of one line of German-speaking philosophy arising from the work of Hegel and Husserl. I am not alone in regarding Wittgenstein and Heidegger as perhaps the two major voices of philosophy in the middle third of the twentieth century. Yet it seems to me that no one—however intelligent or cultivated—is equally at home, say equally creative, with the writing of both, so that the distance between them, in content and in procedure, remains to my mind unmeasured. I might say that to inherit philosophy now means to me to inherit it as split.

Against this rough background, the figure of Emerson represents for me (along with Thoreau) a mode of thinking and writing I feel I am in a position to avail myself of, a mode which at the same time can be seen to underlie the thinking of both Wittgenstein and of Heidegger—so that Emerson may become a site from which to measure the difficulties within each and between both.

The lecture to follow is a continuation of the work of the first chapter of my *Conditions Handsome and Unhandsome*, concerning Emerson's concept of thinking, a concept I call "aversive thinking." That title alludes to a pair of sentences from "Self-Reliance": "Conformity is the virtue most in request. Self-reliance is its aversion." By "self-reliance" I take Emerson to mean the essay of that title, and by synecdoche his individual body of writing. So for him to say "self-reliance is the aversion of conformity" is to say that his writing and the dominantly desired virtue of his society incessantly recoil from, or turn away from one another; but since this is incessant, the picture is at the same time of each incessantly turning *toward* the other. But why call this writing *thinking*?

Emerson characterizes thinking as marked by transfiguration and by conversion. I will merely assert here that these predicates refer essentially to the action of words, under subjection to some kind of figuration, in causing understanding or illumination on a par with that of religion—the religion always under criticism (held in aversion)—in Emerson's thought. My claim is accordingly that the implied sentence "Self-reliance is the aversion of conformity," when itself subjected to the operation of transfiguration and conversion, means something like: To think is to turn around, or to turn back (Wittgenstein says lead back), the words of ordinary life (hence the present forms of our lives) that now repel thought, disgust it. (Repels him, Emerson, of course, but he is also part of that life, which is therefore disgusted with itself.)

The only way to become convinced of such a reading, and its possible significance, is of course to try it out in scores of instances. We will see some cases in what follows from the essay "Fate."

Before beginning on that, I should say why it is just now in my adventure with Emerson that I choose, or feel forced, to emphasize a political theme in his work. I specify a brief answer at the close of these remarks, but I might indicate at once the general stakes in play. I have over the years ever more closely linked Emerson and Heidegger through the intermediary of Nietzsche, who is intimately, pervasively involved in the thinking of each. In *Conditions Handsome and Unhandsome* I associate each of them in a view of the moral life I call Emersonian perfectionism—at a moment in which the revelations of Heidegger's lasting investments in Nazism were producing a new convulsion of response from at least half of the Western philosophical world. Does Heidegger's politics—by association, to say the least—taint Emerson's points of contact with it?

The essay "Fate" is perhaps Emerson's principal statement about the human condition of freedom, even about something Emerson calls the paradox that freedom is necessary; we might formulate this as the human fatedness to freedom. This comes to speaking of the human fatedness to thinking, since "Intellect annuls Fate. So far as a man thinks, he is free. . . . The revelation of Thought takes man out of servitude into freedom." Could it be that the founder of American thinking, writing this essay in 1850, just months after the passage of the Fugitive Slave Law, whose support by Daniel Webster we know Emerson to have been unforgettably, unforgivingly horrified by, was in this essay not thinking about the American institution of slavery? I think it cannot be. Then why throughout the distressed, difficult, dense stretches of metaphysical speculation of this essay does Emerson seem mostly, even essentially, to keep silent on the subject of slavery, make nothing special of it? It is a silence that must still encourage his critics, as not long ago his admirer Harold Bloom and his detractor John Updike, to imagine that Emerson gave up on the hope of democracy.[1] But since I am continuing to follow out the consequences of finding in Emerson the founding of American thinking—the consequence, for example, that his thought is repressed in the culture he founded—the irony of discovering that this repressed thinking has given up on the hope and demand for a nation of the self-governing would be, so I fear, harder than I could digest.

I was myself silent about this question of Emerson's silence when I wrote an essay in 1983 mostly on Emerson's "Fate" (I called it "Emerson, Coleridge, Kant"[2]), my first somewhat extended treatment of an Emersonian text. It was seeming to me so urgent then to see to the claim of Emerson to be a philosophical writer, in principle imaginable as founding philosophy for a nation still finding itself, that I suppose I recurrently hoped that Emerson had, for the moment of the essay "Fate," sufficiently excused or justified his silence in saying there, "Nothing is more disgusting than the crowing about liberty by slaves, as most men are." But no sooner would I see this as an excuse or justification for silence than it would seem empty to me, so that I could never appeal to it. Isn't the statement that most men are slaves merely a weak, metaphorical way of feeling and of speaking, one that blunts both the fact of literal slavery and the facts of the particular ways in which we freely sell ourselves out? How is this conventional use of words essentially different from the sort of "[shameful capitulation] to badges and names, to large societies and dead institutions" that had so chagrined Emerson in "Self-Reliance":

If malice and vanity wear the coat of philanthropy, shall that pass? If an angry bigot assumes this bountiful cause of Abolition, and comes to me with his last news from Barbadoes, why should I not say to him, "Go love thy infant; love thy woodchopper; be good-natured and modest; have that grace; and never varnish your hard, uncharitable ambition with this incredible tenderness for black folk a thousand miles off. Thy love afar is spite at home."

It is not news that high philosophy can be used to cover low practice; nor that the love in philanthropy is tainted. Is Emerson so in doubt about the state of his own malice and vanity and anger and bigotry and charity and love that he has to clear them up before he can say clearly that he sides against slavery?

On March 7, 1854, Emerson delivered a lecture called "The Fugitive Slave Law," marking the fourth anniversary of Webster's decisive speech in favor of that legislation. Emerson's lecture goes this way:

Nobody doubts that Daniel Webster could make a good speech. Nobody doubts that there were good and plausible things to be said on the part of the South. But this is not a question of ingenuity, not a question of syllogisms, but of sides. *How came he there?* . . . There are always texts and thoughts and arguments. . . . There was the same law in England for Jeffries and Talbot and Yorke to read slavery out of, and for Lord Mansfield to read freedom. . . . But the question which History will ask [of Webster] is broader. In the final hour when he was forced by the peremptory necessity of the closing armies to take a side,—did he take the part of great principles, the side of humanity and justice, or the side of abuse and oppression and chaos?

So Emerson names and would avoid both those at home who choose to interpret the law so as to take the side on behalf of slavery nearby, as well as those whom in "Self-Reliance" he had named angry bigots incredibly varnishing their uncharitable ambition at home by taking the side against slavery afar. Both may count as what Emerson describes as "crowing about liberty by slaves," and his refusal of crowing (for or against) would perhaps be what strikes one as his essential silence on the subject precisely in an essay on freedom paradoxically entitled "Fate."

The suggestion is that there is a way of taking sides that is not crowing, a different way of having a say in this founding matter of slavery. If Emerson is who I think he is, then how he finds his way to having his say, how he undertakes to think—whether, most particularly, he is serious (as opposed to what?—literary?) in his claim that "so far as a man thinks, he is free"—is as fateful for America's claim to its own culture of thinking as its success in ridding itself of the institution of slavery will be for establishing its claim to have discovered a new world, hence to exist.

We have to ask what kind of writing—philosophical? political? religious?—takes the form of the pent, prophetic prose of "Fate." Emerson speaks there also (as well as later in "The Fugitive Slave Law") of the taking of a side. His formulation in "Fate" is of the capacity, when a person finds himself a victim of his fate—for example, "ground to powder by the vice of his race"—to "take sides with the Deity who secures universal benefit by his pain." This may strike one as the formulation less of a course of action than of inaction. But take Emerson's reference in his phrase "the vice of his race" (by which a person finds himself victimized) to be specified in the description earlier in the essay of "expensive races,—race living at the expense of race." But *which* vice does "expensive" suggest? The literal context of that predicate takes the races in question to be the human race living at the expense of the races of animals that serve us as food: "You have just dined, and however scrupulously the slaughter-house is concealed in the graceful distance of miles, there is complicity, expensive races." It happens that we can produce evidence that this passage about human carnivorousness, and its companion human gracefulness in keeping its conditions concealed from itself, is a parable about the cannibalism, as it were, in living gracefully off other *human* races. The evidence comes from an early paragraph in Emerson's address "On Emancipation in the British West Indies," delivered in 1844, the tenth anniversary of that emancipation legislation, the year of Emerson's breakthrough essay "Experience." In Emerson's West Indies address, he remarks that "From the earliest monuments it appears that one race was victim and served the other races" and that "the negro has been an article of luxury to the commercial nations."

He goes on to say there, "Language must be raked, the secrets of the slaughter-houses and infamous holes that cannot front the day, must be ransacked, to tell what negro-slavery has been."

I propose to take "Fate" pervasively—beyond the reach of the sort of textual intersection I just adduced as evidence—to be something I might call a philosophical enactment of freedom, a parable of the struggle against slavery, not as a general metaphor for claiming human freedom, but as the absolute image of the necessary siding against fate toward freedom that is the condition of philosophical thinking; as if the aspiration to freedom is philosophy's breath.

Doesn't the sheer eloquence of the West Indies address—with its demand to rake language and ransack slaughter-houses to tell of negro slavery—compromise this proposal from the outset? And again, always again, the question returns whether Emerson in "Fate"—the same man who younger, in that earlier West Indies address, confessed himself heartsick to read the history of that slavery—isn't courting the danger of seeming to avoid the sickening facts of the slavery that continues not metaphysically afar but at home.

What is he thinking of—whom is he thinking of—when in "Fate" he says, "In the history of the individual is always an account of his condition, and he knows himself to be party to his present estate"? If the sentences of "Fate" are to be brought to the condition of slavery, are we to imagine this statement about the individual knowing himself to be party to his estate to be said to the individual who is in the condition of enslavement? What would prevent this announcement from constituting the obscene act of blaming the slave for his slavery? (My intermittent sense of this possibility, and of the fact that I had no satisfying answer to it, was brought home to me by a letter from Professor Barbara Packer, whose book *Emerson's Fall* is indispensable to readers of Emerson, following a brief conversation between us concerning Emerson's politics. She writes in her letter of her sense of what I called obscene announcement in "Fate" as something that she had yet to bring under control, and asked for my thoughts. That was in the autumn of 1989. The present version of this essay, meant to collect and incorporate those thoughts, was composed the following year.)

An implication of saying "you know yourself party to your estate"— if it is not pure blame—is that you are free to leave it. John Brown might say something of the sort, without obscenity, to a person in the condition of enslavement, given that he would be saying, if with a certain derange-

ment, "I know the only way to exercise your freedom and leave your estate is to court death, and I'll court it with you." And Walt Whitman
might say something related, as in the altogether remarkable "I Sing the
Body Electric," in which he watches the man's body at auction and the
woman's body at auction, and he declares his love for, his sameness with,
the body—hence, he declares, with the soul—of the slave. What gives to
the knowledge of American slavery the absoluteness of its pain is the
knowledge that these human beings in that condition, in persisting to
live, persist in taking part in every breath in interpreting and preserving
what a human existence can bear. But do we imagine that Emerson, like
John Brown and Walt Whitman, has a way to bear the knowledge of that
pain—he who is habitually supposed to have turned aside from the philosophically tragic sense of life?

Then perhaps Emerson only means to say of us Northerners, neither
slaves nor slave owners, that we are party to our estate—meaning perhaps
that we make ourselves slaves to, let us say, the interests of Southern slave
owners that never even paid for us. But that is not exactly news. Emerson
reports in the West Indies address that when "three hundred thousand persons in Britain pledged themselves to abstain from all articles of island produce . . . the planters were obliged to give way . . . and the slave-trade was
abolished." Such responses to slavery as economic boycott are evidently not
Emerson's business in "Fate." Whom, then, in that mood, is he writing to?
Who are we who read him then?

If "taking sides with the Deity" does not, for Emerson, (just) mean
taking the right side in the crowing about slavery, the side Daniel Webster
failed to take as the armies were closing on the issue, how might it be taken?
Here is more context from "Fate": "A man must ride alternately on the
horses of his private and his public nature. . . . Leaving the daemon who
suffers, he is to take sides with the Deity who secures universal benefit by
his pain." That the human being is the being who *can* take a representative—public—stance, knows the (moral, objective) imperative to the
stance, is familiar and recurrent Emersonian—not to say Kantian—
ground; nothing is a more founding fact for him. I read this Platonic image
here about riding alternately the horses of human nature, so that taking
sides with the Deity is a refusal to take sides in the human *crowing* over slavery. Emerson's turn to take sides with the Deity, like and unlike the political extremity of Locke's appeal to Heaven, is not exactly a call to revolution
but a claim to prophecy.[3] "Leaving the daemon who suffers" means leaving
one's private, limited passions on the subject of slavery, for or against.

What is the alternative horse, the public expression of a beneficial pain (given in the absence of a constituted public, since so much of the human voice, the slave's voice, is unrepresented in that public)? The alternative is, let us say, not venting your pain, but maintaining it; in the present case, writing every sentence in pain. (Freud comparably says: remembering rather than repeating something.) It contains the pain of refusing human sides, shunning argument, with every breath. The time of argument is over. Where is pain's benefit? Is philosophy over?

At the opening of "Fate," Emerson says: "We are incompetent to solve the times. . . . To me . . . the question of the times resolved itself into a practical question of the conduct of life." I have in effect said that in "Fate" the "question of the times"—what Emerson calls in his opening "the huge orbits of the prevailing ideas" whose return and opposition we cannot "reconcile," and what he describes near his close by saying, "Certain ideas are in the air"—is the question of slavery; and certain ideas in the air, accordingly, are emancipation and secession, issues producing the compromise of 1850, which concerned, besides the Fugitive Slave Act, the slave trade and the admission of territories into the union with or without slaves. Setting out the terms for "the greatest debate in Congressional history," Henry Clay prefaces his resolutions of compromise by saying, "It being desirable, for the peace, concord and harmony of the Union of these States to settle and adjust amicably all existing questions of controversy between them, arising out of the institution of slavery, upon a fair, equitable and just basis; therefore"—and then follows with eight paragraphs each beginning with the word "Resolved" or the words "But, resolved."[4] Emerson in effect prefaces "Fate" by speaking, in his opening paragraph, as noted, of our incompetence to *solve* the times, and of *resolving* the question of the times; in the second paragraph he states that "The riddle of the age has for each a private *solution*"; and continuing in effect to reverse or recapture the word "Resolved" Emerson says in the middle of "Fate," "Thought *dissolves* the material universe by carrying the mind up into a sphere where all is plastic"; and in the closing paragraphs he speaks of a "solution to the mysteries of human condition" and of "the Blessed Unity which holds nature and souls in perfect solution." This is not Henry Clay's imagined union.

Of course Emerson is quite aware that compared with Henry Clay, and the Houses of Congress, his words about resolution and unity will sound, at best, or at first, private, not to say ethereal. But he seems somehow also to know that he is speaking with necessity ("Our thought, though it were only an hour old, affirms an oldest necessity"), and speaking with universality (being thrown "on the party and interest of the Universe [i.e., taking sides with the Deity], against all and sundry; against ourselves as much as others"). Now necessity and universality are the marks, according to the Kantian philosophy, of the a priori, that is, of human objectivity; so if Emerson's claim is valid, it is the opposing party who is riding the horse of privacy, of what Emerson also calls selfishness, something he would have taken Henry Clay's use of the word "desirable" to have amounted to.

We of course must ask—since Emerson would also know, as well as what is called the next man, that anyone can *claim* to be speaking on the part and interest of the universe and on the side of the Deity—what the source is of his conviction in his own objectivity, his ability, as he puts it in the poem he composed as an epigraph for "Fate," to read omens traced in the air. I understand the source to be his conviction that his abilities are not exclusive, that he claims to know only what everyone knows.

Toward the close of the essay: "The truth is in the air, and the most impressionable brain will announce it first, but *all* will announce it a few minutes later." Emerson is not even saying that *he* is announcing it first, since the truth that is in the air is also, always already, philosophy; it contains not just the present cries for freedom and union and the arguments against them, but perennial cries and arguments. This is surely something the gesture means that Emerson so habitually enjoys making, of listing his predecessors and benefactors—that they are the benefactors of the race, part of our air, our breath. In the essay "Fate" he cites the names of Napoleon, Burke, Webster, Kossuth; Jenny Lind; Homer, Zoroaster, Menu; Fulton, Franklin, Watt; Copernicus, Newton, Laplace; Thales, Anaximenes, Empedocles, Pythagoras; Hafiz, Voltaire, Christopher Wren, Dante, Columbus, Goethe, Hegel, Metternich, Adams, Calhoun, Guizot, Peel, Rothschild, Astor, Herodotus, Plutarch. And he says: "The air is full of men." (Emerson puts those words in quotation marks without saying who or what he is quoting. *Bartlett's Quotations* contains the line "In the air men shall be seen" in a list of rhymed prophecies attributed to Mother Shipton, according to *Bartlett's* editors a witch and prophetess fabricated in the seventeenth century. I'll have a suggestion about why Emerson might have wanted in this essay to associate himself with such a figure.)

I associate the men in the air with—as in Emerson's epigraph poem—"Birds with auguries on their wings/ [who] Chanted undeceiving things,/Him to beckon, him to warn." The "few minutes later" Emerson calculates between the first announcements of truth and, for example, his own impressionable announcings of it—which the world may measure as millennia but which are a few minutes of eternity—are equally no more than the few minutes between, for example, our reading Emerson's pages (his wings of augury, flapping as we turn them forth and back, before us, above our horizon) and our announcing or pronouncing, if just to ourselves, what is chanted from them (not crowed). I have noted elsewhere another of Emerson's master figures for a page of his writing—that of its representing a "standard," that is, a measure to aspire to, specified concretely as a flag, to which to rally oneself. This idea of a standard—by which "Self-Reliance" alludes at the same time to Kant's idea of humankind's two "standpoints"—takes pages one at a time; whereas "wings" pictures them as paired, bound symmetrically on the two sides of a spine.

As with his great reader Thoreau, Emerson loves playing with time, that is, making time vanish where truth is concerned: "'Tis only a question of time," he says casually a few minutes later in "Fate" than, and as a kind of answer to, the earlier, more portentous phrasing, "the question of the times." (In invoking the idea of the casual, as one characteristic tone he gives his prose, I am thinking of Emerson's characteristic association of that idea with the idea of casualty; as if he misses no opportunity for showing that we do not see our fate because we imagine that it is most extraordinary and not yet; rather than most ordinary and already, like our words.)

Emerson's philosophical sentence strikes the time of conversion and transfiguration that he calls thinking, the time—past crowing—of aversion (inversion, perversion, subversion, "unsettling all things," verses, reversals, tropes, turns, dancing, chanting . . .).

Here are three successive sentences to this effect from "Fate." First, "If the Universe have these savage accidents, our atoms are as savage in resistance." That is, speaking philosophically, or universally, "accidents" are opposed to "necessities," and in thus implying that slavery is accidental, or arbitrary, and resistance to it necessary and natural, Emerson takes away its chief argument. Second, "We should be crushed by the atmosphere, but for the reaction of the air within the body." That is, the ideas that are in the air are our life's breath; they become our words; slavery is supported by some of them and might have crushed the rest of them; uncrushed, they live in opposition. Third, "If there be omnipotence in the stroke, there is omnipotence of recoil." That is, every word is a word spoken *again*, or against again; there would be no words otherwise. Since recoil and aversion have been expressed at any time only by breathers of words, mortals, their strokes may be given now, and may gather together now—in a recoiling—all the power of world-creating words. The sentence introducing the three just cited asserts: "Man also is part of [Fate], and can confront fate with fate." Emerson's way of confronting fate, his recoil of fate, I will now say, is his writing, in every word; for example, in every word of "Fate," each of which is to be a pen stroke, a common stroke of genius, because a counterstroke of fate. You make your breath words in order not to suffocate in the plenum of air. The power he claims for his words is precisely that they are not his, no more new than old; it is the power, I would like to say, of the powerlessness in being unexceptional, or say exemplary. ("We go to Herodotus and Plutarch for examples of Fate; but we are examples.") This unavoidable power of exemplification may be named impressionability, and seen to be responsibility construed as responsiveness, passiveness as receptiveness.

These are various ways of looking at the idea that the source of Emerson's conviction in what I called the objectivity (I might have called it the impersonality) of his prophesying, his wing-reading and omen-witnessing, lies in his writing, his philosophical authorship, a condition that each of his essays is bound to characterize and authenticate in its own terms.

A characteristic of this authorship is announced in the opening paragraph of the quite early "Self-Reliance": "In every work of genius we recognize our own rejected thoughts; they come back to us with a certain alienated majesty." Even from those who remember this sentence, there is, I have found, resistance to taking Emerson to be naming his own work as an instance of the work he is characterizing, resistance to taking that sentence about rejected thoughts as itself an instance of such a rejected thought coming back in familiar strangeness, so with the power of the uncanny. The mechanism of this rejection and return is, I suppose, that characterized by Freud as transference, a process in which another person is magnified by our attributing to him or to her powers present in our repressed desires and who, putting himself or herself aside for a moment, gives us usably what we have shown ourselves unusefully to know. It is an interpretation of Kant's mechanism of projection that he calls the sublime, reading our mind's powers in nature, in the air. Emerson's authorship enacts, I have gone on to claim in the most recent work I have been doing, a relationship with his reader of moral perfectionism in which the friend permits one to advance toward oneself, which may present itself, using another formulation of Emerson, as attaining our unattained self, a process which has always happened and which is always to happen.

The word *majesty* reappears in "Fate," again in a context in which the presence of a "thought and word of an intellectual man . . . [rouses] our own mind . . . to activity": "'Tis the majesty into which we have suddenly mounted, the impersonality, the scorn of egotisms, the sphere of laws, that engage us." A "sphere of laws" into which we have suddenly mounted, as if attaining a new standpoint, suggests Kant's realm of ends—call it the eventual human city—in which the reception of the moral law, the constraint, as Kant names the relation, by the moral imperative, expressed by an "ought," is replaced by the presence of another, like and unlike myself, who constrains me to another way, another standpoint, Kant says (Emerson says, transfiguring Kant, a new standard). This other of myself—returning my rejected, say repressed, thought—reminds me of something, as of where I am, as if I had become lost in thought, and stopped thinking. In "Experience," Emerson expresses finding the way, learning as he more or less puts it, to take steps, as to begin to walk philosophically, in the *absence* of another presence—more accurately, in allowing himself to present himself to the loss of presence, to the death of his young son.

His description of his authorship in that essay takes the form—I have given my evidence for this elsewhere[5]—of fantasizing his becoming pregnant and giving birth to the world, to his writing of the world, which he calls a new America and calls Being. In "Fate" he is giving the basis of his authorship in that passage about riding alternately on the horses of his private and his public nature. Those are descendants of the horses he invokes, in his essay "The Poet," in naming the Poet as one whose relation to language is such that "In every word he speaks he rides on them as the horses of thought." The idea is that the words have a life of their own over which our mastery is the other face of our obedience. Wittgenstein, in *Philosophical Investigations*, affirms this sense of the independent life of words in describing what he does as "leading words back from their metaphysical to their everyday use,"[6] suggesting that their getting back, whatever that achievement is, is something they must do under their own power if not quite, or always, under their own direction. Alternating horses, as in a circus ring, teach the two sides of thought, that objectivity is not a given but an achievement; leading the thought, allowing it its own power, takes you to new ground.

The achievement of objectivity cannot be claimed for oneself, that is, for one's writing. As in "Self-Reliance": "I would write on the lintels of the door-post, *Whim.* I hope it may be better than whim at last." But in the necessity for words, "when [your] genius calls [you]," you can only air your thoughts, not assess them, and you must.

In Emerson's as in Wittgenstein's way of thinking, ethics is not a separate field of philosophical study, but every word that comes from us, the address of each thought, is a moral act, a taking of sides, but not in argument. In Emerson's terms, the sides may be called those of self-reliance and conformity; in Wittgenstein's terms, those of the privacy and emptiness of assertion he calls metaphysical, and the dispersal of this empty assertiveness by what he calls leading words home, his image of thinking. It strikes me that the feature of the intersection of Emersonian with Wittgensteinian thinking that primarily causes offense among professional philosophers is less the claim to know peculiar matters with a certainty that goes beyond reasonable evidence (matters like the location of the Deity's side, or of the temptation to insistent emptiness), and less the sheer, pervasive literary ambition of their writing, than the sense that these locations, diagnoses, and ambitions are in the service of a claim to philosophical authorship that can seem the antithesis of what philosophical writing should be, a denial of rational or systematic presentation apart from which philosophy might as well turn itself into, or over to, literature, or perhaps worse.

The worse one may call esotericism, an effect it seems clear to me both Emerson and Wittgenstein recognized in themselves. Wittgenstein recognizes it in his continuous struggle against his interlocutors, whose role sometimes seems less to make Wittgenstein's thoughts clearer than to allow him to show that his thoughts are *not* clear, and not obviously to be *made* clear. They must be *found* so. Emerson recognizes his esotericism in such a remark from "Fate" as: "This insight [that] throws us on the party of the Universe, against all and sundry . . . distances those who share it from those who share it not." But what is the alternative? At the close of "Experience" Emerson suggests that the alternative to speaking esoterically is speaking polemically (taking sides in argument), which for him, as for Wittgenstein, gives up philosophy, can never lead to the peace philosophy seeks for itself.[7] (The philosopher I am reading who preceded Emerson in contrasting something like the esoteric with the polemical in considering the presentation of philosophy, as a matter internal to the present state of philosophy, is Hegel.) The dissonance between these thinkers and professional philosophers is less an intellectual disagreement than a moral variance in their conceptions of thinking, or perhaps I can say in their concepts of the role of moral judgment in the moral life, in the way each pictures "constraint."

If slavery is the negation of thought, then thinking cannot affirm itself without affirming the end of slavery. But for thinking to *fail* to affirm itself is to deny the existence of philosophy. It is accordingly no more or less certain that philosophy will continue than that human self-enslavement will end. Philosophy cannot abolish slavery, and it can only call for abolition to the extent, or in the way, that it can call for thinking, can provide (adopting Kant's term) the incentive to thinking. The incentive Emerson provides is just what I am calling his authorship, working to attract our knowledge that we are rejecting, repressing thinking, hence the knowledge that thinking must contain both pain and pleasure (if it were not painful it would not require repression; if it were not pleasurable it would not attract it).

The linking of philosophical thinking with pain is expressed in an Emersonian sentence that seems a transcription at once of Plato and of Kant: "I know that the world I converse with in the city and in the farms, is not the world I *think*." To think this other world, say the realm of ends, is pleasure; to bear witness to its difference from the actual world of cities and farms is pain. Here, perhaps, in this pleasure and pain, before the advent of an imperative judgment, and before the calculation of the desirable, is the incentive to thinking that Kant sought. The pain is a function of the insight that there is no reason the eventual world is not entered, not actual, hence that I must be rejecting it, rejecting the existence of others in it; and the others must be rejecting my existence there.

I note that it is from here that I would like to follow on with Emerson's understanding of the origination of philosophy as a feminine capacity, as following his claim, toward the end of "Fate," that I excerpted earlier: "The truth is in the air, and the most impressionable brain will announce it first, but all will announce it a few minutes later." He continues: "So women, as *most* susceptible, are the best index of the coming hour. So the great man, that is, the man most imbued with the spirit of the time, is the impressionable man"—which seems to divine that the great man is a woman. The idea that philosophical knowledge is receptive rather than assertive, that it is a matter of leaving a thing as it is rather than taking it as something else, is not new and is a point of affinity between Wittgenstein and Heidegger. Emerson's thought here is that this makes knowledge difficult in a particular way, not because it is hard to understand exactly, but because it is hard to bear; and his suggestion, accordingly, is that something prepares the woman for this relation to pain, whereas a man must be great to attain it. I grant that this may be said stupidly. It may be used—

perhaps it most often is, in fact—to deny the actual injustice done to actual women. Must it be so appropriated? By philosophical necessity? But I associate Emerson's invocation of the feminine with a striking remark of Hélène Cixous, in which she declares her belief that, whereas men must rid themselves of pain by mourning their losses, women do not mourn, but bear their pain. The connection for me here is that the better world we think, and know not to exist, with no acceptable reason not to exist, is not a world that is *gone*, hence is not one to be mourned, but one to be borne, witnessed. The attempt to mourn it is the stuff of nostalgia. (In the closing paragraph of "Experience," I remember: "Patience, patience, we shall win at the last." I had not until now been able to understand this as the demand upon Emerson's writing, and his readers, to let the pain of his thoughts, theirs, collect itself.)

Is philosophy, as Emerson calls for it—we must keep reposing the question, without stopping it—an evasion of actual justice? It hasn't kept Emerson from sometimes writing polemically, as his West Indies and his Fugitive Slave Law addresses attest. His direct idea, to repeat, is that polemic is an evasion, or renunciation, of philosophy. How important a loss is the loss of philosophy?

I think sometimes of Emerson, in his isolation, throwing words into the air, as aligned with the moment at which Socrates in the *Republic* declares that the philosopher will participate only in the public affairs of the just city, even if this means that he can only participate in making—as he is now doing—a city of words. As if without the philosopher's constructions, the actual human city would not only lack justice in fact, but would lose the very concept, hence the imagination, of justice. Whether you think keeping that imagination alive is a valuable activity depends on how you think the reign of justice can come about.

I began, in effect, by saying that for Emerson the loss of philosophy is the loss of emancipation—of the imagination of the possibility of emancipation as such—from all forms of human confinement, say enslavement. I make explicit now, again, for a moment the thought about thinking that I claim is implicit throughout Emerson's writing (not solely in "Fate," however painfully there)—the thought that human freedom, as the opposition to fate, is not merely called for by philosophical writing but is instanced or enacted by that writing: the Emersonian sentence is philosophical in showing within itself its aversion to (turning away in turning toward) the standing conformation of its words, as though human thinking is not so much to be expressed by language as resurrected with it.

Let us accordingly transfigure once again: "In the history of the individual is always an account of his condition, and he knows himself to be party to his present estate." The days of the individual are told, counted out, in his condition by the words he suffers, and in his estate by the statements he utters: to know himself, as philosophy demands—or say to acknowledge his allegiances—is to take his part in each stating and in each silence.

In my encounter in 1983 with the essay "Fate," I did not speak of Emerson's philosophical authorship and esotericism, and I did not see the connection between Emerson's mode of thinking and his moral perfectionism, his constraint of his reader through his conviction in the magnified return of the reader's own rejected thoughts. It is as if in my desperateness to show Emerson capable of rigorous, systematic thinking, against the incessant denial of him as a philosopher, I felt I could not at the same time show his practice of thinking as one of transfiguring philosophy, in founding it, finding it, for America. I could not, as it were, *assume* his right to speak for philosophy. My primary focus in my earlier encounter with "Fate" is on Emerson's use of the term condition, and his relation of it to the term *terms* (meaning words and meaning stipulations) and the term *dictation*, which I claim shows Emerson turning the *Critique of Pure Reason* on itself, taking its fundamental term *condition* in its etymological significance as speaking *together*, so suggesting that the condition of the possibility of there being a world of objects for us is the condition of our speaking together; and that is not a matter of our sharing twelve categories of the understanding but of our sharing a language, hence the task of philosophy is not the deriving of privileged categories but of announcing the terms on the basis of which we use each term of the language. Any term may give rise to what Wittgenstein calls a grammatical investigation, but beyond *condition* and its relatives, my earlier essay got just to the idea of "character" as, as always in Emerson, meaning the fact of language as well as the formation of an individual. But even that distance allowed me to summarize the essay's word as saying that character is fate, that the human is fated to significance, to finding it and to revealing it, and—as if tragically—fated to thinking, or to repressing thinking. Emerson—the American who is repeatedly, famously, denied the title of philosopher and described as lacking the tragic sense—writes an essay on freedom entitled "Fate" and creates the mode of what we may perhaps call the tragic essay.

If I now add the use of the word *constitution* in the essay "Fate" to the terms whose terms I demand, Emerson's claim for his philosophical authorship becomes unpostponable. Along with *condition* and *character,* other philosophical terms Emerson allows the reader to find unobtrusive are *possibility* and *accident,* and *impression* and *idea. Constitution* appears in "Fate" only a few times, but its placement is telling, and the essay's array of political terms or projects magnifies its force: I cited earlier the term *resolved;* and we have heard of our being party to our estate; and then a not notably obtrusive sentence speaks of "this house of man, which is all consent, inosculation and balance of parts"—where "consent" works to associate "balance of parts," with "checks and balances," and "house" thus names each of the branches of Congress. Here is an example of what I called "placement":

Jesus said, "when he looketh on her, he hath committed adultery." But he is an adulterer before he has yet looked on the woman, by the superfluity of animal and the defect of thought in his constitution. Who meets him, or who meets her, in the street, sees that they are ripe to be each other's victim.

In "Emerson, Coleridge, Kant," I read this as the claim that most of what we call marriage is adultery, not a thought original with Emerson. Now, according to my implied hypothesis that every metaphysical claim in "Fate" about freedom, and its deprivation, is to be read also in a social register, as applying also to the institution of slavery, I read the phrase "the defect of thought in his constitution" to refer to the famous defect in the Constitution of the United States concerning those persons who are, let's say, interminably unfree, a defect which adulterates our claim to have established a just and tranquil human society, corrupts it, makes it spurious. I'll come back in a moment to the passage I mean.

From at least as early as "Self-Reliance," Emerson identifies his writing, what I am calling his philosophical authorship, as the drafting of the nation's constitution; or, I have come to say, as amending our constitution. When he says there, "No law can be sacred to me but that of my nature," he is saying no more than Kant had said—that, in a phrase from "Fate," "We are as law-givers," namely, to the world of conditions and of objects, and to ourselves in the world of the unconditioned and of freedom. But the next sentence of "Self-Reliance" takes another step: "Good and bad are but names readily transferable to that or this; the only right is what is after my constitution; the only wrong what is against it." (The anticipation of Nietzsche's genealogy of morals is no accident.) Such a remark seems uniformly to be understood by Emerson's readers so that "my constitution" refers to

Emerson's personal, peculiar physiology and is taken to be the expression of his incessant promotion of the individual over the social. Such an understanding refuses the complexity of the Emersonian theme instanced in his saying that we are now "bugs, spawn," which means simultaneously that we exist neither as individual human beings nor in human nations.

The promise that we are capable of both is the fervent Emersonian theme to the effect that each of us is capable of speaking what is "true for all men." This capacity Emerson envisions in endless ways, often as speaking with necessity (a transfiguration of what philosophers, especially of what Kant, means by necessity). The theme is fervently announced in Emerson's various formulations of the vision that the innermost becomes the outermost: In "The American Scholar," "[The scholar] is one who raises himself from private considerations and breathes and lives on public and illustrious thoughts [as if they were air]"; in "Self-Reliance," "To believe your own thought, to believe that what is true for you in your private heart is true for all men—that is genius," specifically, it is that which in every work of genius comes back to us with the alienated majesty of our own rejected thoughts. Speaking what is "true for all men," what in "Fate" Emerson speaks of as "truth com[ing] to our mind," is the event of insight he describes as "throw[ing] us on the party and interest of the Universe . . . against ourselves as much as others." "[Throwing us] on the party . . . of the Universe,"—as if to say taking its part (as if taking sides with the Deity)—puts me in mind of what Kant calls "[speaking] with the universal voice," which is the essential feature in making an aesthetic judgment (going beyond a mere expression of individual taste), namely, that it demands or imputes or claims general validity, universal agreement; a claim made in the face of the knowledge that this agreement is in empirical fact apt not to be forthcoming. Moral judgment also speaks with—or, rather, listens to—what we might call the universal voice, in the form of the capacity to act under the constraint of the moral imperative, the imperative of the universal (of the universalizable). Emerson is, I am suggesting, appealing to something of the kind in simply claiming as a fact that we can, in thinking generally, judge the constitution of the world and of the lives complicitous with it from a standpoint "all and sundry" may be expected to find in themselves. The great difference from aesthetic and moral judgment is that the constitutional judgment demanding the amending of our lives (together) is to be found by each of us as a rejected thought returning to us. This mode of access to what I am calling "constitutional judgment" seems to me no less well characterized by Emerson than moral or aesthetic judgments are by philosophers generally. (If Emerson's "representativeness," his universalizing, is not to go unexamined, neither should his habitually condemned "individualism." If he is to be taken as an instance of "humanism" [as if he doesn't really mean much definite by being "thrown" on "the interest of the Universe"], then he is at the same time to be taken as some form of antihumanist, working "against ourselves," against what we understand as human [under]standing.)

It is the appeal to what we have rejected, as it were forgotten, say displaced, that gives to Emerson's writing (and to Wittgenstein's) the feel of the esoteric, of work to whose understanding one is asked to convert. It is an obvious sign of danger for professional, university philosophy, and it should be. Emerson ought to have to make his way, to bear the pain of his arrogating his right to speak for philosophy in the absence of making himself curricular, institutionalizable, polemical. Which is another way of saying that it does not follow from his institutionalized silencing that he has failed to raise the call for philosophy and to identify its fate with the fate of freedom. The fact of his call's repression would be the sign that it has been heard. The apparent silence of "Fate" might become deafening.

The absoluteness of the American institution of slavery, among the forms human self-enslavement takes, hence the absoluteness of philosophy's call to react to it, recoil from it, is announced, as I have more or less said, in the sentence cited earlier from the West Indies address: "Language must be raked, the secrets of the slaughter-houses and infamous holes that cannot front the day, must be ransacked, to tell what negro-slavery has been." I take the idea of raking language to be another announcement, in a polemical context, of Emerson's philosophical authorship, of what cannot be undertaken polemically.

A surface of the idea of raking language is a kind of Emersonian joke, namely, that we are to respond to the fact, be responsible to it, that the largely unquestioned form or look of writing is of being raked on a page, that is, raked in parallel straight lines, and then to recognize that bringing what writing contains to light, letting these words return to us, as if to themselves, to mount suddenly to their majesty, to the scorn of egotisms, is to let the fact of them rouse our mind to activity, to turn it to the air. Perhaps we are to think that the fact of language is more telling than any fact uttered within it, as if every fact utters the fact of language: against this fatedness to language, to character, against, that is, what I earlier called our condemnation to significance, it figures that it is we who are raked. To think of language as raking and recoiling is to think of it, though it may look tranquil, as aimed and fired (at itself, at us) as if the human creature of conditions, fated to language, exists in the condition of threat, the prize of unmarked battles, where every horizon—where the air of words (of what might be said) gravitates to the earth of assertion (of what is actually said)—signifies a struggle between possession and dispossession, between speech and silence, between the unspeakable and the unsilenceable. (Here I am letting myself express a little, as earnest of wishing to describe better than I can, the anguish I sense in Emerson's language in "Fate.")

The particular direction in the raking of language I emphasize now is its office in *telling*, which is to say, in counting and recounting—"[telling] what negro-slavery has been" is how Emerson put it—hence in telling every enslavement. An origin of the word "raking" is precisely the idea of reckoning, of counting, as well as recking, paying attention. Of the endless interest there may be in thinking of language itself as a matter of counting, I confine attention momentarily here to the connection between counting or telling and the writing of the American Constitution.

When in the second paragraph of "Experience" Emerson asks, bleakly, "How many individuals can we count in society?" he is directing our attention back, wherever else, to the famous paragraph containing what I earlier quoted Emerson as calling "the defect of thought in [our] constitution." That famous paragraph is the fifth—it is also just the fifth sentence—of the Constitution of the United States: "Representatives and direct Taxes shall be apportioned among the several States which may be included within this Union, according to their respective Numbers, which shall be determined by adding to the whole number of free Persons, including those bound to service for a Term of Years, and excluding Indians not taxed, three fifths of all other Persons." The paragraph goes on to specify the calculation of democratic representation, and I find the comic invoking in "Fate" of the new science of statistics, in its attention to populations, to be another allusion to the "defect," the lack of philosophical necessity, in our constitutional counting. In the large we do not see how many we are; in the small we do not know, as Emerson puts it in "The American Scholar," whether we add up to what the "old fable" calls "One Man." As if we do not know whether any of us, all and each, count. We are living our skepticism.

So again, Emerson's simultaneous use of the idea of "my constitution"—his transfiguration of these words—so that we know they name at once his makeup and the makeup of the nation he prophesies, is a descendant of Plato's use of his *Republic*—his city of words—to form a structure at once of the soul and of its society. That is part of my cause in finding Emerson's philosophical prose, his authorship, to earn something like Plato's description (a city of words) for itself—as I find Thoreau's *Walden* to do—hence to imagine for itself the power to amend the actual city in the philosophical act of its silence, its power of what Emerson calls patience, which he seeks as the most active of intellectual conditions. (Even one who recognizes this possibility of his or her own constitution as entering into an imagination of the constitution of the just city may find no city even worth rebuking philosophically—through the proposal of a shared imagination—but purely polemically. This condition may sometimes be pictured as a form of exile rather than of Emerson's agonized membership. Yet it is not clear how different these forms are. I have elsewhere identified Emerson's idea of American membership, his philosophical stance toward America, as one of immigrancy.[8])

Nothing less than Emerson's peculiar claim to amendment would satisfy my craving for philosophy. But nothing so much creates my fears for it. I am aware that I have mentioned the name of Heidegger once or twice in these remarks, but cited no word of his. And yet in my present return to Emerson's "Fate" and my sense of its tortured, philosophical silence about the tyranny of the institution of slavery—in its effort, as I have more or less put the matter, to preserve philosophy in the face of conditions that negate philosophy—I am aware of a kind of preparation for some explicit coming to terms on my part with Heidegger's relation with the tyranny of Nazism, an explicitness I have, with growing discomfort, postponed over the years. Here is motivation for the present essay I cited at the outset. It is to pose for myself the following questions: Am I prepared to listen to an argument in Heidegger's defense that he was, after his public falling out of favor with the regime, attempting to preserve philosophy in the face of conditions that negate philosophy? If not, how am I prepared to understand, as in his 1936 lectures on Nietzsche and in his contemporaneous "Origin of the Work of Art," his call of a people to its historical destiny, and his announcement of a form of the appearance of truth as the founding of a political order? Such questions press me now not alone because of the oddly late and oddly stale recent accounts of Heidegger's extensive involvements with Nazism, and the inundation of responses to these revelations by so many of the major philosophical voices of Europe, but because of the pitch to which my sense of Nietzsche's absorption in Emerson's writing has come, and of Heidegger's absorption or appropriation, in turn, of Nietzsche.

Only some three years ago did I for the first time read all the way through Heidegger's sets of lectures on Nietzsche, delivered from 1936 to 1940, surely the most influential interpretation of Nietzsche to have appeared for serious philosophers in Europe. Emerson's presence in Nietzsche's thought as Heidegger receives it—in certain passages of Nietzsche that Heidegger leans on most heavily—is so strong at certain moments that one has to say that Nietzsche is using Emerson's words; which means that Heidegger in effect, over an unmeasured stretch of thought, is interpreting Emerson's words. Here are two instances: in volume 2 of the English translation of the Nietzsche lectures, Heidegger notes that Nietzsche's "early thought . . . was later to become the essential center of his thinking." Heidegger mentions two school essays of Nietzsche. In a footnote the translator notes in passing that the essays exhibit the "influence" of Emerson and quotes two sentences from the longer of the essays, "Fate and History":

Yet if it were possible for a strong will to overturn the world's entire past, we would join the ranks of self-sufficient gods, and world history would be no more to us than a dream-like enchantment of the self. The curtain falls, and man finds himself again, like a child playing with worlds, a child who wakes at daybreak and with a laugh wipes from his brow all frightful dreams.

Compare this with a sentence from the next to last paragraph of "Fate": "If we thought men were free in the sense that in a single exception one fantastical will could prevail over the law of things, it were all one as if a child's hand could pull down the sun." Nietzsche is not "influenced" by Emerson but is quite deliberately transfiguring Emerson, as for the instruction of the future. This happens early and late. In the section from book 3 of *Thus Spoke Zarathustra* called "The Convalescent," of which Heidegger's reading is among the high points of his opening set of Nietzsche lectures, Nietzsche says this: "To every soul belongs another world; for every soul, every other soul is an afterworld."[9] In Emerson's "Fate" we find: "The hero is to others as the world." The relation of transfiguration here is the clearer the more one goes into what Emerson means by the hero (who is in principle every soul) and into his view of how souls touch.[10]

So I am faced with the spectacle of Heidegger's in effect—unknowingly—facing certain of Emerson's words, guiding himself in these fateful years by signs from, of all places on earth, the waste of America. How do I guide myself? Do I guide myself by the thought that since Emerson is the philosopher of freedom I can, in his mediation through Nietzsche to Heidegger, in principle trust to our eventual success in showing Heidegger's descent into the allegiance with tyranny to be an aberration of his philosophical genius—hence redeemable? Or must I guide myself instead by the thought that, since Heidegger is so radically, unredeemably compromised, and since Emerson is mediated by philosophers of the powers of Nietzsche and of Heidegger, it is not even to be trusted that we will eventually succeed in showing Emerson's genius to be uncompromised by this mediation, so that the way of philosophy I care about most is as such compromised?

11

What's the Use of Calling Emerson a Pragmatist?

In general I applaud the revival of interest in John Dewey and William James, on various intellectual and political grounds, and seek to learn what is at stake for others in their revival. But I also wish to suspend applause—doubtless more a transcendentalist than a pragmatist gesture on my part—for ideas that seem to be gaining prominence within this movement, expressed by writers and thinkers I admire, according to which Emerson is to be understood as a protopragmatist and Wittgenstein as, let us say, a neopragmatist. Perhaps I will be taken as struggling merely over labels, but sometimes labels should be struggled over.

In the course of working out certain implications of the teachings of the later Wittgenstein and of J. L. Austin, I have, in more recent years, variously recurred to an idea that their sense of the ordinary or everyday in language—as goal and as procedure in philosophy—is well thought of in connection with emphases in Emerson and in Thoreau on what they call the common, the familiar, the low, the near (what Emerson means by "having the day"). As Wittgenstein increasingly was called a pragmatist (or cited for his affinities with pragmatism), I wanted to ask whether John Dewey's reputation as the spokesman, even as the provider of a metaphysics, for the common man might throw some light on the dishearteningly dark matter of the philosophical appeal to the ordinary. Naturally I have felt that the appeal to the ordinary possesses political implications that have barely been touched. Yet I have not heretofore thought that the question of Dewey's relation to that appeal's implied politics of the ordinary—which intuitively seems to mean its pertinence to the democratic ideal—demanded thematizing. In particular, I mean the intuition that the democratic bearing of the philosophical appeal to the ordinary and its methods is at least as strong as, and perhaps in conflict with, its bearing on Dewey's homologous appeal to science and what he calls its "method."

To attest my good faith in this struggle over terms such as *pragmatism, transcendentalism,* and *ordinary language philosophy,* I acknowledge that if Emerson is the founder of the difference in American thinking, then later American thinkers such as Dewey and James are going to be indebted to Emerson. What I deny is that their thinking, so far as it is recognizable as something distinctly called "pragmatism," captures or clarifies or retains all that is rational or moral in the Emersonian event. I quote from my title essay in *Must We Mean What We Say?*: "Wittgenstein's role in combating the idea of privacy . . . and in emphasizing the functions and contexts of language, scarcely needs to be mentioned. It might be worth pointing out that these teachings are fundamental to American pragmatism; but then we must keep in mind how different their arguments sound, and admit that in philosophy it is the sound which makes all the difference." The remarks to follow may be taken as a brief gloss on that observation.

One further prefatory remark. It has been said that pragmatists wish their writing, like all good writing, to work—that is, to make a difference. But does writing (or art more generally) work in the ways that logic or technology work, and do any of these work in the way social organization works? Emerson's essay "Experience" may be understood as written to mourn the death of his young son. Freud speaks of mourning as work, something Emerson quite explicitly declares it to be; and Freud speaks in these terms also of an aspect of dreaming.[1] Does the writing of Dewey or James help us understand this idea of work? If it is a viable idea, is it less important than what they understand work to be?

I will formulate in what follows a few differences between Dewey and James, who are uncontentiously pragmatists, and Emerson and Wittgenstein, who are only contentiously so, although I know these differences may be dismissible, roughly on pragmatic grounds. I will then sketch what I consider to be my stake in these matters.

The following sentence from Dewey's *Experience and Education* is, I assume, characteristic of what makes him Dewey: "Scientific method is the only authentic means at our command for getting at the significance of our everyday experiences of the world in which we live."[2] Perhaps Emerson was wrong to identify mourning as a pervasive character of what we know as experience, and perhaps, in any case, philosophy need not regard it as part of "the significance of our everyday experiences." Yet Emerson finds a work of what he understands as mourning to be the path to human objectivity with the world, to separating the world from ourselves, from our private interests in it. That understanding offers the possibility of moral relationship. According to Wittgenstein, "Concepts . . . are the expression of our interest, and direct our interest."[3] But interest is to be distinguished from whim, something I have regarded as the task to which Emerson dedicates his writing. Does science have anything different to say about mourning? Is it supposed to? Might one say that science has its own understanding of objectivity, call that "intersubjectivity"? It is an understanding that neither Emerson nor Wittgenstein can assume to be in effect; the human subject has first to be discovered, as something strange to itself.

Dewey's remark about scientific method being the authentic means for getting at the significance of our everyday experiences in effect insists that the works of men, requiring human intelligence, are part of this everyday. Of some of these works Emerson writes: "In every work of genius we recognize our own rejected thoughts; they come back to us with a certain alienated majesty." Do not be put off by Emerson's liberal use of "genius." For him genius is, as with Plato, something each person has, not something certain people are. Emerson's remark about genius is a kind of definition of the term: If you find the return of your thoughts to be caused by a work in this way, then you are apt, and in a sense justified, to attribute this return to the genius of the work. You might even say that this kind of reading requires what Emerson calls "experimenting," something Thoreau calls "trying" people. Does what you might call "science," or its philosophy, have an understanding of this use of experimentation, experimentation as provocation? Is this use less important than the understanding science requires? How do the uses get close enough even to seem to conflict—close enough, perhaps, for someone to wish to call Thoreau's use a metaphorical one?

Dewey writes that pragmatism "is the formation of a faith in intelligence, as the one and indispensable belief necessary to moral and social life."[4] Compare this with Emerson: "To believe your own thought, to believe that what is true for you in your private heart is true for all men— that is genius." Emerson expresses what he calls the ground of his hope that man is one, that we are capable of achieving our commonness, by saying that "the deeper [the scholar] dives into his privatest, secretest presentiment, to his wonder he finds, this is the most acceptable, most public, and universally true."[5] Is this route to the universal compatible with what Dewey means by science and its method? This is evidently the most privileged route he envisions to the commonness of the human species, or at least to the reform of certain groupings of them and hence to the possibility of democracy.

I realize I have been shading these comparisons between Emerson and Dewey so as to emphasize a certain air of conflict in philosophy between the appeal to science and the appeal to ordinary language. This is where I came into philosophy. The earliest papers I still use were defenses of Austin's and Wittgenstein's appeals to the ordinary, papers that were attacked as irrational for apparently denying the findings of empirical science (e.g., of Noam Chomsky's new linguistics). Like most issues in philosophy, this one was not exactly settled; rather, each side continued to feel misunderstood, each took what it needed from the exchange, and each went its way. But the issue in various ways still concerns me, perhaps because I still want to understand the source of that philosophical hostility.

The philosophical appeal to the ordinary, to words we are given in common, is inherently taken in opposition to something about my words as they stand. Hence they are in opposition to those (typically philosophers) with whom I had hitherto taken myself to be in a state of intersubjectivity. This appeal presents proposals for what we say, which, requiring something like experimentation, are trials that inherently run the risk of exasperation. The appeal challenges our commonality in favor of a more genuine commonality (surely something that characterizes Dewey's philosophical mission), but in the name of no expertise, no standing adherence to logic or to science, to nothing beyond the genius that fits me for membership in the realm of ends.

William James characteristically philosophizes off of the language of the street, which he respects and wishes to preserve, or to satisfy by clarifying the desire it expresses. This mode of philosophizing seems to me quite uncharacteristic of Dewey. In Dewey's writing, the speech of others, whose ideas Dewey wishes to correct, or rather to replace, especially the speech of children, hardly appears—as though the world into which he is drawn to intervene suffers from a well-defined lack or benightedness. Contrast this with a memorable outburst from Emerson: "Every word they say chagrins us . . . and we know not where to begin to set them right." Before Emerson can say what is repellent in the thoughts or noises of others, he has to discover or rediscover a language in which to say it. This turns out to require an inheritance of philosophy that gives back life to the words it has thought to own—a language in which the traditional vocabulary of philosophy is variously brought to earth, concepts such as "experience," "idea," "impression," "understanding," "reason," "universal," "necessity," or "condition." Emerson retains stretches of the vocabulary of philosophy but divests it of its old claims to mastery. This is why his writing is *difficult* in a way no other American philosopher's (save Thoreau's) has been, certainly not that of James or of Dewey. Are these different responses to language not philosophically fundamental? They seem so to me.

I suggested that I also rather cringe at the idea of thinking of Wittgenstein as a sort of pragmatist, or as having a significant pragmatist dimension to his thought. Hilary Putnam, who is more confident here than I, ends the middle of three lectures entitled *Pragmatism* identifying a central—perhaps, he says, the central—emphasis of pragmatism: its emphasis on the primacy of practice.

I think we must agree that something like this emphasis is definitive for pragmatism. Then look at two passages from Wittgenstein that, I believe, are taken to suggest his affinity with pragmatism. There is, first, the always quoted passage from the *Investigations*: "If I have exhausted the grounds I have reached bedrock, and my spade is turned. Then I am inclined to say: 'This is simply what I do.'"[6] I shall not go over my own grounds for the view of this remark I have urged elsewhere, but merely repeat my conclusion, namely, that this passage does not represent a call for the display of a practice at this crossroads. On the contrary, it expresses silence, the recognition that all invocable practices have been canvassed, thus preparing one, providing words, for suffering, awaiting, an inevitable crossroads in the act of teaching. The one who has reached bedrock here describes himself as "inclined to say" something, which at the same time implies that he finds the words that occur to him to be unsayable, empty, their time gone. Saul Kripke is the most prominent of those who understand that passage to be equivalent to asserting a practice.[7]

A second passage, or pair of passages, this time from *On Certainty*, have recently been taken to declare Wittgenstein's pragmatist leanings: "So I am trying to say something that sounds like pragmatism. Here I am being thwarted by a kind of *Weltanschauung*."[8] But isn't this to say that sounding like pragmatism is not welcome but burdensome to Wittgenstein? It thwarts his making himself sufficiently clear. (I think I know just how that feels.) The previous section reads: "I am in England.—Everything around me tells me so. . . . —But might I not be shaken if things such as I don't dream of at present were to happen?"⁹ This conjunction of sections sounds like a combination expressed at §89:

One would like to say: "Everything speaks for, and nothing against, the earth's having existed long before." . . . Yet might I not believe the contrary after all? But the question is: What would the practical effects of this belief be?—Perhaps someone says: "That's not the point. A belief is what it is whether it has any practical effects or not." One thinks: It is the same adjustment of the human mind anyway.

It is fairly clear that Wittgenstein is dismissing, through interpreting the fantasy of, the one who thinks that practical effects are impertinent to what it is one believes, and indeed to whether one may seriously be said to believe something. At the same time, he is casting suspicion on the introduction of the concept of "believing the contrary."

Questioning the practical effects of a belief does sound like William James, for instance, in this passage from "What Pragmatism Means": "The whole function of philosophy ought to be to find out what definite difference it will make to you and me, at definite instants of our life, if this world-formula or that world-formula be the true one."¹⁰ But Wittgenstein's passage had better not be taken to encourage James's evident faith in practicality.

Wittgenstein's case about the earth's existence long before is one in which someone has been led to forget how specialized, even how *weak*, a consideration is in question in saying, in reasonably clear circumstances, "Everything speaks for and nothing speaks against." It is perhaps enough to voice the consideration when the issue is, say, a choice to buy rather than rent a house, under circumstances in which: we already accept that we must do one or the other (that is, the basic decision to move has already been made); the length of stay is not fixed, but the family is committed to at least three years; buying, especially with help available from an institution, will almost certainly save money in the long run; it is not that much more trouble; and so, obviously, on. "Obviously" implies that there is a notable lack of enthusiasm over either prospect. If it were a great house, and an amazing bargain, where the family could at once imagine friends happily visiting, then perhaps it would be smitten, and would forget the mild balancing springs of advantages and disadvantages. In other circumstances, to give "everything for and nothing against" as a conclusive reason—say for a couple living together or just going away together for a weekend—would be discouraging. (I take it that *desiring* to be or to go together is not one among other reasons for doing either but is rather the condition for anything counting as a reason, for or against.) And if one is led (for some undetermined reason) to offer so weak and summary a support for so presumably massive a structure as the existence of the earth long before, one places the ensuing, forced invocations of the practical effects of a belief in a perfectly impotent position; they are mere words. (Compare what Wittgenstein writes in the *Philosophical Investigations*: "[A] hundred reasons present themselves, each drowning the voice of the others."[11])

One moral to draw is that, as my *Claim of Reason* claims, throughout his *Investigations* Wittgenstein is in struggle with the threat of skepticism, as Emerson is (after the small book *Nature*). In contrast, neither James nor Dewey seems to take the threat of skepticism seriously. This is hasty. James's treatment of the "sick soul" intersects with something I mean to capture in the concept of skepticism. But on James's account, it does not seem imaginable that *everyone* might be subject to this condition. That is, James perceives the condition as being of a particular temperament, not as something coincident with the human as such, as if, as with the skeptical threat that concerns me, it is the necessary consequence of the gift of speech. Or shall we, rather than drawing a moral, lay down definitions that distinguish skeptical pragmatists from nonskeptical pragmatists? To what end? Pragmatism seems designed to refuse to take skepticism seriously, as it refuses—in Dewey's, if not always in James's case—to take metaphysical distinctions seriously.

However, I do not wish either to draw or to define lines, but here merely to state differences. I know, as I said, that each of the differences I have mentioned can be rejected or reduced in significance. What is important to me is what I find to be at stake in asserting the differences.

I end by noting, against the idea of pragmatism's attention to practice, Emerson's peroration to "Experience": "I have not found that much was gained by manipular attempts to realize the world of thought. . . . Patience and patience, we shall win at the last." It is hard not to take this plea of Emerson's for suffering and for waiting as pretty flatly the negation of the primacy of practice. Yet things are not so simple. Patience, as in the more obvious case of Thoreau's visible withdrawal or disinvestment from his neighbors, can be exercised aggressively, as an agent of change. Without pursuing the decisive matter of how change is to come, I will let this apparent difference of practice and patience, action and passion, we might say, project a difference in the audiences (that is, in the conceptions of audience) at work in the writing of Dewey and of Emerson.

Dewey seeks to address a situation of unintelligence, which I suppose is to say one that negates whatever predicates of intelligence a philosopher holds dearest, hence a situation that variously manifests superstition, bigotry, gullibility, and incuriousness. In a similar vein Emerson discerns a scene of what he variously calls conformity, timidity, and shame, something he describes as secret melancholy. It is the condition Thoreau will more famously name quiet desperation, which Thoreau perceives to characterize the lives of the mass of men. The connection between massive unintelligence and general despair is that both are barriers to the future, to the new day whose appearance both Emerson and Dewey, in their ways, would hasten. But the ways are as different as the accompanying ideas of the future; they amount to different ideas of thinking, or reason. I once characterized the difference between Dewey and Emerson by saying that Dewey wanted to get the Enlightenment to happen in America, whereas Emerson was in the later business of addressing the costs of the way it has happened. And again, one may deny that the differences between Enlightenment and post-Enlightenment projects are decisive enough to dislodge the idea of Emerson as a pragmatist, or perhaps take pragmatism as, in James's term, mediating between the two.

To my mind, to understand Emerson as essentially the forerunner of pragmatism is perhaps to consider pragmatism as representing more effectively or rationally what Emerson had undertaken to bring to these shores. This is the latest in the sequence of repressions of Emerson's thought by the culture he helped to found, of what is distinctive in that thought. Such a repression has punctuated Emerson's reputation from the first moment he could be said to have acquired one. So my question becomes: What is lost if Emerson's voice is lost?

In its call for intelligent action, Dewey's writing is self-evidently and famously active. And famous problems with it are, first, that you do not know what in particular he wants you to do and, second, that you do not know whether it is rational to expect the mass of men and women to exercise intelligence in their politics any more than in their religions. You might say that Dewey's writing is a wager on democracy, a wager that is rational not because of the weight of evidence that his writing will prove effective, but because it is worthy of being listened to, because there is some reason to believe that it will be listened to, and because there is no other future worth wagering on and working to achieve.

Emerson's writing, too, is a wager, not exactly of itself as the necessary intellectual preparation for a better future, but rather of itself as a present step into that future, two by two. It cannot be entered alone. ("Two . . . abreast" is the attitude between neighbors that Robert Frost advises in "Mending Wall.") Emerson writes in "Self-Reliance": "But do your work, and I shall know you." Your work now, in reading him, is the reading of his page, and allowing yourself to be changed by it. I have, accordingly, wished to place Emerson's writing in a tradition of perfectionist writing that extends in the West from Plato to Nietzsche, Ibsen, Kierkegaard, Wilde, Shaw, Heidegger, and Wittgenstein. Both Dewey and Emerson are necessary for what each of them thinks of as democracy. To repress Emerson's difference is to deny that America is as transcendentalist as it is pragmatist, that it is in struggle with itself, at a level not articulated by what we understand as the political. But what Dewey calls for, other disciplines can perhaps do as well, maybe better, than philosophy. What Emerson calls for is something we do not want to hear, something about the necessity of patience or suffering in allowing ourselves to change. What discipline will call for this if philosophy does not?

Old and New in Emerson and Nietzsche

It is rarely apparent to me initially what has taken me back, or on, to a text of Nietzsche; but for some years it has become familiar to me that, however I get there, what I find eventually takes me further back to Emerson. One of the most memorable of such encounters for me was being struck a few years ago by Nietzsche's characterization of the philosopher in *Beyond Good and Evil*—a book that calls itself in its subtitle *Prelude to a Philosophy of the Future*—as a man of tomorrow and the day after tomorrow. I suppose I had previously taken that phrase to suggest something like a man who is not satisfied merely by a current taste for the new, or fashionably modern, but one who persists beyond that in transforming himself, which will mean isolating himself, to meet (not for himself alone) the oncoming of a world that has broken from its yesterdays, epitomized, of course, in the image of the death, which is to say our killing, of God. But what struck me now, I mean then, was that the phrase "tomorrow and the day after tomorrow," translating the German *Morgen und Übermorgen*, puts in play the prefix *Über-*, so characteristic a site for Nietzschean inflection, marking a distinction homologous to that between *Mensch* and *Übermensch*. To what end? Take *Morgen* in its sense of morning, as well as of tomorrow, and we may discern in *Übermorgen* an idea of an after-, or over-, or super-morning. Why posit such a thing, or event? *Is* it meant?

That it is meant is confirmed for me in taking the idea to be alluding to Emerson's prophecy, in the essay "Circles" (an essay quoted explicitly at the conclusion of Nietzsche's untimely meditation on Schopenhauer), that there is always "another dawn risen on mid-noon." The idea of a man of the day after tomorrow is roughly that the further- or over-morning is the day realized, reconceived, by the further- or over-man; and contrariwise, that the over-man is one who realizes such a day. (For me, perhaps the most comprehensive working out of the idea is Thoreau's *Walden,* epitomized in its closing line, "The sun is but a morning star.")

It is true that Wordsworth in *The Prelude,* and Milton before him in *Paradise Lost,* had proposed new dawns at noon, which Emerson certainly would have known. Is there a way to tell that Nietzsche, if he also knew this, is specifically (also) invoking Emerson? Does it matter? Light is thrown on these questions, if answers to them are not quite given, in noticing that the phrase "a man of tomorrow and the day after tomorrow" is repeated, the year after *Beyond Good and Evil* appeared, in section 2 of a new Preface to *Human, All Too Human* (in 1886), where, as in *Beyond Good and Evil,* Emersonian master tones are also surely at issue. (The phrase is repeated yet again the year after *Human, All Too Human,* in the Preface to a new edition of *The Gay Science* in 1887.[1]) The eight paragraphs making up the new Preface to *Human, All Too Human* constitute the text of Nietzsche I shall refer to most often here.

In that new Preface, the phrase "a man of tomorrow and the day after tomorrow" characterizes those figures for whom Nietzsche is writing— he dedicates *Human, All Too Human* to them in its subtitle, *A Book for Free Spirits*—figures whom this Preface further announces, most ambiguously, as nonexistent or, more precisely, as having been invented by Nietzsche for his companionship "in the midst of bad things." When he says that "there are no such 'free spirits,'" he at once modifies this to read "were none," a hedge which may mean either that he will himself claim to be one, or that his book may, since its publication eight years earlier, have created one or more such, or that they simply have the existence they now have, namely, as "phantoms." Since he claims he "already see[s] them coming," he can hardly deny them, nor can he fail to confess the sense that he is "perhaps . . . doing something to hasten their coming when I describe before the fact the fateful conditions that I *see* giving rise to them, the paths on which I *see* them coming." Evidently this book is written in order to create, or hasten the creation of, the one for which it is written. But how can it so much as "hasten" this coming, since to be effective it must be understood, and it in effect says that it cannot be understood unless its work of hastening creation has already happened, that is, been understood. I have sometimes called this the paradox of reading, to which texts of a certain ambition are necessarily subject; Nietzsche all but calls his book a book for phantoms. (I understand Emerson to be announcing the idea of, let's say, anticipating existence, or say virtuality, in his prefatory poem to "Fate," which speaks of omens, hints, auguries, and of dawn as signifying the shadows of evening.)

As a book for phantoms is pretty much how I have interpreted the moment in "Self-Reliance" at which Emerson declares "Man is timid . . . ; he dares not say 'I think,' 'I am,' but quotes some saint or sage." If you will grant that Emerson is here invoking by quoting Descartes's cogito argument, then Emerson is saying, or showing, two things: first, that mankind is, or has become, unable to use this argument, hence he does not know he exists, he haunts his existence, as if he is a phantom (he says of us that "we glide ghost-like"); second, that Emerson, like Nietzsche, shows himself not exempt from the condition he describes, since he too, instead of saying something, quotes what he would say, in this instance from Descartes. The paradox of reading—namely, that to understand from a work of a certain ambition how to read it is already to have understood how to read it—occurs in Emerson as the paradox of writing such a work, namely, that to find how to write a work of a certain ambition is already to have found it written; all its words are the words of others. But what, at best, would this show about Nietzsche's relation to Emerson on this point of the transition into, the coming into existence of, a new man in a new dawn? Isn't the most this would indicate about the relation of Nietzsche's phantom of existence to Emerson's, not that Nietzsche had Emerson's passage in mind as he wrote, but that passages in Nietzsche's texts, under a certain interpretation, may provide or confirm the route to a certain interpretation of passages in Emerson's, and contrariwise? But if it happened that in each case these are the interpretations that satisfy us best, I do not know that I could ask more from the intuition of one writer's having another "in mind." But we can be less controversial.

In *Beyond Good and Evil* the phrase "a man of *Morgen* and *Übermorgen*" is used to characterize the philosopher of the future (which is to say, the philosopher in the future whose philosophical task will be, or will have been, the future), since that "extraordinary furtherer of man . . . has always found himself, and *had* to find himself, in contradiction to his today."[2] I have in effect argued over the years that Emerson's phrase for "being in contradiction to his today" is his definition of self-reliance—and above all, self-reliant thinking and writing—as being found in "aversion to the demand for conformity." Nietzsche, in section 1 of the new Preface to *Human, All Too Human*, also explicitly, in connection with conformity, invokes the image of turning, as in Emerson's "aversion," challenging his reader to a "reversal [*Umkehrung*] of one's habitual estimation and esteemed habits."

As early as "The American Scholar," Emerson had identified thinking as being turned, turned around or turning something toward something else—the two characteristics of thinking he names there as "conversion" and "transfiguration," conversion suggesting disorientation, being reversed, and transfiguration (incorporating figuration as a term of rhetoric) suggesting the manifesting of the reverses of thought in the refiguration or defiguration of words. I have taken the idea of turning in Emerson's linking of self-reliance and aversion (taking "self-reliance" as the title of an essay of his, hence as a representative title for his writing as such), to characterize something of his manner with words (as duplicitous as Nietzsche's), as when he turns our attention to the hand in *unhandsome* (to characterize a violence in our grasp of concepts), or to the partiality of thinking (to capture both the incompleteness and the desire in what thinking should be), or to the sound of casualty in *casualness* (to emphasize the fatality of the everyday). I need this in order to make plausible hearing Nietzsche's idea of linking the philosopher with the wanderer (at the close of *Human, All Too Human*) as a response to Emerson's linking of thinking with walking in the essay "Experience," as when he says, in the essay's concluding paragraph, "Patience and patience, we shall win at the last," a form of words about which I claim that "last" contains both its sense of enduring, bearing up, and at the same time its sense of a shoemaker's form, implying that our task is to last as on a long path (an image featured in the new Preface to *Human, All Too Human*, as we saw). Patience and suffering [*Geduld* and *leidend*] occur explicitly, in paragraph 5 of that Preface, as necessary "steps onward" of the free spirit in its journey of convalescence, following on an event Nietzsche calls "the great separation."

I expect to encounter less difficulty with the observation that in the same paragraph Nietzsche announces what can be taken to be the dominant theme of Emerson's "Experience," the question of the near. Nietzsche says of the free spirit: "He almost feels as if his eyes were only now open to what is *near*." And it is more or less obvious, in paragraph 7, where the free spirit can finally say, "Here is a *new* problem" (presumably the problem of the new), and Nietzsche continues, "Here is a long ladder on whose rungs we ourselves have sat and climbed. . . . Here is a Higher, a Deeper, a Below-us, an enormous long ordering, a hierarchy which we *see*: here—is *our* problem," that he is presenting a version or vision of the opening image of Emerson's "Experience," that of "find[ing] ourselves on a stair; there are stairs below us, which we seem to have ascended; there are stairs above us, many a one, which go upward and out of sight."

But perhaps I am counting on a prior connection I have urged that I can neither doubt nor prove, namely, that the second sentence of Nietzsche's *On The Genealogy of Morals*, "We [men of knowledge] have never sought ourselves—how could it happen that we should ever *find* ourselves?" is an explicit response to the opening sentence of "Experience" ("Where do we find ourselves?"), perhaps Emerson's most extended discussion of the old and the new. ("Experience" speaks of old and new testaments, old and new births, old and new Englands, old and new worlds, old and new philosophy.) The theme is, however, no more explicit there than in "Circles," with its dawns at mid-noon and its repeated calls for "newness," where we also find Emerson identifying himself as an "experimenter," "an endless seeker, with no Past at my back." In section 4 of Nietzsche's new Preface to *Human, All Too Human*, this seed of thought becomes "this morbid isolation, . . . the desert of these experimental years [*Versuchsjahre*]," and "the dangerous privilege [given to the free spirit] to live *experimentally*," from which "It is still a long way" to the "*mature* freedom of the spirit." Which suggests that we had better remind ourselves that for each resonance between Nietzsche and Emerson there are differences to be articulated, of varying magnitudes, having pervasively to do with differences between what is called the old and what is called the new world. For both, the difference between old and new implies a matter of the life and death of thinking, hence, of human existence; in both this involves a criticism of Christianity using some perspective of the East, and in both there is a contest joined with despair, in Emerson's case threatening inanition (conformity), in Nietzsche's case nihilism. But what for Nietzsche causes a great separation (as from the past, requiring a reconception of time) and a volcanic earthquake of the spirit (requiring a long path of convalescence), requires in Emerson merely what he calls, in "Circles," "obeying his whims," the thought that produces the idea of himself as experimenter. (Though "*Whim*," in "Self-Reliance," is preceded by the as it were private separation Emerson echoes as his "shun[ning] father and mother

and wife and brother when my genius calls me.") As though the great separation was accomplished for Emerson as the birthright of Americans, by
the fact of sailing away from the old world, leaving the past behind them.
But this is not so simple a difference, in light of the deep melancholy of the
essay "Experience," related to the discovery that America remains unapproachable, one might almost say undiscovered, evidently because we have
made nothing new of it, in it.

I pass, for another day, thinking a little further about the eight paragraphs of Nietzsche's Preface, and Emersonian echoes in their ideas of the
lightning flash (in "Self-Reliance": "to detect and watch that gleam of light
which flashes across his mind from within"), of originality as pregnancy (in
"Experience," among other allusions, there is "the crescive self"), of im-
moralism (in "Self-Reliance," again: "if I am the Devil's child, I will live
then from the Devil"), of one's highest moments (power as elevation), of
perspective (Emerson says "partiality"), of being heard poorly (Emerson
thematizes the necessary condition of being misunderstood), as well as of
the concentration of Emersonianisms in the last sentence of *Human, All
Too Human*, in its characterization of the wanderer and the free spirits like
him: "Born out of the mysteries of the dawn, they ponder how the day can
have such a pure, transparent [Emerson's eyeball], transfigured [one of
Emerson's two characteristics of thinking], and cheerful face [the familiar
charge against Emerson's lack of the tragic sense] between the hours of ten
and twelve—they seek the *philosophy of the forenoon*"[3]—this last trio
(transparency, transfiguration, cheerfulness) perhaps being the most undoubted pact of ideas that show Emerson to have been on Nietzsche's
mind in this book about dawn and noon.

I pause, before drawing a moral or two from my perhaps obsessive
interest in Emerson's text, to pick up the suggestion, or prompting, that I
sketch a possible line of relation between my remarks on Emerson here and
those of David Owen and Aaron Ridley in their discussion of Emerson's
"Fate."[4] I do not quarrel with their proposal that, in Emerson, "Fate, or
more precisely, the fateful constraints on human agency are, at the same
time, the conditions of that agency." I do, I believe, quarrel with, or question, the claim they make for it, that it "resolves the so-called paradox of
fatalism and self-creation." After all, or before all, the opening paragraph
of Emerson's "Fate" declares that "we cannot resolve" something that
sounds awfully like this paradox of fatalism, namely, what Emerson will
call or, rather, what he says he will "hazard": "the contradiction,—freedom

is necessary." But my resistance to this proposal more generally is that if it did resolve the matter Emerson is interested in, that would to my mind make uninterestingly mysterious the torrent of reference and agonized prose of Emerson's essays, nowhere more intense than in "Fate." What is it then that motivates the prose—some inability to be more straightforward, or some attempt to convince through multiplying illustrations? (My sense of a quarrel here may just express my impression that Nietzsche's appropriation of Emerson is more often engaged, not surprisingly, by those seeking illumination about Nietzsche, whereas my emphasis is, if anything, likely to fall on what it betokens about Emerson.)

I have two excuses for breaking into this discussion just here. One excuse is, I must confess, to reaffirm certain ideas I advance in the two essays I have published on Emerson's "Fate." The earlier ("Emerson, Coleridge, Kant"[5]) deals most directly with the ideas of contradiction and condition, emphasizing that both terms contain the idea of speaking ("contradiction" of speaking against, "condition" of speaking with); the later of my essays deals with Emerson's idea of "solving [or resolving] the times." In the later ("Emerson's Constitutional Amending"[6]), I read "Fate" as taking the riddle or problem we are incompetent to solve—this is in 1850, the year "Fate" was composed and the year Daniel Webster, to Emerson's dismay, was supporting the passage of the Fugitive Slave Law—to be the persistence of slavery, the absolute negation of freedom. Our incompetence is described, in Emerson's opening paragraph, as tied to our apparent obligation to "accept an irresistible dictation" (a third major term in which Emerson emphasizes speech). The specific dictation referred to, my essay claims, is what Emerson calls our or my or his "constitution," by which Emerson invariably (so far as I have discovered) means simultaneously the Constitution of the United States and the state of my or our or another's individual health—both of which (because of "[a] defect . . . in [our] constitution") require further amending, simultaneously. (The defect is our constitutional accommodation of slavery.)

That we are to resist—"antagonize" is the repeated term in "Fate"—this (and any and all) supposedly irresistible dictations is to be seen in the light of the emphasis in Emerson's essay on a further chain of terms referring to modes and perspectives of speech—for example, announcing, expressing, harping on, crowing, planting oneself, calling things, prophesying, along with repeated uses of the term "speaking" itself. In that light, when Emerson says he will "hazard the contradiction,—freedom is necessary," he is announcing a metaphysical proposition demonstrated not in this paradox alone but in principle in every sentence of his writing, which I would like to describe as a continuous resistance to dictation, an aversiveness to conformity, not an acceptance but an exploration of, or experimenting with, the conditions and contradictions of speech. "The revelation of Thought [that] takes man out of servitude into freedom" is in effect a criterion for determining of each sentence whether it indeed expresses a complete thought (an old definition of a sentence); the revelation is unpredictable and interminable. (Why is such a criterion necessary? An answer would be: because, as in "Self-Reliance," "every word they say chagrins us." But why and how has *that* calamity happened, that we have become unhappy with language as such?) Put otherwise, the paradox that freedom is necessary is an instance of the injunction in "Self-Reliance" to speak with necessity ("to sink darts in their ears"). Call this the discovery of free speech. No wonder Emerson's writing can set sensible people's teeth on edge.

I said I had a second excuse for breaking in here. It is that the topic I was focused on, and reading for, on the present occasion—the topic of the new and the old—is inscribed in "Fate" almost as incessantly as in "Experience" ("Things ripen, new men come"; "that new piece of music which [each man's] life is"; "The new forgets the old"). In particular, we find in "Experience" a version, so I suppose, of the new dawn at noon of "Circles." In "Fate" it is termed "the day of days, the great day of the feast of life," and we are said "rightly [to] say of ourselves we were born and afterwards we were born again, and many times," the result of which is that "we are as lawgivers" (namely, precisely what Kant claims for us). Emerson reformulates this result in the phrase "we speak for Nature" (a sort of summary of the *Critique of Pure Reason* together with the *Critique of Judgment*: if Nature were not made for the conditions of human judgment, there would be no Nature for us). A way of stating Emerson's claim as a philosopher is to say that he undertakes to show that the universality and necessity Kant seeks in judgments (of objects, of duty, and of the beautiful) is not a metaphysical, or postmetaphysical, task alone, but throughout what we may call a moral one—coming to speak with necessity, judging the world. (I would be glad to know if this fits what Owen and Ridley have in mind in speaking, on their opening page, of "an ethics of the ordinary.")

I must stop. Suppose all that I have said, and suggested, were agreeable. What is the good of it? It would perhaps be worth the continuing trouble or patience involved if all it proved were that Nietzsche was one of Emerson's two great readers of the nineteenth century (the other being Thoreau)—a most ambiguous heritage, as I have noted elsewhere, since Heidegger, in 1942, especially singles out early Nietzsche, which Heidegger would not have known is Nietzsche at his most purely Emersonian, as the greatest Nietzsche. But there are more private encouragements I take from Nietzsche's transfigurations of Emerson, considered as an extreme, or eccentric, example of philosophy's history, or its denial of history, as a process of commenting on, recasting, surmounting what it can see of its past. One such encouragement is the chance to see that Emerson has his own way of revising, or re-seeing, the philosophical past. Another is the terrible difficulty I would like it to make for the process of absorbing Emerson into the image of a proto-pragmatist—unless of course you wish to claim that Nietzsche is also a pragmatist. A yet further encouragement, I guess the most important for me (not me alone, I trust), is the bearing this has on possibilities for writing something to be called philosophy now, and here. This is bound, for those who cannot feel free of the issue, to cause controversy.

An instance of what I mean is indicated by noting that the opening sentence of the Preface to the second volume of *Human, All Too Human* runs as follows: "One should speak only where one *may* not be silent." (I do not allow myself to speak much about Wittgenstein's *Tractatus*, but I assume this sentence of Nietzsche's has been adduced in conjunction with the interestingly different positioning of speech and silence in the famous concluding entry of the *Tractatus*: "What we cannot speak about we must pass over in silence." Nietzsche's variation could be an epigraph for Wittgenstein's *Philosophical Investigations*). Nietzsche continues: "And [one should] only speak about that which one has overcome—all else is chatter, '*Literatur.*'" Overcoming, I recall, in paragraph 1 of the new Preface to *Human, All Too Human*, is figured as turning around, a figure I earlier linked with Emerson's signature idea of thinking and speaking in "aversion" to conformity's demands. The ideas of philosophy as turning itself, and us, around, and as returning words from fixations, conceived as overcoming temptations, are critical in Wittgenstein's *Investigations*. Philosophers will disagree about how important they are, or how they are important. Reading Wittgenstein against the interactions of Nietzsche and Emerson, I have taken such ideas to be paramount in guiding myself through the *Investigations*. In that text, overcoming temptation (particularly the temptation to the absolute, as I have characterized Wittgenstein's image of metaphysics there) is a cause Wittgenstein can have had for his suggestion that the *Investigations* might be read from a religious perspective. If Nietzsche's and Emerson's work may usefully be thought of as therapeutic, then so may Wittgenstein's be.

I hope I need not be told that such appropriations, as of Wittgenstein with Emerson and Nietzsche, can be made not as a way of inheriting the tasks of philosophy but as a mode of avoiding them, for making philosophy into "*Literatur.*" I hope as well that the consequent difficulty sometimes in telling, or risking, differences between philosophy and literature, or, for that matter, between what Nietzsche means by the chatter he calls "*Literatur*" and what we may call literature, is not taken as a justification for avoiding questions of difference, hence omens and moments of sameness.

13

Henry James Reading Emerson
Reading Shakespeare

I do not know whether, when Henry James accepted the assignment of composing an Introduction to *The Tempest* for Sidney Lee's edition of Shakespeare in 1907, he had been offered his choice among the plays, but he uses the occasion to challenge what he calls "the accepted, imposed view" (famously associated when James wrote with the critical work of George Brandes) that the production represents Shakespeare's "farewell to the stage"—to challenge not the truth of it (James accepts that there are no facts to adduce against it, which is the reason he calls the view "imposed," uncontested), but, so to speak, the weight of it, whether we understand what we have accepted. This is his response to those who will object to his persistent or recurrent desire—he knows it must seem to advanced critics "morbid"—to touch, or glimpse, the man in the artist. In the next to last paragraph of his Introduction he gives voice to the impatience he knows his toying with morbidity will inspire: "You speak [he imagines his critics crying] of his career as . . . *the* conspicuously transcendent adventure . . . of the mind of man; but no glimmer of any such story, of any such figure or 'presence,' to use your ambiguous word, . . . can be discerned in any quarter. So what is it you propose we should do? What evidence do you suggest that, with this absence of material, we should put together?"[1] James had a few pages earlier already confessed that he has no answer. His problem is that he has an ungovernably recurrent question:

There are moments, I admit, in this age of sound and fury . . . when we are willing to let it pass as a mystery [namely, the eternal mystery, . . . the complete rupture, for our understanding, between the poet and the man]. But there are others when, speaking for myself, its power to torment us intellectually seems scarcely to be borne; and we know these moments best when we hear it proclaimed that a comfortable clearness reigns.[2]

James cites the example of the critic Mr. Halliwell-Phillips, for whom "it is all our fault if everything in our author's story, and above all in this last chapter of it, be not of a primitive simplicity. The complexity arises from our suffering our imagination to meddle with the Man at all; who is quite sufficiently presented to us on the face of the record." Halliwell-Phillips is said by James to propose that Shakespeare, or, rather, as James refers to him, "the supreme master of expression," "had made, before fifty, all the money he wanted; therefore what was there more to express?"[3] To which James tartly responds: "This view is admirable if you can get your mind to consent to it." So James displays his position as caught between an insupportable mystery and an insufferable mindlessness.

This argumentative rhythm, as I might express the matter, is bound to catch my attention, since it is quite congruent with the rhythm of the skeptical problematic. The philosopher has a recurrent intuition of a reality unknown, perhaps unknowable, beyond or behind or within the things and persons we apprehend with our senses, an intuition which mostly, being human, he can put aside, but which sometimes, he being human, torments him, a torment most surely inflamed when one not of his mood or of his flesh comforts him with the assurance that the matter is simple, that things and persons are certainly there, or uncertainly there, and the complexities are produced by the philosopher's own meddling imagination, or morbid reason. Yet it is not this resemblance that for the moment emphatically captures my interest, but rather resonances with what James says here, and says elsewhere, about the work of Shakespeare and about the task of a criticism of the future that should be worthy of it, in relation to some things I have said about certain philosophical criticisms or attitudes toward Shakespeare's achievement, specifically those of Emerson and of Wittgenstein. And the resonances are magnified through the fact that James's torment about how Shakespeare can be imagined to choose silence after his late, most perfect, command of expression is itself expressed by James precisely in his late work, after indeed almost everyone agrees that James had achieved the summit of what Americans have achieved in the form of the novel with his concluding trilogy around the turn of the century—*The Ambassadors, The Wings of the Dove, The Golden Bowl*—after which, so the received agreement mostly continues, his inspiration notably declined.

Emerson and Wittgenstein as readers of Shakespeare figure in some work of mine, first presented in a lecture in 1996[4] (a year or so before I knew of James's Introduction to *The Tempest*) on what I perceive as a problem in the study of Shakespeare comparable in its torment to James's in seeking the man in the artist—perhaps it is the same problem rephrased— namely, the necessity and the impossibility of praising Shakespeare accurately. It is a problem whose complexity is variously reflected within Shakespeare's work, as in Joel Fineman's study of the Sonnets, so relentlessly manifesting the narcissistic compulsion and the idolatrous implications of hyperbolic praise, and in Kenneth Burke's reading of Mark Antony's speech of praise over Caesar's body in which Antony famously denies that he has come to praise, and notoriously in the history of the search for the real author of the works called Shakespeare's (a history containing such figures as Freud and the logician Cantor, no less), a history which perfectly avoids the tormented task James attests to, which is seriously to conceive how *any* mortal can have achieved it.

Wittgenstein avoids the task a different way, namely, by confessing that, while he can understand how someone can call what Shakespeare creates supreme art, he himself does not like it, a sentiment whose interest for me is that it is Wittgenstein who has expressed it. But why bother to express this sentiment, as one among only the dozen or so brief entries explicitly about Shakespeare found in Wittgenstein's notebooks and included in the collection translated under the title *Culture and Value*? Wittgenstein is explicit concerning his suspicion of the way Shakespeare is conventionally praised, a pressing matter also for Henry James, as we saw. But he says a little more in articulation of his distaste, within his admission of recognizing Shakespeare's extreme creativity. He suggests that his uniqueness lies in his perhaps being a "creator of language" rather than a poet.[5] Perhaps what causes Wittgenstein's distaste, then, is a function of the idea of creating language as something private or personal, as if this must be opposed to Wittgenstein's insistence on the publicness and commonness of language.

But we might also take the concept of creation in opposition to the concept of chaos and hear Wittgenstein say, from the same collection, in other connections, two years earlier, "When you are philosophizing you have to descend into the old chaos and feel at home there."[6] He is evidently characterizing his late way of bringing words back to their homes, their home language games, back to the order he calls the ordinary, back, as if anew, from chaos. If this is philosophy's creativity—say it is discovering language's own creativity, dispersing chaos—then it is open to language to be discovered further, further than bringing words home as language games discern home. I hazard the thought that what Wittgenstein senses in Shakespeare's language is the continuous threat of chaos clinging to his creation, an anxiety produced as the sense that it is something miraculous that words can mean at all, that there are words.

In contrast to Wittgenstein's unhappy sense of Shakespeare's uniqueness, when Emerson casts Shakespeare as one of his six Representative Men, the piece of human greatness Shakespeare represents to Emerson he introduces by stressing that Shakespeare is unoriginal. Put positively, this means that it is Shakespeare who best shows that "The greatest genius is the most indebted man," representative in exhibiting best a quality each member of the human species possesses. More specifically, "Shakespeare's principal merit may be conveyed in saying that he of all men best understands the English language, and can say what he will." Like Wittgenstein's reflections, this one of Emerson's seems bland or vague enough, until one catches the implication that the rest of us are in various states of ignorance of our language and are unable to say what we will, chronically inexpressive, as if we are all to some extent aphasic (which is something that Lacan almost says). I put this thought with Emerson's saying, "This power of expression, or of transferring the inmost truth of things into music and verse, makes [Shakespeare] the type of the poet and has added a new problem to metaphysics." The new problem I take Emerson to have articulated a paragraph earlier in saying, "Shakespeare is as much out of the category of eminent authors, as he is out of the crowd. He is inconceivably wise; the others, conceivably. . . . He was the farthest reach of subtlety compatible with an individual self,—the subtlest of authors, and only just within the possibility of authorship." The uniqueness, the limit of possibility, the call for a difference of category, are evidently what Emerson records as posing a new problem to metaphysics.

It is the problem I understand Henry James wishing to bring to life again as a problem of what he calls "criticism," call it the problem of finding categories in which to account for our sense of reading in Shakespeare's texts the work of "the supreme master of expression."[7] It is this master whose career James described as "*the* conspicuously transcendent adventure of the mind of man," an accomplishment whose value, or philosophical exemplariness, I imagine as measured by what I took to be Wittgenstein's anxiety in experiencing Shakespeare's capacity to register the threat of chaos clinging to the creativity of language. It is an anxiety I understand to be enacted in Wittgenstein's focal problematic of the idea of a private language, which I claim is a fantasy that expresses at once a fear of inexpressiveness (or suffocation) and of exposure (Freud sees it as incessant self-betrayal) suffered by creatures possessed of language, creatures called by Emerson "victims of expression."

In relating James's sense of the problem posed by Shakespeare to Emerson's speaking of that achievement as posing a new problem in metaphysics, I meant to be urging not merely some connection for my purposes, but a fact of history. James's demand for the man in the poet can be understood as a sort of gloss on Emerson's claim, in his *Representative Men*, for (as the title of Emerson's pertinent chapter of that book expresses it) "Shakespeare, or The Poet" as a Representative Man. Whether one takes James's putting a criticism of the future in the place of Emerson's invocation of metaphysics to be an amendment or an admiring rebuke (suggesting that Emerson's intuitions had not found their proper tuition in Emerson's descriptions) may be worth further consideration. That James knew, and was remembering, Emerson's chapter should not need much verification: terms common to both their texts, such as "torment," "wonder," "expression," "[the delay of an adequate] criticism," in their respective contexts, ought to be enough, to begin with.

There is another late text by James on the mystery of Shakespeare's authorship, from 1903, this time a short story entitled "The Birthplace," that pairs with James's Introduction. It supplies much of the ground gone over in the later critical Introduction, but emphasizes what in the Introduction he calls "critical complacencies" less than pious insufficiencies of praise, especially as based on crumbs, or what James calls "pebbles," of history.

"The Birthplace" is about the keeping of a museum or shrine established to preserve and celebrate the memory and existence of one identified as "The Supreme Author," always capitalized (as are all pronouns referring back to Him) but never named, and unmistakably tipped off to us as the one sought by the name Shakespeare. It is the text I know that best isolates and analyzes the compulsion to praise Shakespeare, and while it obviously deals in some parody of a banal religiosity, the smile gets wiped off its face.

Everything in the story suggests allegorical overtones, but the overall fable concerns a needy couple mysteriously picked, having no specific expertise or experience for the position, to manage the shrine, who vow, out of their ecstasy in finding themselves so perfectly saved, or rescued economically, to become worthy of the task—namely, to become (especially this will concern the man of the couple, Morris Gedge) expert in the works of the supreme man. After beginning by following the pattern of the pair of sisters who preceded them as directors, which was to learn from the visitors to the shrine what they wanted to hear and then provide it for them, the man becomes as it were a true believer, that is, becomes filled with the conviction in the supremacy of the creator of the works and at the same time with the knowledge of the radical disparity between that conviction and anything actually known about the history of the creator's life. If, however, he were to reveal the truth of this disparity to the crowd of visitors, reveal that, in effect, his sense of supremacy is based on faith alone, their disappointment would show in the reduction in their number, hence in the receipts to the shrine (the principal among the governors of the shrine is frank to call it The Greatest Show on Earth), the consequence of which will be, the principal warns him, the removal of the couple from this refuge of perfect livelihood. (Both the crowd and the governors of the shrine are called Them by the narrator of the story. The concept of "the show," meaning something like the world as appearance—derived, I suppose, from Hegel—is also associated with Shakespeare in Emerson's *Representative Men*, in its Introduction.) Into this pressed situation an American couple appears at the shrine, late enough one day to be admitted as the last and sole visitors. A relation is formed between Morris Gedge and this pair, one that Gedge thinks of as forming "the good society," based on their shared knowledge and their agreement that he must learn to survive—as it were possessed on earth by conviction in heaven—by giving the congregation what it can stand and can use in the way of spiritual nourishment without causing himself to starve spiritually. This little society empowers Gedge to improvise lectures/sermons to the crowd, which allow them to form pictures of the historical Supreme Author without his actually committing himself to any assertion concerning this figure. When the principal summons him for a private conference, the little group (including now Gedge's wife) fears that his ruse has been recognized, but when he returns it is to reveal, to their amazement, that they have been given a raise.

The few sentences there is time to consider here I take from the initial interview with the American couple, the husband speaking first:

"I'm interested," he explained, "in what I think *the* interesting thing—or at all events the eternally tormenting one. The fact of the abysmally little that, in proportion, we know."

"In proportion to what?" his companion [that is, his wife] asked.

"Well, to what there must have been—to what in fact there *is*—to wonder about. . . . He escapes us like a thief at night, carrying off—well, carrying off everything. And people pretend to catch Him like a flown canary."

A little later Gedge observes:

"Luckily it doesn't at all affect the *work*!"

[Gedge's wife intervenes:] "It's our unfortunate ignorance, you mean, that doesn't?"

"Unfortunate or fortunate. I like it so," said the husband. "'The play's the thing.' Let the author alone."

[Gedge replies:] "That's just what They won't do—nor let *me* do. It's all I want—to let the author alone. Practically . . . there *is* no author; that is for us to deal with. There are all the immortal people—*in* the work; but there's nobody else."

"Yes," said the young man [i.e., the husband]—"that's what it comes to. There should really, to clear the matter up, be no such Person."

"As you say," Gedge returned, "it's what it comes to. There *is* no such Person."

The evening air listened, in the warm thick midland stillness, while the wife's little cry rang out. "But *wasn't* there—?"

"There was somebody," said Gedge. . . . "But They've killed Him. And, dead as He is, They keep it up. . . . They kill Him every day."

There are at least four distinct positions here involved in coming to terms with our relation to the work that art does (and hence to the demands of religion, and most generally to the understanding of the existence of others). If we say that Gedge's wife is in the most primitive position (taking our ignorance of origins to be simply an empirical matter), then we can say that the American husband is in the most civilized, combining interest with torment, and "liking" the fact of our empirical ignorance. He is as far as you can go in the way of spectatordom: when he says "The play's the thing," the tone of enjoyment I get from it brings into view the theory that the thing of art is its invitation to and provision of play, an oasis of freedom within human life, and the cost of letting the artist alone is to let him or her indeed escape us like a thief in the night. (Rather, perhaps, than coming to us like a thief in the night, as happened to Nicodemus.) It is the equivalent in art, or say it is an allegory, of a view of religion that would take the absconding or disappearance of God to provide a kind of thrill to the practices of observance. It suggests that humankind would rather praise the void than to be void of praise.

This teasing of mine of the end of Nietzsche's *Genealogy of Morals* is meant to underline the Nietzschean moment with which my citation of the James story ended: "They kill him everyday." Is it known whether Henry James read Nietzsche? His brother William cites *The Genealogy of Morals* in his *Varieties of Religious Experience*. And George Brandes, whom Henry cites in connection with Shakespeare, wrote the first book on Nietzsche. In particular, had he read the for us inescapable parable of the Madman crying in the public square, that is, I take it, one driven mad by still seeking a public divinity? I recall his words: "Whither is God? . . . I shall tell you. *We have killed him*—you and I."[8] If Henry James had not heard of Nietzsche's Madman, the issue remains at least as pressing to understand how James had arrived at a thought shared with autograph Nietzsche. There is another source that might have inspired him to the thought, to which I will come back in a moment.

I note, no doubt superfluously, that James's discussion anticipates quite uncannily the recently famous discussion of the death of the author in—to cite the obvious warhorses here—Roland Barthes's "The Death of the Author" from 1968 and Michel Foucault's answer, "What Is an Author?" from the following year. Both of these texts insist on the pertinence of Nietzsche's annunciation of the death of God. James's achievement goes for me beyond what I get out of these texts of Barthes and Foucault in its commitment to find the implication, and sustaining, of world catastrophe in what we do every day, in the way, for example, we as it were capitalize persons, or, as Wittgenstein puts the matter, we sublime, hence metaphysicalize, our concepts. Wittgenstein's is the most original and convincing account I know of how it is that words are driven away from us, from our everyday needs, into an uncontrollable structure of transcendent service.

Gedge's triumph only serves to isolate him further, from the different wordless, breathless satisfactions his circus virtuosity affords the American husband and Gedge's wife. Henry James, in his search, as it were in his own person, for the man in the poet, in his Introduction to *The Tempest*, may be seen to take his point of departure from Gedge's isolation at the end of "The Birthplace," but to go quite beyond Gedge in his recognition of his own possession of the unquenched desire to face the fact of the human creator's existence, to come close. And beyond also in his provision of grounds for hope that the future will take us further by means of a new criticism. Having again noted that, although "recorded circumstances [of Shakespeare's life] . . . are supremely dim and few," "they . . . throw us back on the work itself with a rebellious renewal of appetite and yearning," James remarkably continues:

> The secret that baffles us being the secret of the Man, we know, as I have granted, that we shall never touch the Man *directly* in the Artist. We stake our hopes thus on indirectness . . . try to look on it as helpful for the Criticism of the future. That of the past has been too often infantile. . . . The figured tapestry, the long arras that hides him, is always there, with its immensity of surface and its proportionate underside. May it not then be but a question, for the fullness of time, of the finer weapon, the sharper point, the stronger arm, the more extended lunge?

Why is the proposed criticism figured in violent terms, as if it threatens to kill the man James seeks? It will help here if we go further into James's recollections of Emerson. For the moment I leave Emerson's *Representative Men*, noting just two further fingerprints of it in James's "The Birthplace": (1) The Shakespeare Society is explicitly invoked in Emerson's chapter on Shakespeare, which notes that they "have inquired in all directions, advertised the missing facts [of Shakespeare's biography], offered money for any information that will lead to proof," and observes that "whatever scraps of information concerning his condition these researches may have rescued, they can shed no light upon that infinite invention which is the concealed magnet of his attraction for us." (2) The American wife introduces the one writer explicitly named in "The Birthplace," in response to her husband's gladness in noting that the unnamed supreme poet escapes us like a thief, by saying, "It's rather a pity, you know, that He *isn't* here. I mean as Goethe's at Weimar. For Goethe *is* at Weimar." Now Goethe appears as one of Emerson's six Representative Men, standing for The Writer, about whom Emerson announces, "I dare not say that Goethe ascended to the highest grounds from which genius has spoken. . . . He is the type of culture, the amateur of all arts, and sciences, and events; artistic, but not artist; spiritual, but not spiritualist." He is, in short, the type of the conceivably wise, not, as with Shakespeare, the inconceivably.

But the Emerson texts I ask attention to now are ones perhaps less, let us say, direct in their bearing on James's address to Shakespeare, surely at any rate they are not explicitly so. The first is the further source that I suggested a moment ago may have a bearing on the portrait of us as killers of God, Emerson's "Divinity School Address" from 1838. In that text Emerson declares to Harvard's small graduating class of aspiring preachers, in defining for them their "holy office . . . the first in the world" (one he had renounced for himself half a dozen years earlier), his conviction "of the universal decay and now almost death of faith in society"; and he specifies two defects of historical Christianity that cause it to participate in this near death: first, "It has dwelt, it dwells, with noxious exaggeration about the *person* of Jesus," something that "corrupts all attempts to communicate religion"; second, "Men have come to speak of the revelation as somewhat long ago given and done, as if God were dead." This second defect suggests that James would not have needed Nietzsche's prompting to the idea of the death of God, but that he took it from the same source I assume Nietzsche took it from, and he modified it, as Nietzsche did, so that it registers the character of our everyday lives ("They kill him every day"), perhaps not so much the cause of their desperation as what that desperation causes, which may therefore be confronted by an alteration of our direction, or say a change of heart. James's continuation of Emerson's marking these two defects in historical Christianity suggests that neither the carrying on of the mission of religion by art, nor the carrying on of the mission of art in the absence of religion, is hopeful.

The first defect, the noxiously exaggerated attention to the *person* of Jesus, seems the immediate and massive point on which James is taking issue, affirming precisely what Emerson decries, that the quest for the man in the work is the hope of the revelatory criticism of the future. But the continuations of Emerson in James and the complexities in each are too arresting to let us stop with so flat a contradiction. Look again at James's demand that the response, in the form of a new criticism, to the supreme dimness and dearth of historical facts concerning Shakespeare "throws us back on the work itself with a rebellious appetite and yearning," which, in conceding that "we shall never touch the Man *directly* in the Artist," at the same time "stake[s] our hopes on indirectness," but in some form that will express a sense of lunging more strongly, with a finer, sharper weapon, further into the tapestry that seems to hide his work, that is, his labor, to reach the proportionate underside. But how are we to understand an indirectness, a reconciliation to something that is not quite touchable, that is expressed in an image of lethal violence?

Notice that the violence begins already with the description of our motivation to enter the work. We are, James says, thrown back, which is to say, repulsed by something we already in some way have engaged; and then the rebelliousness he finds to ensue is one, I suppose, that struggles against the terms of that former, unsatisfied engagement and yields a renewed appetite and yearning, an imperative readiness for understanding. I use the idea of "understanding" with the weight and complexity I have found it to have in Emerson's essays "Self-Reliance" and "Fate," where it encodes a way of standing toward the world, of bearing up under and countering its pressure, exhibiting the form and power of revelation.

This discovering of understanding is continued in his essay "Experience," where, in particular, the revelatory relation to the world is characterized as mastering what may be called "indirectness." This ambitious text undertakes a criticism of philosophy's, especially empiricism's and Kant's, conceptions of experience. Empiricism based our human access to experience of the world on what it called "impressions," from which our ideas are formed; and now Emerson asks whether anything any longer reliably makes an impression upon us, hence whether our ideas of the world—for example, that of America—are sound. He takes as his most extreme case of experience the death of his young son Waldo and finds that his grief eludes him; it illuminates nothing, neither the world that was nor the different world that is. He says about it, among other things, "I cannot get it nearer to me," meaning at once Waldo, America, and the world. I argue in "Finding as Founding" that this formulation is not a fixed description of metaphysical loss or limitation, but that it is a prompting recognition of something concerning Emerson's master tone of the near (one of the conceptual inflections of his problematic of the common, the low, the familiar, the everyday).

In specifying his inability to get something nearer, he is leaving a direction open. *I* cannot get "it" nearer (as, in general, in "Experience" I do not get, but I am and I have—this is part of a contesting of Kant's idea of thinking as active, Heidegger says grasping, as opposed to sensing as receptive); if it is to become nearer, *it* must come nearer, draw closer. But what can this mean? With respect to approaching America it means: I cannot approach it alone; the eventual human community is between us, or nowhere. With respect to nature, having spoken of objects slipping through our clutching fingers as the unhandsome part of our condition, Emerson says this: "Nature does not like to be observed. . . . Direct strokes she never gave us power to make; all our blows glance, all our hits are accidents. Our relations to each other are oblique and casual." Unpacking a little: glancing is a way of observing, an oblique way, one in which you do not see a thing coming, cannot predict it (as empiricists would prefer); a casual way, meaning a way of casualty, of fateful accident, means that no glancing hit is in itself essential. Such a picture of getting to know makes it indirect, negates the direction in which philosophy takes knowledge to come, namely, by what Emerson calls manipular efforts, which he says he distrusts; it requires what he calls, at the close of his text, "Patience, patience." Indirection thus negates the active direction of knowing and names the direction in which an approach is awaited from the object. This seems to make sound sense where the object is another subject, an other. Does it make much sense where the object is a text, say one of Shakespeare's? James evidently thinks so, given his insistence on coming close to the man behind the text. What sense?

Something it means is that you had probably better not expect that the text will speak to you all the time, nor equally clearly each time it stirs. And it probably means you had better learn to glimpse times or places in which it has spoken to you which you may rather have slighted, even repeatedly. And probably it means, too, that any idea worth your best patience is one that presents itself as a surprise, an accident, something you did not see coming. Whether a critical text in response to a text is apt to prove very orderly if composed according to such constraints, even perhaps including some indication of the sense of danger approaching from a certain region or of an anxiety in continuing to miss something, is, I suppose, not James's problem. If an Emerson essay or a Henry James Introduction or longish short story are instances of such responsive texts, it is hard to put any limit on the form such texts may take. When Emerson lists what it is that "the researches of antiquaries, and the Shakespeare Society" have set out with "keen . . . hope to discover," he instances such questions as "whether the boy Shakespeare poached or not, whether he held horses at the theatre door, whether he kept school, and why he left in his will" this and that—sounding like he would be content to join the mood of Morris Gedge and the American couple at its most mocking. But though Emerson says that "It is the essence of poetry to . . . abolish the past, and refuse all history," he also says, "We are very clumsy writers of history," something his essay "History" elaborates. What, then, might a tactful writing of history be—one, said otherwise, that touches indirectly?

It may be only fair, before looking for a conclusion, to show my hand explicitly and cite an occasion fresh in my experience in which I found myself in an accident of response to a line of Shakespeare. It happened in reading a collection of essays by the remarkable Shakespearean Harry Berger and coming upon his citation of Lear's declaration, in the storm scene, in rejecting the grudging hospitality of his daughters: "No, rather I abjure all roofs, and choose/To wage against the enmity o' th' air." Something in the citational exhibiting of the words, and doubtless in the mood Berger had created in respect to them, showed me that I did not know that I took their point. "To wage" means to engage or battle, but suggests also the pledge to take a chance or risk. But how does "the enmity o' th' air" figure in? What is in the suggestion that Lear will combat the air and take his chance in it, at once an active and a passive response? One can be content to take him simply to mean that he will take what precautions there are of shelter and clothing in the open and thus expose himself to the elements, daring them. But earlier in this scene Lear has recorded his sense of suffocation ("Hysterica passio, down thy rising sorrow," well studied by Janet Adelman in her *Suffocating Mothers*), sensing that I take the enmity of the air as encompassing not only a disturbed sky, but the mortal's condition of living in the medium of air, subject to the necessity of breathing. This may be seen as part of the philosophical effect the storm has on Lear's imagination, driving him to meditate somewhat hysterically upon "unaccommodated man."

Such thoughts are linked in my mind with my reading of Emerson's "Fate," in "Emerson's Constitutional Amending," where Emerson is considering our capacity to receive and contain philosophical ideas. In conjunction with his saying "Certain ideas are in the air" and "A breath of will blows eternally through the universe of souls in the direction of the Right and Necessary. It is the air which all intellects inhale and exhale, and it is the wind which blows the worlds into order and orbit," Emerson comments: "We should be crushed by the atmosphere, but for the reaction of the air within the body. . . . If there be omnipotence in the stroke, there is omnipotence of recoil." I shall not argue that Lear was on Emerson's mind in composing "Fate," but simply indicate what, to my mind, connects such passages by allowing myself to quote a summary moment from my *The Claim of Reason*: "the fantasy of a private language . . . turns out, so far, to be a fantasy, or fear, either of inexpressiveness, one in which I am not merely unknown, but in which I am powerless to make myself known; or one in which what I express is beyond my control."[9] Taking a fear of inexpressiveness to be a sense of suffocation, we have the fear of death from a lack of air presented as a fear of being buried alive within the casing of the body. If Wittgenstein's idea, so articulated, confirms Lear's and Emerson's idea of the fear of breath as a fear of speech, Wittgenstein's idea receives, in return, amplification from Lear and from Emerson's "Fate," so that the fear of breathing is seen as a projection onto language of a fear of its insufficiency, as if it is language itself that has shrunk from its responsibilities of reference and expression. As if the world and my desires in it are too monstrous for telling, and the burden of language, of bearing meaning, of making myself intelligible, crushes me. This is a reasonable portrait of something, as I have roughly urged elsewhere, that philosophical skepticism dreams of explaining as an intellectual lack in human knowledge rather than a perpetual contending with the fate or condition of finitude.

Even if one accepts such a proposal, doesn't it show at most an effort to have my encounters with Shakespeare produce some philosophical outcome, making, in this case, as Walter Benjamin puts the matter, tragedy a chapter of the history of philosophy? This aside, is some idea of seeking the man in the author of the text pertinent, or even indispensable, in this desire for philosophical exchange? The idea, as James describes it, puts us in a certain relation to the work, specifically, the relation, as I might put it, rephrasing an earlier suggestion, to something uttered, made. Doesn't that sound really too trivial to cause the supreme notes of praise that the likes of Emerson and Henry James are compelled to sound in speaking of the texts of Shakespeare? But this omits the quality of their wonder and torment in the disproportion between what is uttered and our ignorance of the utterer, the conditions of its utterance. It is a wonder that these things can have reached language at all, that a language we almost share can have yielded such provocations, ones which seem to ask a response in kind of which we do not know ourselves capable. This is not the mood we will always bring to these texts, or to anything else. But when the mood is upon us it will not be satisfied by the citing of historical facts or by the construction of remarkable intentions; such activities are then distractions, not to say evasions. In case one craves the mood, finds indeed in it the most serious or guiding moments in which a text reveals itself, I would not be talked out of it by a theory of a text's work that shows the appeal to its utterance, or utterer, to be metaphysically improper. This has force only to the extent that we have a concept of a text's properties (of, one may dangerously say, the text itself) that otherwise accounts for this material object's yielding an indefinite lifetime of further revelations, all felt to be in it, there (virtually?).

The search for the utterer, or maker (not necessarily a single one, nor among them anyone inhumanly transparent to herself or to himself), has a double function, one expansive and one restrictive: to mark that a text is written unsurveyably beyond itself (not merely so that it is preserved in another age or a foreign place, but that it continues to find *meaning* there); and yet that not every expansion of a text can be pertinent to a given response, so that to say and to hear something is to allow something else not to be said and not to be heard, is not to say and to hear something else, until the present needs it, namely, the present of another age or another place, for example, your present. (The idea of writing as "unsurveyably beyond itself" is formulated by Emerson in "Self-Reliance" in the form: "Character teaches above our wills," where "character" refers, as always in Emerson, simultaneously to the force of personhood and to writing [expression].) The "relation" to the text proposed in the Emersonian/Jamesian search is, let us say, that of indirection, reversing the conventional direction of what James daringly calls "appreciation": it is not for the text to answer the questions you put to it, but for you to respond to the questions you discover it asks itself (of itself, of you). Without you, Lear's isolation, his breathlessness, would go unrelieved. And what, since noting that condition may well isolate you, will relieve you?

Among the issues we have barely touched on here, especially concerning James's sense of the violence of serious criticism, of the criticism for which he calls upon the future, one is to consider why James's phantasm of this violence—the longer plunge with the finer point through to the underside of the arras—takes the form of Hamlet's mania in his mother's chamber. It happens that in Emerson's chapter on Shakespeare, as Emerson is considering how criticism has failed these texts, we find this:

not until two centuries had passed, after his death, did any criticism which we think adequate begin to appear. It was not possible to write the history of Shakespeare till now . . . : it was with the introduction of Shakespeare into German by Lessing, and the translation of his works by Wieland and Schlegel, that the rapid burst of German literature was most intimately connected. It was not until the nineteenth century, whose speculative genius is a sort of living Hamlet, that the tragedy of Hamlet could find such wondering readers.

Against Emerson's sketch of the conditions of, let's say, philosophical criticism, James's desire for Hamlet's powers of penetration attests to the persistent inadequacy of speculation to contain his wondering reading. Since systematic philosophy and the German language are fields Henry James had early and explicitly consigned to his brother William, we have here, in the year after returning from his months in America, the late period which also produced his nonfictional masterpiece *The American Scene* and his unfinished autobiography, more autobiography to consider, to glimpse the man in James's kind of critic. To help us this history will have to throw light on James's incorporation of Hamlet's displeasure, or disgust, with his contemporaries, who deny the presence of the past and the absence of the present, and who lack the heart to be tormented by the imperatives and the disappointments of speech.

Notes

The following abbreviations have been used for citations from Emerson. All quotations are drawn from *The Complete Works of Ralph Waldo Emerson*, Concord Edition (Boston: Houghton, Mifflin and Company, 1903–4). A concordance for this edition is available on-line at http://www.walden.org/emerson/concordance/. Numbers for each citation refer to volume, page, and the line on which the quotation opens.

AmS	*The American Scholar* (vol. 1)
CbW	*Considerations by the Way* (vol. 6)
Cir	*Circles* (vol. 2)
Exp	*Experience* (vol. 3)
F	*Fate* (vol. 6)
Hist	*History* (vol. 2)
MoS	*Montaigne; or, The Skeptic* (vol. 4)
NER	*New England Reformers* (vol. 3)
SR	*Self-Reliance* (vol. 2)
Trans	*The Transcendentalist* (vol. 1)

PREFACE

1. Cavell, *The Senses of Walden*, p. 33.

INTRODUCTION

1. Franz Liszt, "Études d'exécution transcendante d'après Paganini" (1851).
2. "Patience, patience, we shall win at the last" (Exp 3.85.14).

CHAPTER I

1. See Cavell, *The Senses of Walden*, pp. 32–33.
2. Cavell draws his Emerson citations mainly from a facsimile of the first edition of *Essays* (1841) and *Essays: Second Series* (1844). Citation references are based on the *Complete Works* (1903–4), in which Emerson's revisions from 1847 are registered. On the few occasions when the editions differ, this has been noted.

3. Emerson quotes Galileo, who, confronted with imminent persecution, denied his claim that the earth moves around the sun. Rumor has it, however, that Galileo appended a concluding remark to his confession: "Pero si muove [And yet it does move]." See Porte's note in Emerson, *Essays and Lectures*, p. 1144.

4. Heidegger, *The Piety of Thinking: Essays.*

5. "Always" at the beginning of this sentence was dropped in the revised edition of 1847.

6. Arvin, "The House of Pain: Emerson and the Tragic Sense."

7. Nietzsche, *Thus Spoke Zarathustra*, p. 27.

8. See, especially, "Knowing and Acknowledging," in Cavell, *Must We Mean What We Say?* pp. 238–66, and "The Knowledge of Existence," in Cavell, The *Claim of Reason*, pp. 231–43.

9. "Every thing the individual sees without him corresponds to his states of mind, and every thing is in turn intelligible to him, as his onward thinking leads him into the truth to which that fact or series belongs" (Hist 2.23.16).

10. Wittgenstein, *Philosophical Investigations*, §155.

11. Emerson alludes to the following biblical passages: "He that loveth father or mother more than me is not worthy of me: and he that loveth son or daughter more than me is not worthy of me" (Matthew 10:37); "And thou shalt write them upon the posts of thy house, and on thy gates" (Deuteronomy 6:9); "For the Lord will pass through to smite the Egyptians; and when he seeth the blood upon the lintel, and on the two side posts, the Lord will pass over the door, and will not suffer the destroyer to come in unto your houses to smite you" (Exodus 12:23).

12. Emerson's phrase is actually "secret melancholy": "We adorn the victim with manual skill, his tongue with languages, his body with inoffensive and comely manners. So have we cunningly hid the tragedy of limitation and inner death we cannot avert. Is it strange that society should be devoured by a secret melancholy which breaks through all its smiles and all its gayety and games?" (NER 3.268–69.27). For "quiet desperation," see Thoreau, *Walden*, chap. 1, par. 9.

13. Heidegger, *What Is Called Thinking?*, p. 144.

14. The revised edition of 1847 reads: "for the inmost in due time becomes the outmost" (SR 2.45.11).

CHAPTER 2

1. See "Must We Mean What We Say?," "The Availability of Wittgenstein's Later Philosophy," and "Austin at Criticism," in Cavell, *Must We Mean What We Say?* pp. 1–43, 44–72, 97–114. See also Cavell, *The Claim of Reason*, pp. 3–125, 168–90.

2. "Instead of the sublime and beautiful, the near, the low, the common, was explored and poetized" (AmS 1.110.22).

3. This idea first appears in "The Aesthetic Problems of Modern Philosophy" (1965): "philosophy concerns those necessities we cannot, being human, fail to

know. Except that nothing is more human than to deny them" (Cavell, *Must We Mean What We Say?* p. 96). Compare *The Claim of Reason*: "And to trace the intellectual history of philosophy's concentration on the meaning of particular words and sentences, in isolation from a systematic attention to their concrete uses would be a worthwhile undertaking. . . . A fitting title for this history would be: Philosophy and the Rejection of the Human" (pp. 206–7).

4. "Let us rise early and fast, or break fast, gently and without perturbation; let company come and let company go, let the bells ring and the children cry,—determined to make a day of it" (Thoreau, *Walden*, chap. 2, par. 22).

5. See "Baudelaire and the Myths of Film," in Cavell, *The World Viewed*, pp. 41–46.

6. "If any man come to me, and hate not his father, and mother, and wife, and children, and brethen, and sisters, yea, and his own life also, he cannot be my disciple" (Luke 14:26).

7. "And the disciples came, and said unto him, Why speakest thou unto them in parables? He answered and said unto them, Because it is given unto you to know the mysteries of the kingdom of heaven, but to them it is not given" (Matthew 13:10–11).

8. "For whosoever hath, to him shall be given, and he shall have more abundance: but whosoever hath not, from him shall be taken away even that he hath. Therefore, speak I to them in parables: because they seeing see not; and hearing they hear not, neither do they understand" (Matthew 13:12–13).

9. Deuteronomy 11:18–20.

10. Deuteronomy 11:21.

11. "And he said unto another, Follow me. But he said, Lord, suffer me first to go and bury my father. Jesus said unto him, Let the dead bury their dead: but go thou and preach the kingdom of God. And another also said, Lord, I will follow thee; but let me first go bid them farewell, which are at home at my house. And Jesus said unto him, No man, having put his hand to the plough, and looking back, is fit for the kingdom of God" (Luke 9:59–62).

12. "For the poor always ye have with you; but me ye have not always" (John 12:8).

13. Cf. John 12:26, Matthew 16:24, and Mark 8:34.

CHAPTER 3

1. "[O]ver-simplification, schematization, and constant obsessive repetition of the same small range of jejune 'examples' are not only not peculiar to this case, but far too common to be dismissed as an occasional weakness of philosophers" (J. L. Austin, *Sense and Sensibilia*, p. 3).

2. Cavell, *The Claim of Reason*, p. 243.

3. "The Avoidance of Love," Cavell, *Must We Mean What We Say?* p. 325.

4. "Ending the Waiting Game: A Reading of Beckett's *Endgame*," in Cavell, *Must We Mean What We Say?* pp. 115–62.

5. Cavell, *The Senses of Walden*, p. 33.

6. Kuklick, *The Rise of American Philosophy: Cambridge, Massachusetts, 1860–1930*, p. 10.

7. "Heidegger writes philosophy according to the myth of having read everything essential, Wittgenstein according to the myth of having read essentially nothing" (Cavell, *This New Yet Unapproachable America*, p. 19).

8. Thoreau, *Walden*, chap. 3, par. 4.

9. *Ibid.*, chap. 4, par. 1.

10. *Ibid.*, chap. 8, par. 3.

11. *Ibid.*, chap. 4, par. 12.

12. *Ibid.*, chap. 8, par. 3.

13. *Ibid.*, chap. 1, par. 63.

14. See Chapter 6, below, for a fuller discussion of this claim.

15. Thoreau, *Walden*, chap. 12, par. 11.

16. See ibid., the opening paragraphs of chap. 2.

17. See Chapter 2, p. 23 and Chapter 2, note 3.

CHAPTER 4

1. See Chapter 1, above.

2. See Chapter 6, below.

3. Kant, *Prolegomena to Any Future Metaphysics*, sec. 32, pp. 61–62.

4. Thoreau, *Walden*, chap. 1, par. 3.

5. See Chapter 2, p. 26.

6. "The Politics of Interpretation ('Politics as Opposed to What?')," in Cavell, *Themes Out of School*, pp. 27–59.

7. The famous teacher at the University of California, Berkeley, was Benjamin Lehman.

8. Whicher, *Freedom and Fate: An Inner Life of Ralph Waldo Emerson* and *Selections from Ralph Waldo Emerson: An Organic Anthology*; Bloom, "The Central Man," "Emerson: The American Religion," "Emerson: The Glory and the Sorrows of American Romanticism," "Emerson and Influence," "Emerson and Whitman: The American Sublime," "The Internalization of Quest Romance," and "Mr. America."

9. This reference has not surfaced, but of interest is Nietzsche's reflection on Emerson's sense of his age: "—Emerson has that good-natured and brilliant cheerfulness that deters all seriousness; he simply does not know how old he already is and how young he will still be—he could say of himself, in the words of Lope de Vega, 'yo me sucedo a mi mismo' ['I am my own successor']" (Nietzsche, *Twilight of the Idols*, "Raids of an Untimely Man," §13).

10. Wittgenstein, *Philosophical Investigations*, §445.

11. Kant, *Critique of Pure Reason*, A 93; B 126.

12. "The Availability of Wittgenstein's Later Philosophy," in Cavell, *Must We Mean What We Say?* pp. 44–72.

13. Wittgenstein, *Philosophical Investigations*, §90.

14. Kant, *Critique of Pure Reason*, A 56; B 80–81.

15. "The book of Nature is the book of Fate" (F 6.15.13).

16. The saying "Character is fate" is often attributed to Friedrich von Hardenberg (Novalis), who wrote: "I often feel, and ever more deeply realize, that fate and character are the same conception" (Novalis, *Heinrich von Ofterdingen* [1802], bk. 2).

17. See Chapter 3, above.

18. Coleridge, *Biographia Literaria*, chap. 22.

19. *Ibid.*, chap. 12.

20. *Ibid.*, chap. 9, par. 6.

21. See: Abrams, "English Romanticism: The Spirit of the Age"; for works by Bloom, n. 8 of this chapter, above; Hartman, *Wordsworth's Poetry, 1787–1814*; and de Man, *Allegories of Reading: Figural Language in Rousseau* and *Blindness and Insight: Essays in the Rhetoric of Contemporary Criticism*. For more on de Man's *Allegories of Reading*, see "The Politics of Interpretation," esp. pp. 41–48, in Cavell, *Themes Out of School.*

22. In McFarland, *Reading Coleridge: Approaches and Applications.*

23. "Outside language games" is a close paraphrase of a line from the fourth paragraph of §47 of Wittgenstein's *Philosophical Investigations*: "—Asking 'Is this object composite?' *outside* a particular language-game is like what a boy once did, who had to say whether the verbs in certain sentences were in the active or passive voice, and who racked his brains over the question whether the verb 'to sleep' meant something active or passive."

CHAPTER 5

1. "We can only obey our own polarity" (F 6.3.15); "We are sure that, though we know not how, necessity does comport with liberty, the individual with the world, my polarity with the spirit of the times" (F 6.4.16).

2. See Hintikka, "Cogito, Ergo Sum: Inference or Performance?" and Williams, "The Certainty of the *Cogito*."

3. "Ghostlike we glide through nature, and should not know our place again" (Exp 3.45.16).

4. Wittgenstein, *Philosophical Investigations*, §525.

5. Thoreau, *Walden*, chap. 3, par. 3.

6. "But greater is that in which you do not wish to have faith—your body and its great reason: that does not say 'I,' but does 'I'" (Nietzsche, *Thus Spake Zarathustra*, p. 34).

7. For earlier remarks on this subject, see "The Politics of Interpretation," in Cavell, *Themes Out of School*, pp. 27–59. For more recent comments, see Chapter 5, p. 226.

8. The first edition of *Essays* (1841) has "But do your thing, and I shall know you." This is revised in 1847 to the passage as quoted.

9. Wittgenstein, *Philosophical Investigations*, §133, beginning at the second paragraph.

10. Cavell's original note reads: "I find it hard not to imagine that this surmise has to do with the history of the frantic collection of statistical tables cited in Ian Hacking's 'Making Up People,' and 'Prussian Statistics,' Emerson's essay 'Fate' self-consciously invokes the new science of statistics as a new image of human fate—a new way in which others are finding us captured by knowledge and which Emerson finds a further occassion for ignorance."

11. See "Hamlet's Burden of Proof," in Cavell, *Disowning Knowledge*, pp. 179–91.

CHAPTER 6

1. Cavell, "Declining Decline: Wittgenstein as a Philosopher of Culture," *This New Yet Unapproachable America*, pp. 29–75.
2. *Ibid.*
3. Exp 3.48.23.
4. Kant, *Critique of Pure Reason*, A 69; B 94.
5. Wittgenstein, *Philosophical Investigations*, §373.
6. Allen, *Waldo Emerson*, pp. vii–viii.
7. Cavell, *The Senses of Walden*, p. 104.
8. Cavell here compresses two of Emerson's sentences into one: "The virtue in most request is conformity. Self-reliance is its aversion" (SR 2.50.4).
9. A line Nietzsche quotes—and italicizes—in "Schopenhauer as Educator" (Nietzsche, *Untimely Meditations*, p. 193).
10. See §6.43 of Wittgenstein's *Tractatus Logico-Philosophicus*.
11. Kant, *Critique of Pure Reason*, A 158; B 197.
12. *Ibid.*, A 145; B 185.
13. Jeremiah 1:4–7, 9.
14. February 4, 1842, in Emerson, *Letters*, 7: 485.
15. Wittgenstein, *Philosophical Investigations*, §217.

CHAPTER 7

1. Jaspers, *Nietzsche*, p. 386.
2. Emerson refers to Montaigne's words, not sentences (MoS 4.168.11).
3. SR 2.64.6.
4. SR 2.50.4.
5. Kant, "Conjectural Beginning of Human History," pp. 56–57.
6. Heidegger, *What Is Called Thinking?* p. 29.
7. *Ibid.*, p. 6.
8. Cavell used this line as the epigraph for *The Claim of Reason*.
9. Heidegger, *What Is Called Thinking?* p. 16.
10. Lewis, *The Collected Papers*.
11. See Chapter 4, above.
12. See Chapter 6, above.

13. AmS 1.96.5.

14. See "The Importance of Importance: *The Philadelphia Story*," Cavell, *Pursuits of Happiness*, p. 155.

15. SR 2.49.8.

16. Rawls, *A Theory of Justice*, p. 256.

17. SR 2.62.9 and Exp 3.82.2.

18. See Chapter 5, above.

19. See §50 of Rawls, *A Theory of Justice*: "The Principle of Perfection," pp. 325–32.

20. *Ibid.*, p. 325.

21. *Ibid.*, p. 331.

22. Nietzsche's lines appear in ibid., p. 325, n. 51.

23. See Kant, *Religion within the Limits of Reason Alone*, p. 109.

24. Nietzsche, *Untimely Meditations*, p. 162.

25. Cavell will develop further the idea of "arrogation of voice" in his *A Pitch of Philosophy: Autobiographical Exercises*. See, in particular, the first chapter: "Philosophy and the Arrogation of Voice," pp. 1–51.

26. SR 2.51.25.

27. Nietzsche, *Untimely Meditations*, p. 163.

28. *Ibid.*; Cavell's emphasis.

29. See Chapter 6, above.

30. Matthew 8:22.

31. Nietzsche, *Untimely Meditations*, p. 162.

32. Hurka, "The Well-Rounded Life."

33. See, for example: Weiskell, *The Romantic Sublime*; Bloom, "Mr. America"; Hertz, *The End of the Line*; and Cavell, "Psychoanalysis and Cinema: Moments of Letter from an Unknown Woman," in Cavell, *Contesting Tears: The Hollywood Melodrama of the Unknown Woman*, pp. 81–114.

34. "The Politics of Interpretation (Politics as Opposed to What?)," in Cavell, *Themes Out of School*, pp. 27–59.

35. The sentence "You are constrained to accepted his standard" appears in "Self-Reliance" in the first edition of *Essays* (1841), but apparently was edited out of the 1847 revision. Here is its original placement: "[The true man] measures you, and all men, and all events. You are constrained to accept his standard. Ordinarily every body in society reminds us of somewhat else or of some other person" (SR 2.60.27; Emerson, *Essays*, p. 50).

36. See the second section of Kant, *Foundations of the Metaphysics of Morals*.

37. AmS 1.114–15.26.

38. Mill, *On Liberty*, chap. 3, par. 6.

CHAPTER 8

1. This address was composed for and delivered at the honors convocation at Iona College in October 1985. The published form of the text given below is reprinted from the January/February 1986 issue of *The American Poetry Review*.

2. Bloom, "Mr. America"; Updike, "Emersonianism."

3. "Ending the Waiting Game: A Reading of Beckett's *Endgame*," Cavell, *Must We Mean What We Say?* p. 135.

4. Cavell, *Must We Mean What We Say?* pp. 136–37.

5. Trans 1.339–40.24.

6. John 12:8.

7. Deuteronomy 11:18; 11:20.

8. See "The Fugitive Slave Law" (address at Concord, May 3, 1851), *Collected Works*, 11: 177–214.

CHAPTER 9

1. Kateb, *The Inner Ocean: Individualism and Democratic Culture.*

2. The subtitle of Nietzsche's autobiographical *Ecce Homo* reads: *How One Becomes What One Is*. In the concluding paragraph of the seventh essay of *The Conduct of Life*, "Considerations by the Way," Emerson writes of "the courage to be what we are" (CbW 6.278.21).

3. See Chapter 6, p. 113.

4. In 1847, Emerson amended this passage to read: "working wherever a man works" (SR 2.60.24).

5. See the poem "Blight," which begins: "Give me truths;/For I am weary of the surfaces,/And die of inanition" (Emerson, *Collected Poems and Translations*, p. 111).

6. Cf. Epictetus, *Encheiridion*, §43, p. 26.

CHAPTER 10

1. See Chapter 8, above.

2. See Chapter 4, above.

3. See Locke, *Second Treatise*, chap. 4, §168, and, chap 19, §242.

4. See Commager, *Documents of American History*, p. 319.

5. See Chapter 6 above, passim, but esp. p. 000.

6. Wittgenstein, *Philosophical Investigations*, §116.

7. Ibid., §133.

8. See Chapter 2, pp. 30–1, above.

9. Nietzsche, *Thus Spake Zarathustra*, p. 217.

10. Exp 3.48.18.

CHAPTER 11

1. Freud, "Mourning and Melancholia," pp. 152–54.

2. Dewey, *Experience and Education*, p. 59.

3. Wittgenstein, *Philosophical Investigations*, §570.

4. Dewey, "The Development of American Pragmatism," pp. 34–35.

5. AmS 1.106.7.

6. Wittgenstein, *Philosophical Investigations*, §217.

7. See Kripke, *Wittgenstein on Rules and Private Language*, and "The Argument of the Ordinary: Scenes of Instruction in Wittgenstein and Kripke," in Cavell, *Conditions Handsome and Unhandsome*, pp. 64–100.

8. Wittgenstein, *On Certainty*, §422.

9. *Ibid.*, §421.

10. W. James, "What Pragmatism Means," p. 141.

11. Wittgenstein, *Philosophical Investigations*, §478.

CHAPTER 12

1. "This whole book is nothing but a bit of merry-making after long privation and powerlessness, the rejoicing of strength that is returning, of a reawakened faith in a tomorrow and the day after tomorrow, of a sudden sense and anticipation of a future, of impending adventures, of seas that are open again, of goals that are permitted again, believed again" (Nietzsche, *The Gay Science*, Preface for the Second Edition (1887), §1, p. 32).

2. Nietzsche, *Beyond Good and Evil*, §212, p. 137.

3. Nietzsche, *Human, All Too Human*, §9, p. 267.

4. Owen and Ridley's discussion was read, as Cavell's discussion here was, at the panel they organized for the Nietzsche Society at the American Philosophical Association, Eastern Division, in December 2001.

5. See Chapter 4, above.

6. See Chapter 13, above.

CHAPTER 13

1. H. James, Introduction, p. 442.

2. *Ibid.*, p. 438.

3. *Ibid.*, p. 439.

4. Cavell, "Skepticism and Iconoclasm."

5. Wittgenstein, *Culture and Value*, p. 84.

6. *Ibid.*, pp. 75–76.

7. H. James, Introduction, p. 439.

8. See Nietzsche, *The Gay Science*, §125, pp. 181–82.

9. Cavell, *The Claim of Reason*, p. 351.

Works Cited

Abrams, M. H. "English Romanticism: The Spirit of the Age." In *English Romanticism*, ed. Northrop Frye. New York: Columbia University Press, 1971.

Adams, James Truslow. "Emerson Re-Read." *The Atlantic Monthly*, October, 1930. Reprinted in *The Recognition of Ralph Waldo Emerson: Selected Criticism since 1837*, ed. Milton R. Konvitz, pp. 182–93. Ann Arbor: The University of Michigan Press, 1972.

Adelman, Janet. *Suffocating Mothers: Fantasies of Maternal Origin in Shakespeare's Plays, 'Hamlet' to 'The Tempest.'* New York: Routledge, 1992.

Allen, Gay Wilson. *Waldo Emerson.* New York: Viking Press, 1986.

Arnold, Matthew. *Culture and Anarchy.* Ed. J. Dover Wilson. Cambridge: Cambridge University Press, 1986.

————. *Discourses in America* (1885). Reprinted in *The Recognition of Ralph Waldo Emerson: Selected Criticism Since 1837*, ed. Milton R. Konvitz, pp. 66–74. Ann Arbor: The University of Michigan Press, 1972.

Arvin, Newton. "The House of Pain: Emerson and the Tragic Sense." *The Hudson Review*, vol. 12 (Spring, 1958). Reprinted in *Emerson: A Collection of Critical Essays*, ed. Milton R. Konvitz and Stephen E. Whicher. Englewood Cliffs., N.J.: Prentice-Hall, 1962.

Austin, J. L. *Philosophical Papers.* 3d ed. Ed. J. O. Urmson and G. J. Warnock. New York: Oxford University Press, 1979.

————. *Sense and Sensibilia.* Ed. G. J. Warnock. New York: Oxford University Press, 1975.

————. "Three Ways of Spilling Ink." In *Philosophical Papers*, 2d ed., pp. 272–87. New York: Oxford University Press, 1970. Also in *Philosophy Today*, no. 1, ed. Jerry H. Gill (New York: The Macmillan Company, 1968).

Barthes, Roland. "The Death of the Author." In *Image, Music, Text*, trans. Stephen Heath, pp. 142–48. New York: Hill and Wang, 1997.

Berger, Harry, Jr. *Making Trifles of Terrors: Redistributing Complicities in Shakespeare.* Ed. and introd. Peter Erickson. Stanford: Stanford University Press, 1997.

Bible. King James Version. Nashville: Thomas Nelson Publishers, 1984.

Bloom, Harold. "The Central Man." Chap. 16 of *The Ringers in the Tower: Studies in Romantic Tradition.* Chicago: University of Chicago Press, 1971.

———. "Emerson: The American Religion." Chap. 6 of *Agon.* New York: Oxford University Press, 1982.

———. "Emerson: The Glory and the Sorrows of American Romanticism." In *Romanticism: Vistas, Instances, Continuities,* eds. David Thorburn and Geoffrey Hartman, pp. 155–76. Ithaca: Cornell University Press, 1973.

———. "Emerson and Influence." Chap. 9 of *A Map of Misreading.* New York: Oxford University Press, 1975.

———. "Emerson and Whitman: The American Sublime." Chap. 9 of *Poetry and Repression: Revisionism from Blake to Stevens.* New Haven: Yale University Press, 1976.

———. "The Internalization of Quest Romance." In *Romanticism and Consciousness: Essays in Criticism,* ed. Harold Bloom, pp. 3–23. New York: W. W. Norton and Company, 1970.

———. "Mr. America." *The New York Review of Books,* November 22, 1984.

Burke, Kenneth. *The Philosophy of Literary Form: Studies in Symbolic Action.* Rev. ed. New York: Vintage Books, 1957.

Cavell, Stanley. *The Claim of Reason: Wittgenstein, Skepticism, Morality, and Tragedy.* Oxford: Oxford University Press, 1979/1999.

———. *Conditions Handsome and Unhandsome: The Constitution of Emersonian Perfectionism.* Chicago: University of Chicago Press, 1990.

———. *Contesting Tears: The Hollywood Melodrama of the Unknown Woman.* Chicago: University of Chicago Press, 1996.

———. *Disowning Knowledge: In Six Plays of Shakespeare.* Cambridge: Cambridge University Press, 1987.

———. *Must We Mean What We Say?* New York: Charles Scribner's Sons, 1969. Reprint, Cambridge: Cambridge University Press, 1976.

———. "Night and Day: Heidegger and Thoreau." In *Appropriating Heidegger,* eds. James E. Faulconer and Mark A. Wrathall, pp. 30–49. Cambridge: Cambridge University Press, 2000.

———. *A Pitch of Philosophy: Autobiographical Exercises.* Cambridge: Harvard University Press, 1994.

———. *Pursuits of Happiness: The Hollywood Comedy of Remarriage.* Cambridge: Harvard University Press, 1981.

———. *The Senses of Walden: An Expanded Edition.* Chicago: The University of Chicago Press, 1992. (*Senses* was first published in 1972 by Viking Press. "Thinking of Emerson" was first published by *New Literary History* in 1979. "An Emerson Mood" was delivered as the Scholar's Day Address at Kalamazoo College in 1980. *An Expanded Edition* was first published in 1981 by North Point Press.)

———. "Skepticism and Iconoclasm." In *Shakespeare and the Twentieth Century: The Selected Proceedings of the International Shakespeare Association World Congress*, eds. Jonathan Bates, Jill L. Levinson, and Dieter Mehl. Newark: University of Delaware Press, 1996.

———. *Themes Out of School: Effects and Causes*. San Francisco: North Point Press, 1984.

———. *This New Yet Unapproachable America*. Albuquerque: Living Batch Press, 1989.

———. *The World Viewed: Reflections on the Ontology of Film, Enlarged Edition*. Cambridge: Harvard University Press, 1979.

Coleridge, Samuel Taylor. *Biographia Literaria*. Ed. J. Shawcross. New York: Oxford University Press, 1949.

———. "Othello." In *Coleridge: Shakespeare Criticism*, vol. 1, ed. Thomas Middleton Raysor. London: Everyman's Library, 1960.

———. *The Rime of the Ancient Mariner*. In *The Portable Coleridge*, ed. I. A. Richards, pp. 80–104. New York: Penguin Books, 1978.

Commager, Henry Steele, ed. *Documents of American History*. New York: Appleton-Century-Crofts, 1958.

Days of Heaven. Dir. Terrence Malick, perf. Richard Gere, Brooke Adams, Sam Shepard, and Linda Manz. Paramount, 1978.

Dickstein, Morris, ed. *The Revival of Pragmatism: New Essays on Social Thought, Law, and Culture*. Durham: Duke University Press, 1998.

de Man, Paul. *Allegories of Reading: Figural Language in Rousseau, Nietzsche, Rilke, and Proust*. New Haven: Yale University Press, 1979.

———. *Blindness and Insight: Essays in the Rhetoric of Contemporary Criticism*. Minneapolis: University of Minnesota Press, 1983.

Dewey, John. *Art as Experience*. In Vol. 10: *1934* of *The Later Works of John Dewey: 1925–1953*, introd. Abraham Kaplan. Carbondale: Southern Illinois University Press, 1989.

———. "The Development of American Pragmatism." In *Philosophy and Civilization*. New York: Capricorn Books, 1963.

———. "Emerson: The Philosopher of Democracy." In Vol. 3: *1903–1906* of *The Middle Works of John Dewey: 1899–1924*, introd. Darnell Rucker, pp. 184–92. Carbondale: Southern Illinois University Press, 1981.

———. "An Empirical Survey of Empiricisms." In Vol. 11: *1935–1937* of *The Later Works of John Dewey: 1925–1953*, introd. John J. McDermott, pp. 69–83. Carbondale: Southern Illinois University Press, 1981.

———. *Experience and Education*. In Vol. 13: *1938–1939* of *The Later Works of John Dewey: 1925–1953*, introd. Steven M. Cahn. Carbondale: Southern Illinois University, 1984.

Doney, Willis, ed. *Descartes: A Collection of Critical Essays*. South Bend, Ind.: University of Notre Dame Press, 1967.

Emerson, Ralph Waldo. *Collected Poems and Translations*. Ed. Harold Bloom and Paul Kane. New York: The Library of America, 1994.

———. *The Complete Works of Ralph Waldo Emerson*. Concord Edition. Boston: Houghton, Mifflin and Company, 1903–4.

———. *Emerson in His Journals*. Ed. Joel Porte. Cambridge: Harvard University Press, 1982.

———. *Essays*. Boston: James Munroe and Company, 1841.

———. *Essays; Essays: Second Series*. Facsimile of first editions. Columbus: Charles E. Merrill Publishing Company, 1969.

———. *Essays and Lectures*. Ed. Joel Porte. New York: The Library of America, 1983.

———. *The Journals and Miscellaneous Notebooks of Ralph Waldo Emerson*. 16 vols. Ed. William H. Gilman, et al. Cambridge: Harvard University Press, 1960–82.

———. *Letters*. 10 vols. Eds. Ralph L. Rusk and Eleanor M. Tilton. New York: Columbia University Press, 1939-95.

———. *Selections from Ralph Waldo Emerson: An Organic Anthology*. Ed. Stephen E. Whicher. Boston: Houghton Mifflin Company, 1957.

Epictetus. *Encheiridion*. Trans. Nicholas White. Indianapolis: Hackett Publishing Company, 1983.

Fineman, Joel. *Shakespeare's Perjured Eye: The Invention of Poetic Subjectivity in the Sonnets*. Berkeley: University of California Press, 1986.

Foucault, Michel. "What Is an Author?" In *The Foucault Reader*, ed. Paul Rabinow, pp. 101-20. New York: Pantheon Books, 1984.

Freud, Sigmund. "Mourning and Melancholia." In *Collected Papers*. New York: Basic Books, 1959.

———. "Three Essays on the Theory of Sexuality." In *The Standard Edition of the Compete Psychological Works of Sigmund Freud*, ed. James Strachey, 7: 125–243. London: Hogarth Press, 1953–74.

Frost, Robert. "Mending Wall." In *The Poetry of Robert Frost*, ed. Edward Connery Lathem. New York: Holt, Rinehart and Winston, 1969.

Hacking, Ian. "Making Up People." In *Reconstructing Individualism: Autonomy, Individuality, and the Self in Western Thought*, eds. Thomas C. Heller, Morton Sosna, and David E. Wellbery, pp. 222–36. Stanford: Stanford University Press, 1986.

———. "Prussian Numbers 1860–1882." In Vol. 1: *Ideas in History* of *The Probabilistic Revolution*, ed. Lorenz Krueger, Lorraine J. Daston, and Michael Heidelberger, pp. 377–94. Cambridge: M.I.T. Press, 1988.

Hartman, Geoffrey. *Wordsworth's Poetry, 1787–1814*. New Haven: Yale University Press, 1965.

Heidegger, Martin. *Being and Time*. Trans. John Macquarrie and Edward Robinson. New York: Harper and Row, 1962.

———. *Nietzsche*. Ed. David Farrell Krell. 2 vols. New York: Harper and Row, 1991.

———. *The Piety of Thinking: Essays*. Trans. James G. Hart and John C. Maraldo. Bloomington: Indiana University Press, 1976.

———. *What Is Called Thinking?* Trans. J. Glenn Gray. New York: Harper and Row, 1968.

Hertz, Neil. *The End of the Line*. New York: Columbia University Press, 1985.

Hintikka, Jaakko. "Cogito, Ergo Sum: Inference or Performance?" In *Descartes: A Collection of Critical Essays*, ed. Willis Doney, pp. 108–40. South Bend, Ind.: University of Notre Dame Press, 1967.

His Girl Friday. Dir. Howard Hawks, perf. Cary Grant, Rosalind Russell, Ralph Bellamy, and Gene Lockhart. Columbia, 1940.

Hollingdale, R. J. *Nietzsche: The Man and His Philosophy*. Baton Rouge: Louisiana State University Press, 1965.

Hurka, Thomas. "The Well-Rounded Life." *The Journal of Philosophy* 84 (December 1987): 727–46.

James, Henry. "The Birthplace." In *Complete Stories: 1898–1910*, pp. 441–95. New York: The Library of America, 1996.

———. Introduction to *The Tempest*. In Vol. 8 of *The Complete Works of William Shakespeare*, ed. Sidney Lee. New York: Harper and Brothers, 1907–8.

James, William. "What Pragmatism Means." In *Essays in Pragmatism*, ed. Alburey Castell. New York: Hafner Publishing Company, 1948.

Jaspers, Karl. *Nietzsche: An Introduction to the Understanding of His Philosophical Activity*. Trans. Charles F. Wallraff and Frederick J. Schmitz. Tucson: University of Arizona Press, 1965.

Kant, Immanuel. "Conjectural Beginning of Human History." Trans. Emil Fackenheim. In *Kant: On History*, ed. Lewis White Beck, pp. 56–57. Indianapolis: Bobbs-Merrill, 1981.

———. *Critique of Pure Reason*. Trans. Norman Kemp Smith. New York: St. Martin's Press, 1965.

———. "The End of All Things." Trans. Robert E. Anchor. In *Kant: On History*, ed. Lewis White Beck. Indianapolis: Bobbs-Merrill, 1981.

———. *Foundations of the Metaphysics of Morals*. Trans. Lewis White Beck. Indianapolis: Bobbs-Merrill, 1978.

———. *Kant: On History*. Ed. Lewis White Beck. Indianapolis: Bobbs-Merrill, 1981.

———. *Prolegomena to Any Future Metaphysics*. Trans. Lewis White Beck. Indianapolis: Bobbs-Merrill, 1950.

————. *Religion within the Limits of Reason Alone.* Trans. Theodore M. Green and Hoyt H. Hudson. New York: Harper and Row, 1960.

Kateb, George. *The Inner Ocean: Individualism and Democratic Culture.* Ithaca: Cornell University Press, 1992.

Konvitz, Milton R., and Stephen E. Whicher, eds. *Emerson: A Collection of Critical Essays.* Englewood Cliffs, N.J.: Prentice-Hall, 1962.

Kripke, Saul. *Wittgenstein on Rules and Private Language.* Cambridge: Cambridge University Press, 1982.

Kuklick, Bruce. *The Rise of American Philosophy: Cambridge, Massachusetts, 1860–1930.* New Haven: Yale University Press, 1977.

Lewis, C. I. *The Collected Papers of C. I. Lewis.* Ed. John D. Goheen and John L. Mothershead, Jr. Stanford: Stanford University Press, 1970.

Locke, John. *The Second Treatise of Government.* In *Two Treatises of Government,* 2d ed., ed. Peter Laslett. Cambridge: Cambridge University Press, 1970.

Marx, Karl. "Towards a Critique of Hegel's *Philosophy of Right*: Introduction." In *Karl Marx: Selected Writings,* ed. David McLellan, pp. 63–74. New York: Oxford University Press, 1977.

Matthiessen, F. O. *American Renaissance: Art and Expression in the Age of Emerson and Whitman.* New York: Oxford University Press, 1941.

McFarland, Thomas. *Reading Coleridge: Approaches and Applications.* Ed. Walter B. Crawford. Ithaca: Cornell University Press, 1979.

Mill, John Stuart. *On Liberty.* Ed. Elizabeth Rapaport. Indianapolis: Hackett Publishing Company, 1978.

Nietzsche, Friedrich. *Beyond Good and Evil: A Prelude to a Philosophy of the Future.* Trans. Walter Kaufmann. New York: Vintage Books, 1966.

————. *Ecce Homo: How One Becomes What One Is.* In *Basic Writings of Nietzsche,* trans. Walter Kaufmann. New York: The Modern Library, 1968.

————. *The Gay Science: With a Prelude in Rhymes and an Appendix of Songs.* Trans. Walter Kaufmann. New York: Vintage Books, 1974.

————. *Human, All Too Human: A Book for Free Spirits.* Trans. Marion Faber. Lincoln: University of Nebraska Press, 1986.

————. *Menschliches, Allzumenschliches: Ein Buch für freie Geister.* Munich: Wilhelm Goldmann Verlag.

————. *Thus Spake Zarathustra.* Trans. Walter Kaufmann. New York: Penguin Books, 1966.

————. *Twilight of the Idols; or, How to Philosophize with a Hammer.* Trans. Richard Polt. Indianapolis: Hackett Publishing Company, 1997.

————. *Untimely Meditations.* Trans. R. J. Hollingdale. Cambridge: Cambridge University Press, 1983.

Perry, Bliss. *The Heart of Emerson's Journals.* Boston: Houghton Mifflin Company, 1926.

Plato. *Republic*. Trans. G. M. A. Grube. Indianapolis: Hackett Publishing Company, 1974.

———. Trans. G. M. A. Grube. Rev. C. D. C. Reeve. Indianapolis: Hackett Publishing Company, 1992.

———. *Republic*. Trans. B. Jowett. New York: The Modern Library, 1982.

———. *Symposium*. In *The Collected Dialogues*, eds. Edith Hamilton and Huntington Cairns, trans. Michael Joyce. Princeton: Princeton University Press, 1961.

Poe, Edgar Allen. "The Black Cat." In *Collected Works*, ed. Thomas Ollive Mabbott, 3: 847–59. Cambridge: Harvard University Press, 1978.

———. "The Imp of the Perverse." In *Collected Works*, ed. Thomas Ollive Mabbott, 3: 1217–27. Cambridge: Harvard University Press, 1978.

———. "The Purloined Letter." In *Collected Works*, ed. Thomas Ollive Mabbott, 3: 972–96. Cambridge: Harvard University Press, 1978.

Putnam, Hilary. *Pragmatism: An Open Question*. Oxford: Basil Blackwell, 1995.

Rawls, John. *A Theory of Justice*. Cambridge: Harvard University Press, 1971.

Rousseau, Jean-Jacques. *On the Social Contract*. Trans. Judith R. Masters. New York: St. Martin's Press, 1978.

Santayana, George. "The Genteel Tradition in American Philosophy." In *The Genteel Tradition: Nine Essays by George Santayana*, ed. Douglas L. Wilson, pp. 37–64. Cambridge: Harvard University Press, 1967.

———. *Skepticism and Animal Faith*. New York: Dover Publications, 1955.

Shakespeare, William. *Hamlet*. In *The Complete Works of Shakespeare*. New York: Oxford University Press, 1938.

Sidgwick, Henry. *Miscellaneous Essays and Addresses*. Ed. E. M. Sidgwick and A. Sidgwick. New York: Macmillan, 1904.

Spengler, Oswald. *The Decline of the West*. Trans. Charles Francis Atkinson. New York: The Modern Library, 1962.

Thoreau, Henry David. *Walden; or, Life in the Woods*. New York: The Library of America, 1991.

Tocqueville, Alexis de. *Democracy in America*. Trans. Henry Reeves. Rev. Francis Bowen. Ed. Phillips Bradley. New York: Vintage, 1945.

Updike, John. "Emersonianism." *The New Yorker*, June 4, 1984.

Weber, Max. "Science as a Vocation." In *From Max Weber: Essays in Sociology*, ed. H. H. Gerth and C. Wright Mills, pp. 129–58. New York: Oxford University Press, 1980.

Weiskell, Thomas. *The Romantic Sublime*. Baltimore: Johns Hopkins University Press, 1986.

Whicher, Stephen E. *Freedom and Fate: An Inner Life of Ralph Waldo Emerson*. Philadelphia: University of Pennsylvania Press, 1953.

Whicher, Stephen E., ed. *Selections from Ralph Waldo Emerson: An Organic Anthology*. Boston: Houghton Mifflin Company, 1957.

Whitman, Walt. *Leaves of Grass*. In *Complete Poetry and Selected Prose*, ed. James E. Miller, Jr. Boston: Houghton Mifflin Company, 1959.

Williams, Bernard. "The Certainty of the *Cogito*." In *Descartes: A Collection of Critical Essays*, ed. Willis Doney, pp. 88–107. South Bend, Ind.: University of Notre Dame Press, 1967. For an expanded version of this essay, see "*Cogito* and *Sum*," chap. 3 of *Descartes: The Project of Pure Inquiry* (Atlantic Highlands, N.J.: Humanities Press, 1978), pp. 72–102.

Wittgenstein, Ludwig. *Culture and Value*. Ed. G. H. von Wright. Trans. Peter Winch. Chicago: University of Chicago Press, 1984.

———. *On Certainty*. Eds. G. E. M. Anscombe and G. H. von Wright. Trans. Denis Paul and G. E. M. Anscombe. New York: Harper and Row, 1972.

———. *Philosophical Investigations*. Trans. G. E. M. Anscombe. Englewood Cliffs, N.J.: Prentice Hall, 1958.

———. *Tractatus Logico-Philosophicus*. Trans. D. F. Pears and B. F. McGuinness. London: Routledge, 1995.

Wordsworth, William. "Ode: Intimations of Immortality from Recollections of Early Childhood." In *Selected Poems and Prefaces*, ed. Jack Stillinger, pp. 186–90. Boston: Houghton Mifflin Company, 1965.

———. "Preface to the Second Edition of *Lyrical Ballads*." In *Selected Poems and Prefaces*, ed. Jack Stillinger, pp. 445–64. Boston: Houghton Mifflin Company, 1965.

———. *The Prelude* (Text of 1805). Ed. E. de Selincourt. London: Oxford University Press, 1964.

Books by Stanley Cavell

Must We Mean What We Say? A Book of Essays. New York: Charles Scribner's Sons, 1969. Reprint, Cambridge: Cambridge University Press, 1976.

The World Viewed: Reflections on the Ontology of Film. New York: Viking, 1971. Enlarged edition, Cambridge: Harvard University Press, 1979.

The Senses of Walden. New York: Viking, 1972. Expanded edition, San Francisco: North Point Press, 1981. Reprint, Chicago: University of Chicago Press, 1992.

The Claim of Reason: Wittgenstein, Skepticism, Morality, and Tragedy. Oxford: Oxford University Press, 1979. New edition, 1999.

Pursuits of Happiness: The Hollywood Comedy of Remarriage. Cambridge: Harvard University Press, 1981.

Themes Out of School: Effects and Causes. San Francisco: North Point Press, 1984. Reprint, Chicago: University of Chicago Press, 1988.

Disowning Knowledge: In Six Plays of Shakespeare. Cambridge: Cambridge University Press, 1987.

In Quest of the Ordinary: Likes of Skepticism and Romanticism. Chicago: University of Chicago Press, 1988.

This New Yet Unapproachable America: Lectures after Emerson after Wittgenstein. Albuquerque: Living Batch Press, 1989.

Conditions Handsome and Unhandsome: Constitutions of Emersonian Perfectionism. The Carus Lectures. Chicago: University of Chicago Press, 1990.

A Pitch of Philosophy: Autobiographical Exercises. Cambridge: Harvard University Press, 1994.

Philosophical Passages: Wittgenstein, Emerson, Austin, Derrida. Oxford: Basil Blackwell, 1995.

Contesting Tears: The Hollywood Melodrama of the Unknown Woman. Chicago: University of Chicago Press, 1996.

The Cavell Reader. Ed. Stephen Mulhall. Oxford: Basil Blackwell, 1996. See "Stanley Cavell: A Bibliography, 1951–1995" by Peter S. Fosl, pp. 390–414.

Selected Books and Collections on Cavell

Borradori, Giovanna. *The American Philosopher: Conversations with Quine, David-son, Putnam, Nozick, Danto, Rorty, Cavell, MacIntyre, and Kuhn*. Trans. Rosanna Crocitto. Chicago: University of Chicago Press, 1994.

Cohen, Ted, Paul Guyer, and Hilary Putnam, eds. *Pursuits of Reason*. Lubbock: Texas Tech Press, 1993.

Eldridge, Richard, ed. *Stanley Cavell*. Cambridge: Cambridge University Press, 2003.

Fischer, Michael. *Stanley Cavell and Literary Skepticism*. Chicago: University of Chicago Press, 1989.

Fleming, Richard. *The State of Philosophy: An Invitation to a Reading in Three Parts of Stanley Cavell's* The Claim of Reason. Lewisburg: Bucknell University Press, 1993.

Fleming, Richard, and Michael Payne, eds. *The Senses of Stanley Cavell*. Lewisburg: Bucknell University Press, 1989.

Gould, Timothy. *Hearing Things: Voice and Method in the Writing of Stanley Cavell*. Chicago: University of Chicago Press, 1998.

Hammer, Espen. *Stanley Cavell: Skepticism, Subjectivity, and the Ordinary*. Cambridge: Polity Press, 2002.

Melville, Stephen. *Philosophy beside Itself: On Deconstruction and Modernism*. Oxford: Oxford University Press, 1994.

Mulhall, Stephen. *Stanley Cavell: Philosophy's Recounting of the Ordinary*. Oxford: Oxford University Press, 1994.

Perl, Jeffrey M., ed. Special issue. *Common Knowledge* 5, no. 2 (Fall 1996).

Rothman, William, and Marian Keane. *Reading Cavell's* The World Viewed: *A Philosophical Perspective on Film*. Detroit: Wayne State University Press, 2000.

Smith, Joseph, and William Kerrigan. *Images in Our Souls*. Baltimore: Johns Hopkins University Press, 1987.

Index

nowadays, 40f, 51, 57
Nowhere, 35f, 39, 143
nuclear war, 171

objectivity, 200, 202f, 217
obvious, the, 37
old and new, 122, 125, 129, 138, 228, 231
onwardness, 13, 19 (*see also* thinking)
ordinary, 36, 39, 58, 108ff, 143; appeal to
    the, 215f, 218; Emerson's investment in
    the, 144; political implications of, 215;
    the prize of, 34; (*see also* everyday)
ordinary language, 21, 34; appeal to, 218
ordinary language philosophy, 21, 23,
    89, 216
origin, a common, 32
origins, in Emerson and Thoreau, 60; a
    person's, 30; modern philosophy's,
    108; of thinking, 61; of writing, 127;
    philosophy's 25, 42, 61, 205
other minds, 97
others, belonging to, 31f
Owen, David, 229, 231

Packer, Barbara, 116, 197
partial(ity), 9, 13, 149f, 152, 227, 299 (*see
    also* conversion, thinking,
    transfiguration)
Pascal, Blaise, 69
passiveness, 202; power of, 137f (*see also*
    reception)
passivity, 186
Passover (blood), 29, 54 (*see also* door-
    post)
patience, 136ff, 186, 212, 221ff (*see also*
    suffering)
perception, 19, 28
perfectionism, dimension of any moral
    thinking, 169; Emersonian, 155f, 184,
    193; moral, 144, 153f, 166, 202, 207;
    moral urgency, 162; undemocratic, 157

performing, "I", 94, 255n6
philanthropist, 178
philanthropy, 195
Philosophical Investigations, 203, 233; as
    Kantian, 112f, 117; skepticism, siting
    of, 168; spade is turned, 219 (*see also*
    Wittgenstein)
philosopher, Emerson as, 190; Emerson,
    whether he is, 167, 173; hobo of
    thought, 139
philosophizing, myths of, 46, 254n7
philosophy, and argumentation, 87, 142;
    devoting oneself to, 42; Emerson
    transfiguring, 207; ending, 14, 50, 78,
    138; impoverished idea of, 25; mood
    of, 26, 32; as parody, 100; and poetry,
    76f; professionalizing of, 38, 40, 43,
    66; professors (professionals) of, 50,
    62, 143, 204, 210; replacing, 14, 22;
    and system, 14; task of, 35; and
    theology, 15
philosophy, and literature, 4, 42, 59, 87,
    105f, 108, 140, 168, 204, 233; and
    Beckett, 173; as halves of mind, 33
Plotinus, 111
Poe, Edgar Allen, 99–108 passim;
    autobiography, 105; sound of prose,
    100; "The Imp of the Perverse," 99,
    101f
poetry, 17, 37, 42f
polarity, 68, 73, 79, 84, 84n1, 255n1
politics, of Emerson's writing, 184, 186f,
    189f, 193, 197
poor, 27f, 176f; Emerson's, 30f, 180, 189;
    Jesus's, 28
posture, 90, 92, 94, 96, 98, 138; standing
    and sitting, 91, 93, 164f; standing for
    philosophy, 110
poverty, 13, 18, 110, 133, 138
pragmatism, American, 42, 215–23
    passim; Emerson as a forerunner of, 7;

and skepticism, 221; and
    transcendentalism, 9, 216
pregnancy, 129f, 203, 229
provocation, 145f, 217
Putnam, Hilary, 219

Rawls, John, 154, 156ff, 160, 163, 189
reading, 45f, 50, 54, 95, 174; paradox of,
    94, 226; redemptively, 57; theology of,
    164 (*see also* philosophizing, myths of)
Reagan, Ronald, 172, 177
reception, 17, 133f, 147, 202, 205; pious,
    15; thinking as, 16 (*see also* passiveness)
redemption, 54, 58, 62, 93, 114;
    philosophy's, 65, 76f
repression, 80; and authority, 61
resolution, 199, 229f
responsibility (for discourse), 45f, 75
Ridley, Aaron, 229, 231
romantic, 36; and skeptical, 77
romanticism, 4, 36f, 59, 61, 63, 78, 114,
    137, 142; human doubleness, 64;
    mission, 76; two worlds, use of, 64
Rousseau, Jean-Jacques, 99

Santayana, George, 38, 66
saying, and hearing, 31; and quoting, 91f,
    95
Shklar, Judith, 183
seduction, 166 (*see also* aversion)
self, crescive, 129, 229; further, 159, 161,
    164, 166f; unattained but attainable,
    156, 164, 202
self-reliance, 204; definition of, 226f
"Self-Reliance," 84–99 passim; a study of
    shame, 154; a study of writing, 54f; a
    theory of reading, 94, 128, 181
Senses of Walden, The, 15, 41, 48, 140; a
    central claim of, 41
sentence, Emersonian, 206; topic, 4, 128,
    147; written in pain, 199; written in
    aversion, 231

Shakespeare, William, 234–49 passim
shame, 90f, 98, 154f, 165
Sidgwick, Henry, 162
silence, saying and meaning, 23
sin, philosophy cannot say, 58
skepticism, 69; answer to by Austin and
    Wittgenstein, 21, 113; living, 86, 106,
    211; and melancholia, 64; problematic
    of, 235; recovery from, 58, 78; respect
    for, 118; responses to, 34, 59; and
    revolution, 167; and romanticism, 78;
    and Shakespeare, 126; threat of, 63,
    89, 109, 143, 221; and tragedy, 38f; the
    truth of, 35; turning aside, 108;
    unsolvability of, 112
slavery, 194–201 passim, 205, 208, 210,
    212
Socrates, 26f
solipsism, and realism, 13, 19
sound, of American philosophy, 3; makes
    all the difference, 216; of philosophizing,
    27; of philosophy, 62, 99
standard, 166f, 201, 203 (*see also*
    constraint)
Stroud, Barry, 143
succeeded, 32
success, 135f, 186, 190
succession, 127, 129, 134ff; of moods, 13;
    subjective and objective, 12
successor, 133
suffering, 221, 223 (*see also* patience)
suffocation, 188, 202, 238, 246 (*see also*
    air, breath, breathing)
stand, (*see* posture)
steps, onward, 227; take, 203; two by
    two, 223 (*see also* walk)

thanking, 16, 147, 186 (*see also* thinking)
therapy, 43, 45; edification as, 52
The Winter's Tale, 126
thinking, Emerson laying conditions for,

Cultural Memory | *in the Present*

Stanley Cavell, *Emerson's Transcendental Etudes*

Stuart McLean, *The Event and its Terrors: Ireland, Famine, Modernity*

Beate Rössler, ed., *Privacies: Philosophical Evaluations*

Bernard Faure, *Double Exposure: Cutting Across Buddhist and Western Discourses*

Alessia Ricciardi, *The Ends Of Mourning: Psychoanalysis, Literature, Film*

Alain Badiou, *Saint Paul: The Foundation of Universalism*

Gil Anidjar, *The Jew, the Arab: A History of the Enemy*

Jonathan Culler and Kevin Lamb, eds., *Just Being Difficult? Academic Writing in the Public Arena*

Jean-Luc Nancy, *A Finite Thinking*, edited by Simon Sparks

Theodor W. Adorno, *Can One Live after Auschwitz? A Philosophical Reader*, edited by Rolf Tiedemann

Patricia Pisters, *The Matrix of Visual Culture: Working with Deleuze in Film Theory*

Talal Asad, *Formations of the Secular: Christianity, Islam, Modernity*

Dorothea von Mücke, *The Rise of the Fantastic Tale*

Marc Redfield, *The Politics of Aesthetics: Nationalism, Gender, Romanticism*

Emmanuel Levinas, *On Escape*

Dan Zahavi, *Husserl's Phenomenology*

Rodolphe Gasché, *The Idea of Form: Rethinking Kant's Aesthetics*

Michael Naas, *Taking on the Tradition: Jacques Derrida and the Legacies of Deconstruction*

Herlinde Pauer-Studer, ed., *Constructions of Practical Reason: Interviews on Moral and Political Philosophy*

Jean-Luc Marion, *Being Given: Toward a Phenomenology of Givenness*

Theodor W. Adorno and Max Horkheimer, *Dialectic of Enlightenment*

Ian Balfour, *The Rhetoric of Romantic Prophecy*

Martin Stokhof, *World and Life as One: Ethics and Ontology in Wittgenstein's Early Thought*

Gianni Vattimo, *Nietzsche: An Introduction*

Jacques Derrida, *Negotiations: Interventions and Interviews, 1971–1998*, ed. Elizabeth Rottenberg

Brett Levinson, *The Ends of Literature: Post-transition and Neoliberalism in the Wake of the "Boom"*

Timothy J. Reiss, *Against Autonomy: Global Dialectics of Cultural Exchange*

Hent de Vries and Samuel Weber, eds., *Religion and Media*

Niklas Luhmann, *Theories of Distinction: Redescribing the Descriptions of Modernity*, ed. and introd. William Rasch

Johannes Fabian, *Anthropology with an Attitude: Critical Essays*

Michel Henry, *I Am the Truth: Toward a Philosophy of Christianity*

Gil Anidjar, *"Our Place in Al-Andalus": Kabbalah, Philosophy, Literature in Arab-Jewish Letters*

Hélène Cixous and Jacques Derrida, *Veils*

F. R. Ankersmit, *Historical Representation*

F. R. Ankersmit, *Political Representation*

Elissa Marder, *Dead Time: Temporal Disorders in the Wake of Modernity (Baudelaire and Flaubert)*

Reinhart Koselleck, *The Practice of Conceptual History: Timing History, Spacing Concepts*

Niklas Luhmann, *The Reality of the Mass Media*

Hubert Damisch, *A Childhood Memory by Piero della Francesca*

Hubert Damisch, *A Theory of /Cloud/: Toward a History of Painting*

Jean-Luc Nancy, *The Speculative Remark (One of Hegel's Bons Mots)*

Jean-François Lyotard, *Soundproof Room: Malraux's Anti-Aesthetics*

Jan Patočka, *Plato and Europe*

Hubert Damisch, *Skyline: The Narcissistic City*

Isabel Hoving, *In Praise of New Travelers: Reading Caribbean Migrant Women Writers*

Richard Rand, ed., *Futures: Of Derrida*

William Rasch, *Niklas Luhmann's Modernity: The Paradox of System Differentiation*

Jacques Derrida and Anne Dufourmantelle, *Of Hospitality*

Jean-François Lyotard, *The Confession of Augustine*

Kaja Silverman, *World Spectators*

Samuel Weber, *Institution and Interpretation: Expanded Edition*